G. L. Cady
287 Fourth Av.
New York City
N. Y.

Modern Religious Cults and Movements

Modern Religious Cults and Movements

By

GAIUS GLENN ATKINS, D.D., L.H.D.

Minister of the First Congregational Church, Detroit, Mich.

Author of "Pilgrims of the Lonely Road," "The Undiscovered Country," etc.

NEW YORK   CHICAGO

Fleming H. Revell Company

LONDON   AND   EDINBURGH

New York: 158 Fifth Avenue
Chicago: 17 North Wabash Ave.
London: 21 Paternoster Square
Edinburgh; 75 Princes Street

To E. M. C.

Whose constant friendship through changing years has been like the fire upon his hearthstone, a glowing gift and a grateful memory

Introduction

THE last thirty years, though as dates go this is only an approximation, have witnessed a marked development of religious cults and movements largely outside the lines of historic Catholicism and Protestantism. One of these cults is strongly organized and has for twenty years grown more rapidly in proportion than most of the Christian communions. The influence of others, more loosely organized, is far reaching. Some of them attempt to give a religious content to the present trend of science and philosophy, and, generally, they represent the free movement of what one may call the creative religious consciousness of our time.

There is, of course, a great and constantly growing literature dealing with particular cults, but there has been as yet apparently no attempt to inquire whether there may not be a few unexpectedly simple centers around which, in spite of their superficial differences, they really organize themselves.

What follows is an endeavour in these directions. It is really a very great task and can at the best be only tentatively done. Whoever undertakes it may well begin by confessing his own limitations. Contemporaneous appraisals of movements upon whose tides we ourselves are borne are subject to constant revision. One's own prejudices, no matter how strongly one may deal with them, colour one's conclusions, particularly in the region of religion. The really vast subject matter also imposes its own limitations upon even the most sincere student unless he has specialized for a lifetime in his theme; even then he would need to ask the charity of his readers.

Ground has been broken for such an endeavour in many different directions. Broadly considered, William James' "Varieties of Religious Experience" was perhaps the pioneer work. Professor James' suggestive analyses recognize the greatly divergent forms religious experience may take and establish their right to be taken seriously as valid facts for the investigator. The whole tendency of organized Christianity—and Protestantism more largely than Catholicism—has been to narrow religious experience to accepted forms, but religion itself is impatient of forms. It has its border-lands, shadowy regions which lie between the acceptance of what Sabbatier calls "the religions of authority" on the one hand and the conventional types of piety or practical goodness on the other. Those who find their religion in such regions —one might perhaps call them the border-land people —discover the authority for their faith in philosophies which, for the most part, have not the sanction of the schools and the demonstration of the reality of their faith in personal experience for which there is very little proof except their own testimony—and their testimony itself is often confused enough.

But James made no attempt to relate his governing conceptions to particular organizations and movements save in the most general way. His fundamentals, the distinction he draws between the " once-born " and the " twice-born," between the religion of healthy-minded-ness and the need of the sick soul, the psychological bases which he supplies for conversation and the rarer religious experiences are immensely illuminating, but all this is only the nebulæ out of which religions are organized into systems; the systems still remain to be considered.

There has been of late a new interest in Mysticism, itself a border-land word, strangely difficult of defini-tion yet meaning generally the persuasion that through certain spiritual disciplines—commonly called the mystic way—we may come into a first-hand knowledge of God and the spiritual order, in no sense dependent upon reason or sense testimony. Some modern move-ments are akin to mysticism but they cannot all be fairly included in any history of mysticism. Neither can they be included in any history of Christianity; some of them completely ignore the Christian religion; some of them press less central aspects of it out of all proportion; one of them undertakes to recast Chris-tianity in its own moulds but certainly gives it a quality in so dealing with it which cannot be supported by any critical examination of the Gospels or considered as the logical development of Christian dogma. Here are really new adventures in religion with new gospels, new prophets and new creeds. They need to be twice approached, once through an examination of those things which are fundamental in religion itself, for they have behind them the power of what one may call the religious urge, and they will ultimately stand as they meet, with a measure of finality, those needs of the soul of which religion has always been the expression, or fall as they fail to meet them. But since some limitation or other in the types of Christianity which are dominant amongst us has given them their opportunity they must also be approached through some consideration of the Christianity against which they have reacted. Unsatisfied needs of the inner life have unlocked the doors through which they have made their abundant entry. Since they also reflect, as religion always reflects, contemporaneous movements in Philosophy, Science, Ethics and Social Relationship, they cannot be understood without some consideration of the forces under whose strong impact inherited faiths have, during the last half century, been slowly breaking down, and in answer to whose suggestions faith has been taking a new form.

A rewarding approach, then, to Modern Religious Cults and Movements must necessarily move along a wide front, and a certain amount of patience and faith is asked of the reader in the opening chapters of this book: patience enough to follow through the discussion of general principles, and faith enough to believe that such a discussion will in the end contribute to the practical understanding of movements with which we are all more or less familiar, and by which we are all more or less affected.

G. G. A.

Detroit, Michigan.

Contents

Changed Attention Affects Physical States—
The Power of Faith to Change Mental Atti-
tudes—Demon Possession—The Beginnings of
Scientific Medicine—The Attitude of the Early
and Medieval Church—Saints and Shrines—
Magic, Charms, and the King's Touch: The
Rise of the Faith Healer.

Mesmerism—The Scientific Investigation of
Mesmerism—Mesmerism in America; Phineas
Quimby an Important Link in a Long Chain—
Quimby is Led to Define Sickness as Wrong
Belief—Quimby Develops His Theories—
Mary Baker Eddy Comes Under His Influ-
ence—Outstanding Events of Her Life: Her
Early Girlhood—Her Education: Shaping In-
fluences—Her Unhappy Fortunes. She is
Cured by Quimby—An Unacknowledged Debt
—She Develops Quimby's Teachings—Begins
to Teach and to Heal—Early Phases of
Christian Science—She Writes "Science and
Health" and Completes the Organization of
Her Church.

Christian Science a Philosophy, a Theology, a
Religion and a System of Healing—The
Philosophic Bases of Christian Science—It
Undertakes to Solve the Problem of Evil—
Contrasted Solutions—The Divine Mind and
Mortal Mind—The Essential Limitations of
Mrs. Eddy's System—Experience and Life—
Sense-Testimony—The Inescapable Reality of
Shadowed Experience.

Science and Health Offered as a Key to the
Scriptures—It Ignores All Recognized Canons
of Biblical Interpretation—Its Conception of
God—Mrs. Eddy's Interpretation of Jesus
Christ—Christian Science His Second Coming
—Christian Science, the Incarnation and the
Atonement—Sin an Error of Mortal Mind
—The Sacraments Disappear—The Real Power
of Christian Science.

I

THE FORMS AND BACKGROUNDS OF INHERITED CHRISTIANITY

CHRONOLOGICALLY the point of departure for such a study as this is the decade from 1880 to 1890. This is only an approximation but it will do. It was a particularly decorous decade. There was no fighting save on the outposts of colonial empires, the little wars of Soldiers Three and Barrack Room Ballads—too far away for their guns to be heard in the streets of capital cities, but lending a touch of colour to newspaper head-lines and supplying new material for rising young writers. It was the decade of triumphant Democracy and triumphant Science and triumphant Industrialism and, among the more open-minded, of triumphant Evolution. Western Civilization was sure of its forces, sure of its formulæ, sure of its future; there were here and there clouds no bigger than a man's hand against particularly luminous horizons, but there was everywhere a general agreement that they would be dissolved by the force of benign development. The world seemed particularly well in hand.

The churches generally shared this confidence. Catholicism and Protestantism had reached a tacit working agreement as to their spheres of influence and were even beginning to fraternize a little. The divisive force of Protestantism seemed to have spent itself.

Since Alexander Campbell—dead now for a decade and a half—no Protestant sect of any importance had been established. The older denominations had achieved a distinctive finality in organization and doctrine. Evolution and Biblical criticism were generally the storm centers of controversy and though these controversies were severe enough they produced no schisms in the churches themselves. A few religious leaders were urging a more thoroughgoing social interpretation and application of the teachings of Jesus; such as these were really looked upon with more suspicion than the propagandists of a liberal theology.

We see now with almost tragic clearness that, beneath the surface of the whole interrelated order of that tranquil afternoon of the Victorian epoch, there were forces in action working toward such a challenge of the accepted and inherited as cultures and civilizations are asked to meet only in the great crises of history and bound to issue, as they have issued in far-flung battle lines, in the overthrow of ancient orders and new alignments along every front of human interest. It will be the task of the historians of the future who will have the necessary material in hand to follow these immense reactions in their various fields and they will find their real point of departure not in dates but in the human attitudes and outlooks which then made a specious show of being final—and were not final at all.

Just there also is the real point of departure for a study like this. We may date the rise of modern religious cults and movements from the last decades of the nineteenth century, but they are really reactions not against a time but a temper, an understanding of religion and a group of religious validations which had been built up through an immense labour of travailing generations and which toward the end of the last century were in the way of being more seriously challenged than for a thousand years (and if this seems too strong a statement the reader is asked to wait for at least the attempted proof of it). We shall have to begin, then, with a state of mind which for want of a better name I venture to call the representative orthodox religious consciousness of the end of the nineteenth century. That this consciousness is Christian is of course assumed. It is Protestant rather than Catholic, for Protestantism has supplied the larger number of followers to the newer religious movements.

To begin with, this representative religious consciousness was by no means simple. Professor James Harvey Robinson tells us that the modern mind is really a complex, that it contains and continues the whole of our inheritances and can be understood only through the analysis of all the contributive elements which have combined to make it what it is and that the inherited elements in it far outweigh more recent contributions. The religious mind is an equally complex and deep-rooted inheritance and can best be approached by a consideration of the bases of religion.

Certain Qualities Common to All Religions

We are but pilgrims down roads which space and time supply; we cannot account for ourselves in terms of what we know to be less than ourselves, nor can we face the shadow which falls deeply across the end of our way without dreaming, at least, of that which lies beyond. Whence? Whither? and Why? are insurgent questions; they are voices out of the depths. A very great development of intelligence was demanded before such questions really took definite shape, but they are implicit in even the most rudimentary forms of religion, nor do we outgrow them through any achievement of Science or development of Philosophy. They become thereby, if anything, more insistent. Our widening horizons of knowledge are always swept by a vaster circumference of mystery into which faith must write a meaning and beyond which faith must discern a destiny.

Religion begins, therefore, in our need so to interpret the power manifest in the universe [1] as to come into some satisfying relationship therewith. It goes on to supply an answer to the dominant questions— Whence? Whither? Why? It fulfills itself in worship and communion with what is worshipped. Such worship has addressed itself to vast ranges of objects, fulfilled itself in an almost unbelievable variety of rites. And yet in every kind of worship there has been

[1] I have taken as a working definition of Religion a phrase quoted by Ward Fowler in the introduction to his Gifford Lectures on " The Religious Experience of the Roman People." " Religion is the effective desire to be in right relationship to the power manifesting itself in the Universe." This is only a formula but it lends itself to vital interpretations and is a better approach to modern cults, many of which are just that endeavour, than those definitions of religion just now current which define it as a system of values or a process of evaluation.

some aspiration toward an ideal excellence and some endeavour, moreover, of those who worship to come into a real relation with what is worshipped. It would need a detailed treatment, here impossible, to back up so general a statement with the facts which prove it, but the facts are beyond dispute. It would be equally difficult to analyze the elements in human nature which lead us to seek such communion. The essential loneliness of the soul, our sense of divided and warring powers and the general emotional instability of personality without fitting objects of faith and devotion, all contribute to the incurable religiosity of human nature.

The value which religion has for those who hold it is perhaps as largely tested by its power to give them a real sense of communion with God as by any other single thing, but this by no means exhausts the value of religion for life. All religions must, in one way or another, meet the need of the will for guidance and the need of the ethical sense for right standards. Religion has always had an ethical content, simple enough to begin with as religion itself was simple. Certain things were permitted, certain things prohibited as part of a cult. These permissions and prohibitions are often strangely capricious, but we may trace behind taboo and caste and the ceremonially clean and unclean an always emerging standard of right and wrong and a fundamental relationship between religion and ethics. Religion from the very first felt itself to be the more august force and through its superior authority gave direction and quality to the conduct of its devotees. It was long enough before all this grew into Decalogues and the Sermon on the Mount and the latter chapters of Paul's great letters to his churches and our present system of Christian ethics, but we discover the beginning of the lordship of religion over conduct even in the most primitive cults.

We shall find as we go on that this particular aspect of religion is less marked in modern religious cults and movements than either the quest for a new understanding of God or new answers to the three great questions, or the longing for a more satisfying communion with God. They accept, for the most part, the generally held standards of Christian conduct, but even so, they are beginning to develop their own ethical standards and to react upon the conduct of those who hold them.

As has been intimated, however, the appeal of religion goes far deeper than all this. If it did no more than seek to define for us the " power not ourselves " everywhere made manifest, if it did no more than answer the haunting questions: Whence? and Whither? and Why?, if it did no more than offer the emotional life a satisfying object of worship and communion with the Divine, supplying at the same time ethical standards and guiding and strengthening the will in its endeavour after goodness, it would have done us an immense service. But one may well wonder whether if religion did no more than this it would have maintained itself as it has and renew through the changing generations its compelling appeal. More strong than any purely intellectual curiosity as to a first cause or controlling power, more haunting than any wonder as to the source and destiny of life, more persistent than any loneliness of the questing soul is our dissatisfaction with ourselves, our consciousness of tragic moral fault, our need of forgiveness and deliverance. This longing for deliverance has taken many forms.

Henry Osborn Taylor in a fine passage has shown us how manifold are the roads men have travelled in their quest for salvation.[1] "For one man shall find his peace in action, another in the rejection of action, even in the seeming destruction of desire; another shall have peace and freedom through intellectual inquiry, while another must obey his God or love his God and may stand in very conscious need of divine salvation. The adjustment sought by Confucius was very different from that which drew the mind of Plato or led Augustine to the City of God. Often quite different motives may inspire the reasonings which incidentally bring men to like conclusions. . . . The life adjustment of the early Greek philosophers had to do with scientific curiosity. . . . They were not like Gotama seeking relief from the tedious impermanence of personal experience any more than they were seeking to insure their own eternal welfare in and through the love of God, the motive around which surged the Christian yearning for salvation. Evidently every religion is a means of adjustment or deliverance."

[1] "Deliverance," pp. 4 and 5.

Professor James in his chapter on The Sick Souls deals most suggestively with these driving longings and all the later analyses of the psychology of conversion begin with the stress of the divided self. The deeper teaching of the New Testament roots itself in this soil. The literature of confession is rich in classic illustrations of all this, told as only St. Augustine more than a thousand years ago or Tolstoy yesterday can tell it. No need to quote them here; they are easily accessible for those who would find for their own longings immortal voices and be taught with what searching self-analysis those who have come out of darkness into light have dealt with their own sick souls.

Every religion has in some fashion or other offered deliverance to its devotees through sacrifice or spiritual discipline, or the assurance that their sins were atoned for and their deliverance assured through the sufferings of others. All this, needless to say, involves not only the sense of sin but the whole reach of life's shadowed experiences. We have great need to be delivered not only from our divided selves but from the burdens and perplexities of life. Religion must offer some explanation of the general problem of sorrow and evil; it must, above all, justify the ways of God with men.

Generally speaking, religion is very greatly dependent upon its power so to interpret the hard things of life to those who bear them that they may still believe in the Divine love and justice. The generality of doubt is not philosophical but practical. We break

with God more often than for any other reason because we believe that He has not kept faith with us.
Some of the more strongly held modern cults have
found their opportunity in the evident deficiency of
the traditional explanation of pain and sorrow. Religion has really a strong hold on the average life only
as it meets the more shadowed side of experience with
the affirmation of an all-conquering love and justice
in which we may rest.

Broadly considered, then, the elements common to
all religions are such as these: a satisfying interpretation of the power manifest in the universe, the need
of the mind for an answer to the questions Whence?
and Whither? and Why?, the need of the emotional
life for such peace as may come from the consciousness of being in right relationship and satisfying communion with God, the need of the will and ethical
sense for guidance, and a need including all this and
something beside for spiritual deliverance. The representative religious consciousness of the end of the
nineteenth century in which we find our point of departure for the religious reactions of the last generation naturally included all this, but implicitly rather
than explicitly. The intellectually curious were more
concerned with science and political economies than
the nature or genesis of religion, while the truly devout, who are not generally given to the critical
analysis of their faith, accepted it as a Divine revelation needing no accounting for outside their Bible.
Moreover such things as these were not then and never
can be held abstractly. They were articulate in creeds

and organized in churches and invested with the august sanction of authority, and mediated through old, old processes of religious development.

Christianity Historically Organized Around the Conception of a Transcendant God and a Fallen Humanity

For in its historic development religion has naturally taken distinctly divergent forms, conditioned by race, environment, the action and reaction of massed experience and by the temper and insight of a few supremely great religious leaders. But centrally, the whole development of any religion has been controlled by its conception of God and, in the main, three different conceptions of God give colour and character to the outstanding historic religions. Pantheistic religions have thought of God as just the whole of all that is; they widen the universe to the measure of the Divine, or narrow the Divine to the operations of the universe. Pantheism saturates its whole vague content with a mystical quality of thought, and colours what it sees with its own emotions. The religions of the Divine Immanence conceive God as pervading and sustaining all that is and revealing Himself thereby, though not necessarily confined therein. The religions of the Divine Transcendence have believed in a God who is apart from all that is, who neither begins nor ends in His universe, and from whom we are profoundly separated not only by our littlenesses but by our sin.

All this is a bare statement of what is almost infinitely richer as it has been felt and proclaimed by the devout and we shall see as we go on how the newer religious movements take also their colour and character from a new emphasis upon the nature of God, or else a return to understandings of Him and feelings about Him which have been lost out in the development of Christianity.

Historically Christian theology, particularly in the West, has centered around the conception of a Transcendent God. As far as doctrine goes Christianity took over a great inheritance from the Jew, for arrestingly enough the Jew, though he belongs to the East, had never anything in common with Eastern Pantheism. On the contrary we find his prophets and lawgivers battling with all their force against such aspects of Pantheism as they found about them. The God of the Old Testament is always immeasurably above those who worshipped Him in righteousness and power; He is their God and they are His chosen people, but there is never any identification of their will with His except in the rare moments of their perfect obedience.

True enough, through the insight of the prophets and particularly the experience of psalmists, this conception of the Apart-God became increasingly rich in the persuasion of His unfailing care for His children. None the less, the Hebrew God is a Transcendent God and Christianity inherits from that. Christianity took over what Judaism refused—Jesus Christ and His Gospel. But out of the immeasurable wealth of His teaching apostolic thinking naturally appropriated and made most of what was nearest in line with the prophets and the lawgivers of their race. Judaism refused Christ but the Twelve Apostles were Jews and the greatest of the group—St. Paul—was a Jewish Rabbi before he became a Christian teacher. He had been nurtured and matured in the schools of his people and though he was reborn, in renunciations and obediences distinctly Christian, there were in his very soul inherited rigidities of form in conformity to which he recast his faith.

More distinctly than he himself could ever have known, he particularized the Gospel of Jesus Christ. Doubtless his own experience was the deeper directing force in all this. Theologies always, to begin with, are the molten outpouring of some transforming experience and they are always, to begin with, fluid and glowing.

Such glowing experiences as these are hard to communicate; they, too, soon harden down and we inherit, as cold and rigid form, what was to begin with the flaming outcome of experience. St. Paul's own struggle and the bitterness of a divided self which issued in his conversion naturally gave content to all his after teaching. He worked out his system strangely apart from the other group of disciples; he had probably never heard a word of Christ's teaching directly from Christ's lips; he naturally fell back, therefore, upon his Jewish inheritance and widened that system of sacrifices and atonements until he found therein not only a place for the Cross but the necessity for it. He made much, therefore, of the sense of alienation from God, of sin and human helplessness, of the need and possibility of redemption.

The Incarnation as the Bridge Between God and Man; the Cross as the Instrument of Man's Redemption. The Cross the Supreme Symbol of Western Theology

Here, then, are the two speculative backgrounds of historic Christianity,—God's apartness from man in an inconceivable immensity of lonely goodness, man's alienation from God in a helpless fallen estate. For the bridging of the gulf between God and His world Christianity offers the incarnation; for the saving of man from his lost estate Christianity offers the Cross. The incarnation is the reëntry of God into a world from which, indeed, according to the Christian way of thinking, He has never been entirely separate, but from which He has, none the less, been so remote that if ever it were to be rescued from its ruined condition there was needed a new revelation of God in humanity; and the Atonement is just the saving operation of God thus incarnated.

Eastern Christianity has made most of the incarnation. The great Greek theologies were built around that. They exhausted the resources of a language particularly fitted for subtle definition in their endeavour to explain the mystery of it, and, after more than a century of bitter debate about the nature and person of Christ, contented themselves with affirming the reality both of the human and divine in His nature, neither confounding the persons nor dividing the substance, nor indeed making clear in any truly comprehensible way the truth which they so sought to define, or the faith to which they so passionately held. But though their keen dialectic broke down under the burden they laid upon it, they did, nevertheless, keep alive just that confidence in God as one come into human life and sharing it and using it, without which there would have been in all the faith and thinking of the West for more than a thousand years an unbridged and unbridgeable gulf between God and man.

Indeed, when we turn back again to the great Greek symbols with that conception of the immanence of God which the truer insights of our own time have done so much to supply, we find these old forms and phrases unexpectedly hospitable to our own interpretations. If the Western Church had been more strongly influenced by the philosophical insight of the early Eastern Church, Western Christendom might have been saved from a good deal of that theological hardness from which great numbers are just now reacting.

But Western Christendom took the Cross for the central symbol of its faith. What would have happened to Western Christendom without Augustine we do not know, and it is idle to try to guess, but Europe in its religious thinking followed for a thousand years the direction he gave it. His theology is only the travail of his soul, glowing and molten. His Confessions reveal to us more clearly than any other record we have Paganism becoming Christian. In the travail of his spirit we see something vaster than his own conversion, we see the formulation of new spiritual experiences, the birth of new spiritual relationships, the growth of new moral orders and consecrations. He bridges for us the passages between Paganism and Christianity. He reveals what rebirth meant for men to whom it was no convention but an agonizing recasting of both the inner and outer life. He shows us what it meant to put aside the inheritances and relationships of an immemorial order and to stand as a little child untaught, undisciplined and unperfect in the presence of the new. The spiritual attitude which Augustine attained was to be for long the dominant spiritual attitude of Europe, was to govern medieval conceptions, inspire medieval actions, colour with its flame the mystic brooding of the medieval mind.

In the end the sovereignty of God became for Augustine supreme and over against this he set with strong finality man's hopeless fallen state. He was doubtless in debt to St. Paul for these governing conceptions but they took new character as they passed through the alembic of his own experience. " The one pervading thought of the Greek fathers concerning the redemptive work of Christ is that men are thereby brought into unity with God. They do not hesitate to designate this unity to be as a deification . . . they dwell on the idea that we become partakers of the Divine nature." [1] The emphasis here is not so much upon sin to be atoned for or punishment to be avoided, as reconciliation to be achieved.

After Augustine the interpretations of the Cross

[1] Fisher, " History of Christian Doctrine," p. 162.

take a new direction. Now men are thereby not so much to be made partakers of the divine nature as to be saved from hell. The explanations of the way in which this salvation is really achieved change with the changing centuries but through shifting theologies there is one constant. All men are lost and fore-doomed to an eternal punishment from which they are saved only in that Christ suffered for them and they, through their faith and obedience, have availed them-selves of His vicarious death. The varying theological interpretations are themselves greatly significant as if here were something whose meanings no single ex-planation could exalt, something to be felt rather than understood. The Cross so seen is the symbol at once of love and need, of moral defeat and moral discipline, of suffering helplessness and overcoming goodness. We cannot overstate the influence of this faith upon the better part of Western civilization.

It has kept us greatly humble, purged us of our pride and thrown us back in a helplessness which is, after all, the true secret of our strength, upon the saving mercy of God. The story of it, simply told, has moved the hard or bitter or the careless as nothing else can do. Its assurances of deliverance have given new hope to the hopeless and a power not their own to the powerless. It has exalted as the very message of God the patient enduring of unmerited suffering; it has taught us how there is no deliverance save as the good suffer for the bad and the strong put their strength at the service of the weak; it has taught us that the greatest sin is the sin against love and the really enduring victories for any better cause are won only as through the appeal of a much enduring un-selfishness new tempers are created and new forces are released. Nor is there any sign yet that its empire has begun to come to an end.

The Catholic Church Offered Deliverance in Obedience to the Authority of an Inerrant Church

Nevertheless the preaching of the Cross has not commonly taken such forms as these; it has been rather the appeal of the Church to the individual to escape his sinful and hopeless estate either through an obedient self-identification with the Church's discipline and an unquestioning acceptance of the Church's authority, or else through an intellectual acceptance of the scheme of redemption and a moral surrender to it. Here are really the two lines of approach through the one or the other of which Christianity has been made real to the individual from the time of St. Paul till our own time. During the early formative period of the Church it was a matter between the individual and his God. So much we read in and between the lines of the Pauline Epistles. As far as any later time can accurately recast the thought and method of a far earlier time evangelical Protestant theology fairly interprets St. Paul. Faith—a big enough word, standing for both intellectual acceptance and a kind of mystic receptivity to the love and goodness and justice of God revealed in the Cross of Christ—is the key to salvation and the condition of Christian character. It is also that through which religion becomes real to the individual. But since all this lays upon the individual a burden hard enough to be borne (as we shall see when we come back to Protestantism itself) the Church, as her organization became more definite and her authority more strongly established, took the responsibility of the whole matter upon herself. She herself would become responsible for the outcome if only they were teachable and obedient.

The Catholic Church offered to its communicants an assured security, the proof of which was not in the fluctuating states of their own souls but in the august authority of the Church to which they belonged. As long, therefore, as they remained in obedient communion with their Church their souls were secure. The Church offered them its confessional for their unburdening and its absolutions for their assurance, its sacraments for their strengthening and its penances for their discipline and restoration. It took from them in spiritual regions and maybe in other regions too, the responsibility for the conduct of their own lives and asked of the faithful only that they believe and obey. The Church, as it were, " stepped down " religion to humanity. It did all this with a marvellous understanding of human nature and in answer to necessities which were, to begin with, essential to the discipline of childlike peoples who would otherwise have been brought face to face with truths too great for them, or dismissed to a freedom for which they were not ready.

It was and is a marvellous system; there has never been anything like it and if it should wholly fail from

amongst us there will never be anything like it again.
And yet we see that all this vast spiritual edifice, like
the arches of its own great cathedrals, locks up upon
a single keystone. The keystone of the arch of
Catholic certainty is the acceptance of the authority
of the Church conditioned by belief in the divine character of that authority. If anything should shake the
Catholic's belief in the authority of his Church and
the efficacy of her sacraments then he is left strangely
unsheltered. Strongly articulated as this system is, it
has not been untouched by time and change. To continue our figure, one great wing of the medieval structure fell away in the Protestant Reformation and what
was left, though extensive and solid enough, is still like
its great cathedrals—yielding to time and change. The
impressive force and unity of contemporaneous
Catholicism may lead us perhaps to underestimate the
number of those in the Catholic line who, having for
one reason or another lost faith in their Church, are
now open to the appeal of the newer movements. For
example, the largest non-Catholic religious group of
Poles in Detroit are Russellites. There are on good
authority between three and four thousand of them.

The Protestant Church Made Faith the Key to Salva-
tion with Conversion the Test for the Individual
of the Reality of His Religious Experience

If religion has been made real to the Catholic
through the mediation of his Church, Protestantism,
seeking to recreate the apostolic Church, has made the
reality of religion a matter between the individual and

his God. And yet Protestantism has never dared commit itself to so simple a phrasing of religion as this, nor to go on without authorities of its own. Protestantism generally has substituted for the inclusive authority of the Catholic Church the authority of its own creeds and fundamentally the authority of the Bible. As far as creeds go Protestantism carried over the content of Latin Christianity more largely than we have generally recognized. Luther was in direct line with Augustine as Augustine was in direct line with St. Paul, and Luther's fundamental doctrine—justification by faith—was not so much a rewriting of ancient creeds as a new way of validating their meaning for the individual. Faith, in our common use of the term, has hardened down into an intellectual acceptance of Protestant theologies, but certainly for St. Paul and probably for Luther it was far more vital than this and far more simple. It was rather a resting upon a delivering power, the assurance of whose desire and willingness to deliver was found in the New Testament. It was an end to struggle, a spiritual victory won through surrender.

The Latin Catholic system had come to impose upon such tempers as Luther's an unendurable amount of strain; it was too complex, too demanding, and it failed to carry with it necessary elements of mental and spiritual consent. (St. Paul had the same experience with his own Judaism.) What Luther sought was a peace-bringing rightness with God. He was typically and creatively one of William James' "divided souls" and he found the solution for his fears, his struggles and his doubts in simply taking for granted that a fight which he was not able to win for himself had been won for him in the transaction on the Cross. He had nothing, therefore, to do but to accept the peace thus made possible and thereafter to be spiritually at rest.

Now since the whole of the meaning of the Cross for Christianity from St. Paul until our own time is involved in this bare statement and since our theologies have never been able to explain this whole great matter in any doctrinal form which has secured universal consent, we must simply fall back upon the statement of the fact and recognize that here is something to be defined in terms of experience and not of doctrine. The validating experience has come generally to be known as conversion, and conversion has played a great part in evangelical Protestantism ever since the Reformation. It has become, indeed, the one way in which religion has been made real to most members of evangelical churches. So sweeping a statement must be somewhat qualified, for conversion is far older than Luther;[1] it is not confined to Protestantism and the Protestant churches themselves have not agreed in their emphasis upon it. Yet we are probably on safe ground in saying that religion has become real to the average member of the average Protestant Church more distinctly through conversion than anything else.

Conversion has of late come up for a pretty thoroughgoing examination by the psychologists, and

[1] But rather in the discipline of the Mystic as an enrichment of the spiritual life than as a door to the Communion of the Church.

their conclusions are so generally familiar as to need no restatement here. William James, in a rather informal paragraph quoted from one of his letters, states the psychologist's point of view more simply and vividly than either he or his disciples have defined their position in their more formal works. " In the case of conversion I am quite willing to believe that a new truth may be supernaturally revealed to a subject when he really asks, but I am sure that in many cases of conversion it is less a new truth than a new power gained over life by a truth always known. It is a case of the conflict of two self-systems in a personality up to that time heterogeneously divided, but in which, after the conversion crisis, the higher loves and powers come definitely to gain the upper hand and expel the forces which up to that time had kept them down to the position of mere grumblers and protesters and agents of remorse and discontent. This broader view will cover an enormous number of cases psychologically and leaves all the religious importance to the result which it has on any other theory." [1]

In Luther, Augustine and St. Paul, and a great fellowship beside, this stress of the divided self was both immediate and intense. Such as these through the consciousness of very real fault—and this is true of Augustine and St. Paul—or through a rare spiritual sensitiveness and an unusual force of aspiration—and this is true of many others—did not need any conviction of sin urged upon them from the outside. They had conviction enough of their own. But all these

[1] Letters of William James, Vol. II, p. 57.

have been men and women apart, intensely devout by nature, committed by temperament to great travail of soul and concerned, above all, for their own spiritual deliverance. But their spiritual sensitiveness is by no means universal, their sense of struggle not a normal experience for another type of personality. The demand, therefore, that all religious experience be cast in their particular mould, and that religion be made real to every one through the same travail of soul in which it was made real to them, carries with it two very great dangers: first, that some semblance of struggle should be created which does not come vitally out of experience; and second, that the resultant peace should be artificial rather than true, and therefore, should not only quickly lose its force but really result in reactions which would leave the soul of the one so misled, or better perhaps, so mishandled, emptier of any real sense of the reality of religion than to begin with.

Protestantism Found Its Authority in an Infallibly Inspired Bible

Now this is too largely what has happened in evangelical Protestantism. The " twice-born " have been set up as the standard for us all; they have demanded of their disciples the same experience as those through which they themselves have passed. Since this type of religious experience has always been the more ardent and vivid, since the churches in which least has been made of it have generally tended to fall away into routine and some want of real power, we have had, particularly since Jonathan Edwards in America and the Wesleys in England, a recurrent insistence upon it as the orthodox type of religious experience. Partly through inheritance and partly in answer to its own genius Protestantism has built up a system of theology tending to reproduce the sequence of conviction of sin, aspiration, repentance, and conversion by doctrinal pressure from the outside. The foundations of it all are in the New Testament and somewhat in the Old, but what has been built upon these foundations has been either too extended or too one-sided. In order to include in one general sense of condemnation strong enough to create an adequate desire for salvation, all sorts and conditions of people, theology has not only charged us up with our own sins which are always a sad enough account, but it has charged us up with ancestral and imputed sins.

This line of theology has been far too rigid, far too insistent upon what one may call the facts of theology, and far too blind to the facts of life. It has made much of sin in the abstract and sometimes far too little of concrete sin; it has made more of human depravity than social justice; it has failed to make allowance for varieties of temper and condition; it is partly responsible for the widespread reaction of the cults and movements of our own time.

Since so strongly an articulate system as this needed something to sustain it, Protestantism has constantly supported itself in the authority of the Old and New Testaments. It displaced one authority by another, the authority of the Church by the authority of the

Book, and in order to secure for this authority an ultimate and unquestioned power it affirmed as the beginning and the end of its use of the Scriptures their infallibility. The growth of Protestant teaching about the Bible has necessarily been complicated but we must recognize that Protestant theology and Protestant tradition have given the Bible what one may call read-in values.

At any rate after affirming the infallibility of the text Protestantism has turned back to the text for the proof of its teaching and so built up its really very great interrelated system in which, as has already been said, the power of religion over the life of its followers and the reality of religion in the experiences of its followers locked up on just such things as these: First, the experiences of conversions; second, conversion secured through the processes of Protestant indoctrination, backed up by the fervent appeal of the Protestant ministry and the pressure of Protestant Church life; and third, all this supported by an appeal to the authority of the Bible with a proof-text for every statement.

All this is, of course, to deal coldly and analytically with something which, as it has worked out in religious life, has been neither cold nor analytical. Underneath it all have been great necessities of the soul and issuing out of it all have been aspirations and devoutnesses and spiritual victories and new understandings of God and a wealth of love and goodness which are a part of the imperishable treasures of humanity for three centuries. This faith and experience have voiced themselves in moving hymns, built themselves into rare and continuing fellowships, gone abroad in missionary passion, spent themselves for a better world and looked unafraid even into the face of death, sure of life and peace beyond. But behind the great realities of our inherited religious life one may discover assumptions and processes less sure.

The Strength and Weakness of This Position

Once more, this inherited faith in the Bible and the systems which have grown out of it have been conditioned by scientific and philosophic understandings. The Protestant doctrine of the infallibility of the Bible assumed its authority not only in the region of religion but in science and history as well. The inherited theologies really went out of their way to give the incidental the same value as the essential. There was no place in them for growth, correction, further revelation. This statement may be challenged, it certainly needs to be qualified, for when the time for adjustment and the need of adjustment really did come the process of adjustment began to be carried through, but only at very great cost and only really by slowly building new foundations under the old. In fact the new is not in many ways the old at all, though this is to anticipate.

It is directly to the point here that the whole scheme of religion as it has come down to us on the Protestant side till within the last fifty years was at once compactly interwrought, strongly supported and unexpectedly vulnerable. The integrity of any one part of its line depended upon the integrity of every other part; its gospel went back to the Fall of Man and depended, therefore, upon the Biblical theory of the Creation and subsequent human history. If anything should challenge the scientific or historical accuracy of the book of Genesis, the doctrine of original sin would have either to be discarded or recast. If the doctrine of original sin were discarded or recast, the accepted interpretations of the Atonement went with it. With these changed or weakened the evangelical appeal must either be given new character or lose force. A system which began with the Fall on one side went on to heaven and hell on the other and even heaven and hell were more dependent upon ancient conceptions of the physical structure of the world and the skies above it than the Church was willing to recognize. The doctrine of eternal punishment particularly was open to ethical challenge.

Evangelical Protestantism the Outcome of the Whole Process

Of course all this is rather an extreme statement of the situation fifty years ago. The churches did not all agree in insisting upon a conversion; some evangelic churches were beginning to place their emphasis upon Christian nurture; they sought what is secured for the emotionally twice-born through guided growth and a larger dependence upon normal spiritual conditions, though they were at least one with their brethren in believing that those who come into Christian discipleship must in the end be greatly changed and conscious of the change; they too must possess as an assurance of the reality of their religious life a sense of peace and spiritual well-being.

The high Anglican Church approached the Latin Catholic Church in its insistence upon sacramental regeneration. This wing of the Church believed and believes still that baptism truly administered and the Holy Communion also administered in proper form and accepted in due obedience by priests belonging to some true succession, possess a mystic saving power. Just why all this should be so they are perhaps not able to explain to the satisfaction of any one save those who, for one reason or another, believe it already. But those who cannot understand sacramentarianism may dismiss it far too easily, for though there be here danger of a mechanical formulism, the sacraments themselves may become part of a spiritual discipline through which the lives of men and women are so profoundly changed as in the most clear case of conversion, manifesting often a spiritual beauty not to be found in any other conception of Christian discipleship. Our differences here are not so great as we suppose them.

There have always been liberal reactions within the Church herself, tending either toward relaxation of discipline or the more rational and simple statements of doctrine. What has been so far said would not be true of Unitarianism and Universalism in the last century. But these movements have been somehow wanting in driving power, and so, when all these qualifications are made, evangelical Protestantism has resulted in a pretty clearly recognizable type. The representative members of the representative evangelical churches all had a religious experience; some of them had been converted after much waiting at the anxious seat, or long kneeling at the altar rail; others of them had been brought through Christian teaching to the confession of their faith, but all of them were thereby reborn. They were the product of a theology which taught them their lost estate, offered them for their acceptance a mediatorial and atoning Christ, assured them that through their faith their salvation would be assured, and counselled them to look to their own inner lives for the issue of all this in a distinct sense of spiritual peace and well-being. If they doubted or questioned they were answered with proof-texts; for their spiritual sustenance they were given the services of their churches where preaching was generally central, and exhorted to grow in grace and knowledge through prayer and much reading of their Bible.

The Individual Experience of the Believer the Keystone of Evangelical Protestantism. Its Openness to Disturbing Forces

Now fine and good as all this was it was, as the event proved, not big enough to answer all the needs of the soul, nor strong enough to meet the challenge of forces which were a half century ago shaping themselves toward the almost entire recasting of great regions of human thought. It was, to begin with, unexpectedly weak in itself. Evangelical Protestantism, as has been noted, throws upon the members of Protestant churches a larger burden of individual responsibility than does the Catholic Church. The typical evangelical Protestant has had little to sustain him in his religious life save his sense of reconciliation with God, from whom possibly he never vitally thought himself to have been estranged, and a consequent spiritual peace.

His church promises him nothing except teaching, inspiration, comradeship, an occasion for the confession of his faith and some opportunity for service. His ministers are only such as he; they may exhort but they dare not absolve. He is greatly dependent, then, for his sense of the reality of religion upon his own spiritual states. If he is spiritually sensitive and not too much troubled by doubt, if he possesses a considerable capacity for religious understanding, if his Bible is still for him the authoritative word of God, if his church meets his normal religious needs with a reasonable degree of adequacy, if he is resolute in purpose and if he has no excessively trying experiences in the face of which his faith breaks down, and if the cares of this world, the deceitfulness of riches, or the strain of poverty do not too much distract him (and this is a long and formidable list of ifs) then he is faithful in his church relationships and personally devout. He grows in grace and knowledge and the outcome of it all is a religious character admirable in manifold ways, steadfast and truthful in good works.

The fact that in spite of all hindrances the Protestant churches do go on, registering from decade to decade a varying statistical growth with a strongly organized life and a great body of communicants who find in the religious life thus secured to them the true secret of interior peace and their true source of power, is itself a testimony to the massive reality of the whole system. And yet the keystone of the great structure is just the individual experience of the individual believer, conditioned upon his longing for deliverance and his personal assurance that he has found, through his faith in his church's gospel, what he seeks.

If anything should shake the Protestant's confidence in his creed or his Bible, or if his own inner experiences should somehow fail in their sense of sustaining reality, then all the structure of his religion begins to weaken.

If one may use and press a suggestive figure, here is a religious structure very much like Gothic architecture; its converging arches of faith and knowledge lock up upon their keystones and the thrust of the whole great structure has been met and conquered by flying buttresses. In other words, sustaining forces of accredited beliefs about science, history and human nature have been a necessary part of the entire system and the temple of faith thus sustained may be weakened either through some failure in the keystone of it which is inner experience, or the flying buttresses of it which are these accepted systems of science, history, philosophy and psychology.

Readjustment of Both Catholic and Protestant Systems Inevitable

Out of such elements as these, then, through such

inheritances and disciplines the representative religious consciousness of American Protestantism of the end of the nineteenth century had been created. It rooted itself in elements common to all religion. it inherited practically the whole content of the Old Testament, it invested Hebraic systems of sacrifice with typical meanings and Jewish prophecy with a mystic authority. It was in debt to St. Paul and Augustine for its theology. Its cosmogony was 4,000 years old and practically uninfluenced by modern science, or else at odds with it. It was uncritical in its acceptance of the supernatural and trained on the whole to find its main line of evidence for the reality of religion in the supernatural. It made more of the scheme of deliverance which St. Paul found in the Crucifixion of Jesus than the ethics of the Gospels. It was mystic in its emphasis upon an inner testimony to the realities it offered. For the Protestant it locked up unexpectedly upon the infallible authority of the Bible and for the Catholic upon the inerrancy of the Church. It was out of the current of the modern temper in science and philosophy generally. Its conceptions of the probable fate of the world were Jewish and of the future life were medieval, and perhaps the strangest thing in it all was the general unconsciousness of its dependence upon assumptions open to challenge at almost every point and the process of profound readjustment upon the threshold of which it stood.

It is almost impossible to disentangle the action of the two sets of strain whih have within the last half century been brought to bear upon it. Each has reacted upon the other. Perhaps the best thing to do is to consider the forces which for the last two generations have been challenging and reshaping inherited faiths, and then to consider the outcome of it all in the outstanding religious attitudes of our own time.

II

NEW FORCES AND OLD FAITHS

WITHIN the last fifty years particularly the fundamentals of the Christian faith have not only come up for reëxamination but have been compelled to adapt themselves to facts and forces which have gone farther toward recasting them than anything for a millennium and a half before. The Reformation went deep but it did not go to the bottom. There are differences enough in all reason between Protestantism and Catholicism, but their identities are deeper still. The world of Martin Luther and John Calvin was not essentially different in its outlook upon life from the world of Augustine and Athanasius. The world of Jonathan Edwards was much the same as the world of John Calvin and the world of 1850 apparently much the same as the world of Jonathan Edwards. There was, of course, an immense difference in the mechanism with which men were working but an unexpectedly small difference in their ruling ideas.

The Readjustments of Christian Faith More Far-reaching in the Last Fifty Years Than for a Thousand Years Before; Science Releases the Challenging Forces

We should not, of course, underestimate the contribution of the Reformation to the breaking up of the old order.   It left the theologies more substantially unchanged than Protestantism has usually supposed, but it did mark the rise of changed attitudes toward authority.   The reformers themselves did not accept without protest the spirit they released.   They imposed new authorities and obediences upon their churches; they distrusted individual initiative in spiritual things and the more democratic forms of church organization.   John Calvin sought in his Institutes to vindicate the law-abiding character of his new gospel; Luther turned bitterly against the German peasants in their demand for a most moderate measure of social justice; the Anglican leaders exiled the Pilgrims; the Puritan drove the Quaker out of Boston through an instinctive distrust of inward illumination as a safe guide for faith and religious enthusiasm as a sound basis for a new commonwealth.   But the spirit was out of the bottle and could not be put back.

The right of the individual to make his own religious inquiries and reach his own religious conclusions was little in evidence for almost two hundred years after the Reformation, partly because the reactions of the post-Reformation period made the faithful generally content to rest in what had already been secured, partly because traditional authority was still strong, and very greatly because there was neither in history, philosophy nor science new material upon which the mind might exercise itself.   We may take 1859, almost exactly two hundred years after the final readjustments of the Reformation period, as the point of departure for the forces which have so greatly

modified our outlook upon our world and our understanding of ourselves; not that the date is clean-cut,
for we see now how many things had already begun
to change before Darwin and the Origin of Species.

Darwin's great achievement is to have suggested the
formula in which science and history have alike been
restated. He had no thought at all that what he was
doing would reach so far or change so much. He
simply supposed himself, through patient and exhaustive study, to have accounted for the rich variety of
life without the supposition of a special creation for
each form. But the time was ripe and longing for
what he supplied and his hypothesis was quickly taken
and applied in almost every field of thought. Nor
does it greatly matter that Darwinism has been and
may be still greatly modified. We have come under
the spell of evolution. Our universe is no longer a
static thing; it is growing and changing. Our imaginations are impressed by long sequences of change,
each one of them minute in itself but in the mass capable of accounting for immense transformations. Darwin's initiative released the scientific temper which
has been the outstanding characteristic of our own
age. The physicist, the chemist and the biologist re-
related their discoveries in the light of his governing
principle and supplied an immense body of fact for
further consideration. Geology was reborn, the records of the rocks came to have a new meaning, every
broken fossil form became a word, maybe a paragraph, for the retelling of the past of the earth.

Astronomy supplied cosmic backgrounds for ter-

restrial evolution and Physics became a kind of court
of appeal for both. The physicist proclaimed the conservation of energy, reduced seeming solidities to underlying force and resolved force itself into ultimate
and tenuous unities. The processes thus discovered
and related seemed to be self-sufficient. No need to
bring in anything from the outside; unbroken law, unfailing sequence were everywhere in evidence. Where
knowledge failed speculation bridged the gap. One
might begin with a nebula and go on in unbroken sequence to Plato or Shakespeare without asking for
either material, law or force which was not in the
nebula to begin with. Man himself took his own
place in the majestic procession; he, too, was simply
the culmination of a long ascent, with the roots of
his being more deeply in the dust than he had ever
dreamed and compelled to confess himself akin to
what he had aforetime scorned.

The Reaction of Evolution Upon Religion

All our old chronologies became incidental in a
range of time before which even imagination grew
dizzy. We found fragments of the skulls of our ancestors in ancient glacial drifts and the traditional
6,000 years since creation hardly showed on the dial
upon which Geology recorded its conclusions. There
is no need to follow in detail how all this reacted upon
religion. The accepted religious scheme of things was
an intricately interlocking system irresistible in its
logic as long as the system remained unchallenged in
its crucial points. If these should begin to be doubted

then the Christian appeal would have lost, for the time at least, a most considerable measure of its force. The inner peace which we have already seen to be the keystone of the Protestant arch grew in part out of the sense of a universal condemnation from which the believer was happily saved; this in turn was conditioned by the unquestioned acceptance of the Genesis narrative. We can see clearly enough now that Christianity, and Protestant Christianity especially, really depended upon something deeper than all this. Still for the time being all these things were locked up together and once the accepted foundations of theology began to be questioned far-reaching adjustments were inevitable and the time of readjustment was bound to be marked by great restlessness and confusion.

The evolutionary hypothesis profoundly affected man's thought about himself. It challenged even more sharply his thought about God. Atheism, materialism and agnosticism are an old, old trinity, but they had up to our own time been at the mercy of more positive attitudes through their inability to really answer those insurgent questions: Whence? Whither? and Why? Creation had plainly enough demanded a creator. When Napoleon stilled a group of debating officers in Egypt by pointing with a Napoleonic gesture to the stars and saying, " Gentlemen, who made all these? " his answer had been final. Paley's old-fashioned turnip-faced watch with its analogies in the mechanism of creation had supplied an irresistible argument for a creation according to design and a designing creator. But now all this was changed. If Napoleon could have ridden out from his august tomb, reassembled his officers from the dust of their battlefields and resumed the old debate, the officers would have been apparently in the position to answer—" Sire, they made themselves." Our universe seemed to be sufficient unto itself.

We have reacted against all this and rediscovered God, if indeed we had ever lost Him, but this ought not to blind those who have accomplished the great transition to the confusion of faith which followed the popularization of the great scientific generalizations, nor ought it to blind us to the fact that much of this confusion still persists. Christian theism was more sharply challenged by materialism and agnosticism than by a frankly confessed atheism. Materialism was the more aggressive; it built up its own great system, posited matter and force as the ultimate realities, and then showed to its own satisfaction how everything that is is just the result of their action and interaction. Nor did materialism pause upon the threshold of the soul itself. Consciousness, so conceived, was a by-product of the higher organization of matter, and we ourselves a spray flung up out of the infinite ocean of being to sparkle for a moment in the light and then fall back again into the depths out of which we had been borne.

Those who so defined us made us bond-servants of matter and force from birth to death though they drew back a little from the consequences of their own creeds and sought to save a place for moral freedom and responsibility and a defensible altruism. It is doubtful if they succeeded. Materialism affected greatly the practical conduct of life. It offered its own characteristic values; possession and pleasure became inevitably enough the end of action, and action itself, directed toward such ends, became the main business of life. Science offered so fascinating a field for thought as to absorb the general intellectual energy of the generation under the spell of it; the practical application of science to mechanism and industry with the consequent increase in luxury and convenience, absorbed the force of practical men.

It naturally went hard with religion in a world so preoccupied. Its foundations were assailed, its premises questioned, its conclusions denied, its interests challenged. The fact that religion came through it at all is a testimony both to the unconquerable force of faith and the unquenchable need of the soul for something greater than the scientific gospel revealed or the achievements of science supplied.

The Reaction of Biblical Criticism Upon Faith

The first front along which the older faith met the impact of new forces was scientific; the second drive was at a more narrow but, as far as religion goes, an even more strategic front. The Bible had to submit to those processes of inquiry and criticism which had so greatly altered the scientific outlook. The Old and New Testaments, as has been said, supplied really the basal authority for the whole Protestant order, and speaking merely as a historian one is well within the facts when one says that even before the enlightenment of the last two generations the traditional way of thinking about the Bible had not proved satisfactory. The more free-minded were conscious of its contradictions; they could not reconcile its earlier and later moral idealisms; they found in it as much to perplex as to help them. Some of them, therefore, disowned it altogether and because it was tied up in one bundle with religion, as they knew religion, they disowned religion at the same time. Others who accepted its authority but were unsatisfied with current interpretations of it sought escape in allegorical uses of it. (We shall find this to be one of the distinct elements in Christian Science.) But after all it did answer the insistent questions, Whence? and Whither? and Why? as nothing else answered them. Therefore, in spite of challenge and derelict faith and capricious interpretations and forced harmonies it still held its own. Directly science began to offer its own answers to Whence? and Whither? and Why? curiosity found an alternative. Science had its own book of genesis, its own hypothesis as to the creation of man, its own conclusions as to his ascent. These had a marvellously emancipating and stimulating power; they opened, as has been said, vast horizons; they affected philosophy; they gave a new content to poetry, for the poet heard in the silences of the night:

> " Æonian music measuring out
> The steps of Time—the shocks of Chance—
> The blows of Death."

The challenge of science to the book of Genesis

specifically and to the miraculous narratives with which both the Old and the New Testaments are veined more generally, doubtless stimulated Biblical criticism, but the time was ripe for that also. The beginnings of it antedate the scientific Renaissance, but the freer spirit of the period offered criticism its opportunity, the scientific temper supplied the method and the work began.

Inherited faith has been more directly affected by Biblical criticism than by the result of scientific investigation and the generalizations based thereon. The Bible had been the average man's authority in science and history as well as faith. That statement naturally needs some qualification, for before evolution took the field it was possible not only to reconcile a fair knowledge of the natural sciences with the Bible, but even, as in the argument for design, to make them contributory to Bible teaching. But evolution changed all that and it was really through the impact of the more sweeping scientific conclusions upon his Bible that the average man felt their shock upon his faith. If he had been asked merely to harmonize the genesis of the new science with the genesis of the Old Testament he would have had enough to occupy his attention, though perhaps he might have managed it. The massive mind of Gladstone accomplished just that to its own entire satisfaction.

But the matter went deeper. A wealth of slowly accumulated knowledge was brought to bear upon the Scriptures and a critical acumen began to follow these old narratives to their sources. There is no need here to follow through the results in detail. They[1] were seen to have been drawn from many sources, in some cases so put together that the joints and seams were plainly discernible. One wonders how they had so long escaped observation. The Bible was seen to contain contributory elements from general ancient cultures; its cosmogony the generally accepted cosmogony of the time and the region; its codes akin to other and older codes. It contained fragments of old songs and the old lore of the common folk. It was seen to record indisputably long processes of moral growth and spiritual insight. Its prophets spoke out of their time and for their time. It was plainly enough no longer an infallible dictation to writers who were only the automatic pens of God, it was a growth rooted deep in the soil out of which it grew and the souls of those who created it. The fibres of its main roots went off into the darkness of a culture too long lost ever to be quite completely understood. It was no longer ultimate science or unchallenged history.

We have come far enough now to see that nothing really worth while has been lost in this process of reinterpretation, and much has been gained. If, as the French say in one of their luminous proverbs, to understand is to pardon, to understand is also to be delivered from doubts and forced apologies and misleading harmonies and the necessity of defending the indefensible. In our use of the Bible, as in every other

---

[1] The Old Testament narratives particularly. The results of New Testament criticism have not yet fully reached the popular mind.

region of life, the truth has made us free. It possesses still—the Bible—the truth and revelation and meaning for life it always possessed. We are gradually realizing this and gaining in the realization. But the Bible has been compelled to meet the challenge of an immensely expanded scientific and historical knowledge. We have had to test its supposed authority as to beginnings by Astronomy, Geology and Biology; we have had to test its history by the methods and conclusions of modern historical investigation. The element of the supernatural running through both the Old and New Testaments has been compelled to take into account that emphasis upon law and ordered process which is, perhaps more than any other single thing, the contribution of science to the discipline of contemporaneous thought.

The Average Man Loses His Bearings

The whole process has been difficult and unsettling. There was and is still a want of finality in the conclusions of Biblical scholars. It needed and needs still more study than the average man is able to give to understand their conclusions; it needed and it needs still a deal of patient, hard, clear-visioned thinking to win from the newer interpretations of the Bible that understanding and acceptance of its value which went with the inherited faith. The more liberal-minded religious teachers doubtless very greatly overestimate the penetration of popular thought already accomplished, by what seems to them a familiar commonplace. The New Testament is still, even for the

thoroughgoing consideration of the power of suggestion upon bodily states, and eventually to formulate, as they have been able, both the laws of suggestion and the secret of its power. Telepathy and psychic phenomena generally have also offered a rich field to the student of the abnormal and psychology has broadened its investigations to include all these conditions. That is to say, the border-land phenomena of consciousness as stressed and manifested in the more bizarre cults have really supplied the material upon which the new psychology has been working, and the psychologist to-day is seriously trying to explain a good many things which his predecessors, with their hard and fast analyses of the mind and its laws, refused to take seriously.

They concede that a complete psychology must have a place in it for the abnormal as well as the normal, and for the exceptional as well as for the staid and universally accepted. Those who have been fathering new religions and seeking to make the abnormal normal have been quick to avail themselves of the suggestions and permissions in the new psychology. Once we have crossed the old and clearly defined frontiers, almost anything seems possible. Personality, we are now taught, is complex, far-reaching, and is really, like a floating iceberg, more largely below the sea level of consciousness than above it. How far it extends and what connections it makes in these its hidden depths, no one of us may know. Normal consciousness, to change the figure, is just one brilliantly illuminated center in a world of shadow deepening into darkness. The light grows more murky, the shadows more insistent, as we pass down, or out, or back from that illumined center. We cannot tell how much of the shadow is really a part of us, nor do we dare to be dogmatic about what may, or may not, there be taking place.

Indeed, we may fill the shadows with almost anything which caprice or desire may suggest. Our curiously inventive minds have always loved to fill in our ignorances with their creations. We formerly had the shadowed backgrounds of the universe to populate with the creatures of our fear or fancy, but now, strangely enough, since science has let in its light upon the universe psychology has given us the subconscious as a region not yet subdued to law or shot through with light. And the prophets of new cults and border-land movements have taken advantage of this. "Since there is," they say in substance, "so much in life of which we are not really conscious, and since there are hints within us of strange powers, how can we set limits to what we may either be or do, and may not one man's caprice be as reasonable as another man's reason?"

The popularization of the new psychology has thus created a soil finely receptive to the unusual. Without understanding what has been accomplished in the way of investigation, and with little accurate knowledge of what has actually been tested out, there is amongst us a widespread feeling that almost anything is possible. Here also we may end in a sentence by saying that present-day psychology with its wide sweep of law, its recognition of the abnormal, its acceptance of and insistence upon the power of suggestion, its recognition of the subconscious and its tendency to assign thereto a great force of personal action, has broken down old certainties and given a free field to imagination. It has, more positively, taught us how to apply the laws of mental action to the more fruitful conduct of life, and so supplied the basis for the cults which make much of efficiency and self-development. It has also lent new meaning to religion all along the line.

The Influence of Philosophy and the Social Situation

How far contemporaneous philosophy has affected inherited faith or supplied a basis for new religious development, is more difficult to say. Beyond debate philosophic materialism has greatly influenced the religious attitude of multitudes of people just as the reactions against it have supplied the basis for new religious movements. Pragmatism, affirming that whatever works is true, has tended to supply a philosophic justification for whatever seems to work, whether it be true or not, and it has beside tended to give us a world where little islands of understandings have taken, as it were, the place of a continuous continent of truth. The tendencies of the leaders of new cults have been to take the material which science and psychology have supplied and build them into philosophies of their own; they have not generally been able or willing to test themselves by the conclusions of more disciplined thinkers.

New Thought has undoubtedly been affected by the older idealisms—Berkeley's for example—while James and Royce have supplied congenial material. The movements are generally selective. New Thought uses James' applied psychology and possibly Royce's Absolute, but does not consistently confine itself to any one system. Philosophy also has been itself of late working in a pretty rarified region. Its problems have not been the problems of the common mind. It has been trying to find out how we know, to relate the inner and the outer world, and in general to account for things which the average man takes for granted, and in the understanding of which he is more hindered than helped by the current philosophy of the schools. It takes philosophy a good while to reach the man in the street, and even then its conclusions have to be much popularized and made specific before they mean much for him. We shall know better fifty years from now what philosophy is doing for religion and life than we know to-day. There are, however, as has been said, aspects of philosophy which religion generally is beginning to take into account.

The failure of Christianity to create for itself a distinctly Christian environment has also had much to do with dissolving old religious stabilities. Strongly felt social injustices are releasing forces of discontent and creating a fertile soil for revolutionary experiment, though it must be said that modern religious cults and movements have not gained so much from this particular form of discontent as have those movements which look toward radical social readjustment.

But the whole situation has created a shaken state of public opinion. The fierceness of modern competition, industrially and economically, finally carried through to the tragic competition of a world war, has put our tempers on edge. The extremes of wealth and poverty and the baffling fluctuations in modern industry have brought the existing order into disrepute. The very great number of the socially unfit and the grievous number of social misfits, along with crime and poverty and the deposit of human sediment in our cities, not only trouble men of good will but create a human element easily misled. Such conditions as these are in such painful contrast with the ideals of the Gospel, the spirit of Christianity and even the potential productive force of modern society as to lead many to believe that something is radically wrong. Many are persuaded that Christianity as now organized and led is socially sterile; they have withdrawn themselves from the church; many of them have become its mordant critics; the more extreme of them have disowned religion as well as its organized form, and the violently radical would dethrone any conception of the Divine and take the word God out of our vocabulary. This extreme group has not for the most part associated itself with the new religious movement, but here at least has been a disintegrating force.

An Age of Confusion

In such ways as these, then, the accepted religious order identified with historic Catholicism and Protestantism has in the last fify years been greatly altered.

Science, Biblical criticism, psychology and philosophy, and social unrest have all had their share in making people impatient of the inherited order, or doubtful or defiant of it. We have been asked to relate our old creeds and confidences to new insights and understandings. The old answers to the questions Whence? and Whither? and Why? have been challenged by new answers; our horizons have been pushed back in every direction and a strange sense of mystery both in personality and the external order has perplexed and stimulated us. Along with all this and in no little way growing out of it, has gone impatience of discipline and an undue haste to gain the various goods of life.

Evolution misled us, to begin with. If the longing for deliverance be one of the driving forces in religious life, then the vaster scientific conclusions of the latter part of the nineteenth century offered a new definition of deliverance. It was not, after all, so much in the travail of the soul as in a serene and effortless self-commitment to a power, not ourselves, which makes for righteousness, that we were to be saved. We had only to push out upon tides which asked of us neither rudder nor oar, to be brought to our appointed havens. How greatly we have been disillusioned in all this and how bitterly we have been taught that life is not so much a drifting with the tide as making brave headway against it, we all know well enough to-day. Somewhere back of a vast deal in these modern religious cults and movements, is the smug optimism, now taking one form and now another, which was the misleading bequest of the nineteenth century to the twentieth.

The great scientific discoveries and their application to the mechanism of life led the nineteenth century to believe that nothing was impossible. Everything we touched became plastic beneath our touch save possibly ourselves; there seemed to be no limit to what man might do and he consequently assumed that there was no limit to what he might become. He disassociated his hopes from both his disciplines and experiences; everything seemed not only possible but easily possible. A general restlessness of temper, due in part to the breaking up of the inherited order, in part to the ferment of new ideas and in part to a general relaxing of discipline, began to manifest itself.

The demoralizing influence of migratory populations ought not to be overlooked in this connection. In all the Western nations there has been an outstanding growth of industrial city populations due to changing economic conditions. The steadying influences of old environments have been lost, the influence of the new environment is too stimulating at its best and demoralizing at its worst. Our cities are not kind to home life; too often they do not supply a proper physical setting for it. The specialization of hard driven industries takes the creative joy out of work and leads to an excess of highly commercialized pleasure. The result is the modern city worker, never living long enough in one place to create for himself a normal social environment, always anxious about his economic future, restless, too largely alternating between strenuous work and highly coloured pleasure and much open, through temperament and circumstance, to the appeal of whatever promises him a new experience or a new freedom.

The Lure of the Short Cut

Dean Inge in a recent study of the contribution of the Greek temper to religion has drawn a strong, though deeply shadowed picture of the disorganization of modern life through such influences as these. " The industrial revolution has generated a new type of barbarism, with no roots in the past. For the second time in the history of Western Europe, continuity is in danger of being lost. A generation is growing up, not uneducated, but educated in a system which has little connection with European culture in its historical development. The Classics are not taught; the Bible is not taught; history is not taught to any effect. What is even more serious, there are no social traditions. The modern townsman is *déraciné:* he has forgotten the habits and sentiments of the village from which his forefathers came. An unnatural and unhealthy mode of life, cut off from the sweet and humanizing influences of nature, has produced an unnatural and unhealthy mentality, to which we shall find no parallels in the past. Its chief characteristic is profound secularity or materialism. The typical town artisan has no religion and no superstitions; he has no ideals beyond the visible and tangible world of senses." [1]

[1] " The Legacy of Greece," p. 38.

Writing as an Englishman Dean Inge did not note the equally unsettling influence of migratory races. The European peasant in Detroit or Chicago or New York is still more *déraciné*. He has not only left the soil in whose culture his ancestors had been established for generations, he has left the tradition and the discipline which have made him what he is. The necessary readjustments are immensely difficult. For the first generation they are largely a dumb puzzle, or a dull, aching homesickness or a gray laborious life whose outcome must be often strangely different from their dreams, but for the second generation the whole experience is a heady adventure in freedom not easy to analyze though social workers generally are agreed that the children of the immigrant, belonging neither to the old nor the new, are a disturbing element in American life. A city like Detroit, in which this is being written, where both movements combine, the American country and village dweller coming to a highly specialized industrial center and the European immigrant to an entirely new environment, illustrates the complex issue of the whole process.

It is just to note that the Catholic immigrant, finding in his Church the one homelike thing, is often a better Catholic in America than he was at home. A Protestant writer without accurate information would not dare to generalize on the religious dislocation of the second Catholic generation. But there must be a very great loss. The large non-churched elements in our population must be in part due to Catholic disintegration as they are certainly due to Protestant disintegration. And new movements find their opportunity in this whole group. In general, society, through such influences, has grown impatient of discipline, scornful of old methods, contemptuous of experience and strangely unwilling to pay the price of the best. The more unstable have surrendered themselves to the lure of the short cut; they are persuaded that there are quick and easy roads to regions of well-being which had before been reached only through labour and discipline and much travail of body, mind and soul.

Popular Education Has Done Little to Correct Current Confusions

Nor has the very great extension of popular education really done much to correct this; it seems rather to intensify it, for education shared and shares still the temper of the time. Our education has been more successful generally in opening vistas than in creating an understanding of the laws of life and the meaning of experience; it has given us a love of speculation without properly trained minds; it has furnished us with the catch words of science and philosophy but has not supplied, in the region of philosophy particularly, the corresponding philosophic temper. It has, above all, been fruitful in unjustified self-confidence, particularly here in America. We have confused a great devotion to higher education and the widespread taking of its courses with the solid fruition of it in mental discipline. America particularly has furnished for a long time now an unusual opportunity for bizarre and capricious movements. Nothing overtaxes the credulity of considerable elements in our population. Whatever makes a spacious show of philosophy is sure to find followers and almost any self-confident prophet has been able to win disciples, no matter to what extremes he goes.

This has not been equally true of older civilizations with a more clearly defined culture or a more searching social discipline. Something must be lacking in the education of a people in which all this is so markedly possible. The play of mass psychology (one does not quite dare to call it mob psychology) also enters into the situation. Democracy naturally makes much of the verdict of majorities. Any movement which gains a considerable number of adherents is pretty sure to win the respect of the people who have been taught to judge a cause by the number of those who can be persuaded to adopt it. This generally unstable temper, superficial, restless, unduly optimistic, open to suggestion and wanting in the solid force of great tradition has joined with the recasting of Science, Theology, Psychology and Philosophy, to open the door for the entrance of new religions, and in general, to so unsettle the popular mind as to make almost anything possible.

The Churches Lose Authority

In the field of religion certain well-defined consequences have either followed or accompanied the whole process. There has been, to begin with, a loosening of church ties. The extent of all this has been somewhat covered up by the reasonable growth of the historic churches. In spite of all the difficulties which they have been called upon to face, the statistics generally have been reassuring. The churches are attended in the aggregate by great numbers of people who are untroubled by doubts. Such as these have little sympathy with the more restless or troubled, and little patience with those who try to understand the restless and troubled; they do not share the forebodings of those who look with a measure of apprehension upon the future of Christianity. As far as they recognize disturbing facts at all they are very much like Carlyle who, when told that Christianity was upon its last legs, said, " What of that? Christianity has always been upon its last legs." And perhaps their simple faith and hope are more to the point than many opposing attitudes. The churches have grown faster than the population, or at least they had at the last census. More than that, there has been a marked increase in church activity. The churches are better organized; they are learning the secret of coöperation; they are reaching out in more directions and all of them, even the more democratic, are more hard driven from the top.

The result of all this has been a great show of action, though it is difficult now to say whether the real results of this multiplied activity have been commensurate in spiritual force and ethical fruitage with the intensity of their organized life. (The writer thinks not.) But through all this we discern, nevertheless, a marked weakening of authority as far as the Church goes and a general loosening of ties; though the churches in the regions of finance and organization drive harder than they used to drive, in the matter of creed and conduct they are driving with an easy rein. Denominational loyalties are relaxed; there is much changing from one denomination to another and within the denominations and individual churches there is, of course, a substantial proportion of membership which is only nominal.

Efforts at Reconstruction Within the Church

There are those who view with apprehension the whole future of religion. They believe that the foundations of the great deep are breaking beneath us, that Christianity must be profoundly recast before it can go on prevailingly, and they are reaching in one direction and another for constructive changes, but all this within the frontiers of historic Christianity and the Church. They want church unity but they still want a church; they want a new theology but still a theology; they want new applications of religion but still substantially the old religion. There was more of this during the war than just now. Such a book as Orchard's " Future of Religion," perhaps the most thoughtful analysis of conditions given us for a long time, was born of the war itself and already many of its anticipations seem to miss the point. Such expectations of wholesale religious reconstruction leave out of account the essential conservatism of human nature, a conservatism more marked in religion than anywhere else.

There is also a strong and telling group which is

seeking so to recast and interpret inherited faiths as to make them more consonant to modern needs and more hospitable to new understandings. Such as these have accepted gladly the tested conclusions of science, the results of Biblical criticism and the revealing suggestion of both psychology and philosophy; they have sought to disentangle the essential from the unessential, the enduring from the transient. They have found in science not the foe but the friend of religion. Those intimations of unfailing force, those resolutions of the manifold phases of action and reality toward which science is reaching have seemed to them a discovery of the very presence and method of God, and they have found in just such regions as these new material for their faith. They have dealt reverently with the old creeds, for they have seen that the forms which Christianity has taken through the centuries have grown out of enduring experiences and needs never to be outgrown, and that their finality is the finality of the deep things of the soul itself. They have been able, therefore, to make new truth tributary to old faith and to interpret the central affirmations of Christianity in terms of present-day facts. They have sought to share their conclusions with others and they have really been able to carry Christianity through the transitional period of the last fifty years and continue it open-minded, strongly established, reverent and enriched rather than impoverished.

What they have done has been doubly hard, once through the sheer difficulty of the task itself, and once through the hostile and too often abusive temper with which they and their endeavours have been opposed. None the less, they have saved for Christendom a reasonable faith. Science has of late gone half-way to meet them. It is rather painfully revising a good many of its earlier conclusions and on the whole walking rather humbly just now before its God, recognizing that the last word has not yet really been said about much of anything.

An Age of Doubt and a Twilight-Zone in History

But the apparently unchanged traditions of the older forms of faith and the relatively strong position of the Church must not blind us to the generally disorganized condition of religion to-day. There is much in evidence a body of doubt which clouds the outlook of multitudes upon religion generally. Beyond debate a kind of eclipse of faith began to draw across the Western world so early as the middle of the last century. The militant skepticism of the brilliant group of younger poets who sang their defiances in the first two decades of the nineteenth century to a world which professed itself duly shocked, is wholly different from the sadness with which the more mature singers of two generations later announce their questioning and their disillusionment. The difference is just the difference between Shelley and Matthew Arnold. There is a philosophic depth in this later music which the former wholly lacked. Arnold speaks for his time when he announces himself as standing between two worlds, one dead, the other powerless to be born. A profound disillusionment expressed itself in great ranges of later nineteenth century literature and confirmed the more sensitive and despairing in a positive pessimism, strangely contrasted to the self-assertive temper of the science and industry of the period. It would need a pretty careful analysis to follow all this to its roots. Something of it no doubt was due to the inability of poet and philosopher to reconcile their new understanding of life and the universe with the old religious forms but more of it was likely due to some deep exhaustion of spiritual force, an exhaustion which has from time to time marked transitional periods in the development of cultures and civilizations.

There have always been twilight zones in history, times in which the force of the old had spent itself and nothing new had come to take its place. We are beginning to see now that we too have been passing through a twilight zone whose contrasts are all the more dramatic through the more than tropic swiftness with which the high lights of the Victorian period darkened into the distractions and disillusionments of our own time. The best one can say is that there was on the part of the more sensitive a widespread anticipation of all this, as if the chill of a coming shadow had fallen first of all upon them, and beyond debate, not a little of the doubt which has been so marked a feature of the last two generations in literature generally, and in the attitude of a great number of people toward religion, has been due to just this.

The Hunger of the Soul and the Need for Faith Persist

And yet, since religion is so inextinguishable a thing,

changing forces and attitudes have still left untouched
the hunger of the soul and the need of men for faith.
Indeed the very restlessness of the time, the breaking
up of the old orders, the failure of the old certainties,
has, if anything, deepened the demand for religious
reality and there has been in all directions a marked
turning to whatever offered itself as a plausible substitute for the old, and above all a turning to those
religions which in quite clearly defined ways promise
to demonstrate the reality of religion through some
sensible or tangible experience. If religion will only
work miracles and attest itself by some sign or other
which he who runs may read there is waiting for it
an eager constituency. We shall find as we go on
how true this really is, for the modern religious cult
which has gained the largest number of followers
offers the most clearly defined signs and wonders.

If religion cures your disease and you are twice
persuaded, once that you really are cured and once
that religion has done it, then you have something
concrete enough to satisfy anybody. Or if, perplexed
by death and with no faith strong enough to pierce
that veil through a persuasion of the necessity of immortality established in the very nature of things, you
are offered a demonstration of immortality through
the voices and presences of the discarnate, then, once
more, you have something concrete enough, if only
you were sure of it, to settle every doubt. And finally,
if the accepted religions are too concrete for you and
if you desire a rather vague and poetic approach to
religion made venerable by the centuries and appeal-

ingly picturesque through the personalities of those
who present it, you have in some adaptation of oriental
faith to occidental needs a novel and interesting approach to the nebulous reality which passes in the
Eastern mind for God, an approach which demands no
very great discipline and leaves a wide margin for the
play of caprice or imagination.

*Modern Religious Cults and Movements Find Their
    Opportunity in the Whole Situation. The Three
    Centers About Which They Have Organized
    Themselves*

There has been, then, as the outcome of the complex
of forces which we have been considering, a new approach to religion distinctive in our own time and in
general taking three directions determined by that
against which it has reacted, or perhaps more positively by the varying character of what it seeks. A
pretty careful analysis of modern religious cults and
movements shows that they have organized themselves, in action and reaction, around three centers
definitely related to three outstanding deficiencies of
inherited faith. I say deficiencies, though that is of
course to beg the question. We saw earlier in this
study how religion everywhere and always grows out
of some of the few central and unexpectedly simple,
though always supremely great, needs and how the
force of any religion waxes or wanes as it meets these
needs. Religion is real to the generality of us as it
justifies the ways of God to man and reveals the love
and justice of God in the whole of personal experi-

ence.   Religion is always, therefore, greatly dependent
upon its power to reconcile the more shadowed side of
experience with the Divine love and power and goodness.   It is hard to believe in a Providence whose deal-
ings with us seem neither just nor loving.   Faith
breaks down more often in the region of trying personal experience than anywhere else.

All this is as old as the book of Job but it is none
the less true because it is old.

The accepted theology which explained sin and sorrow in terms of the fall of man and covered each individual case with a blanket indictment justified by the
condemnation of the whole of humanity has lost its
force.   It depended, to begin with, on a tradition of
human beginnings which has not borne examination,
and it was beside, in spite of all the efforts to defend
it, profoundly unethical.   Calvinistic theology, moreover, made a difficult matter worse by assuming for
every individual a predestined fate reaching beyond
death itself which a man was powerless to escape.
Those chapters in the long story of theology which
record the turning and groping of minds—and souls—
enmeshed in this web of their own weaving and more
deeply entangled still in the challenging experiences
of life itself are among the most pathetic and arresting in the whole story of human thought.   We ought
to recognize more clearly than we have generally done
and confess more frankly that our inherited explanations of the problems of pain and sorrow have been
markedly unsatisfactory and have greatly contributed
to the justifiable reaction against them.

One group of modern religious cults and movements, then, has found its opportunity just here. Christian Science and kindred cults are just an attempt to reconcile the love and goodness of God with pain, sickness, sorrow, and to a lesser degree with sin. How they do this remains to be seen, but the force of their appeal depends upon the fact that a very considerable and constantly growing number of people believe that they have really done it. Such cults as these have also found a place for the New Testament tradition of healing; they have also appealed strongly to those who seek a natural or a pseudo-natural explanation for the miraculous elements in religion generally. They have been expectedly reinforced by the feeling for the Bible which strongly persists among those who are not able to find in the inherited Protestant position that real help in the Bible which they had been taught they should there find, and who are not, on the other hand, sufficiently acquainted with the newer interpretations of it to find therein a resolution for their doubts and a vital support for their faith. Finally, Christian Science and kindred cults offer a demonstration of the reality of religion in health and happiness, and generally, in a very tangible way of living. Here, then, is the first region in which we find a point of departure for modern religious cults and movements.

Spiritualism organizes itself around another center. Religion generally demands and offers a faith in immortality. We are not concerned here with the grounds which various religions have supplied for this faith or the arguments by which they have supported it. Generally speaking, any religion loses ground as it fails to convince its adherents of immortality, or justify their longings therefor. Any religion supplying clear and indisputable proof of immortality will command a strong following and any seeming demonstration of immortality not particularly associated with this or that religious form will organize about itself a group of followers who will naturally give up pretty much everything else and center their entire interests upon the methods by which immortality is thus supposed to be demonstrated. Now modern Spiritualism comes in just here. It professes to offer a sure proof of immortality to an age which is just scientific enough to demand something corresponding to scientific proof for the support of its faith and not scientific enough to accept all the implications of science, or to submit to its discipline. Theosophy and kindred cults are generally a quest for deliverance along other than accepted Christian lines; they substitute self-redemption for Christian atonement, and deliverance through mystical disciplines for that forgiveness of sin and assurance of salvation in which Christianity has found its peace.

There is, of course, a vast deal of action and reaction between the newer movements themselves and between the new faith and the old. There are elements common to all religions; there are frontiers where all religions meet and somewhat merge; at some point or other almost every faith touches its contrary or becomes uncertain and shifts its emphasis. Religion is always dependent upon changing tempers and very greatly upon varying personalities; it is always in flux, impatient of definitions and refusing the rigid boundary lines within which we attempt to confine it. Though it be clearly possible, therefore, to find three distinct points of departure for the whole of the border-land cults and religions, there is running through them all a certain unity of driving force. They are in general a quest for a new type of religious reality; they are largely due to certain marked inadequacies of the more accepted religious teachings and to the want of the more accepted religious experiences to satisfy certain types. They have come to light in our own time through the failure of authority in both Catholicism and Protestantism, through the failure of the accepted understandings of the Bible to satisfy those who are still persuaded that it has a real message and through the reaction of the modern spirit upon religious attitudes. They owe much to the deficiency of the traditional explanation of sin, sorrow and suffering; they owe something to the failure of Christianity to create a Christian environment; and they owe not a little to the natural longing for some positive assurance of life after death, as well as to the quest of the soul for deliverance and its longing for a satisfying communion with God. And they are reinforced in every direction by the restless and unsettled temper of a time subject to great changes of habit and outlook through the breaking up of old industrial and social orders and the impact of new forces driving in from every direction.

We shall need to relate these conditioning causes more definitely to the various cults and movements as we go on to study them, but here at least are the backgrounds against which they must be studied and the lines of testing down which they must be followed. We shall begin in our more detailed study of these movements with the modern religious quest for health and healing. But even here we shall find it worth while to trace broadly the history of faith and mental healing.

III

FAITH HEALING IN GENERAL

THOSE cults which are either founded upon faith healing or involve it have a long ancestry. George Barton Cutten's very suggestive book [1] makes that clear enough and supplies an informing mass of detail. Medical Science and Psychology have been slow to take into account the facts thus submitted, but they have of late made amends for their somewhat unaccountable delay, and we have now reached certain conclusions about which there is little controversy except, indeed, as to the range of their application. Beneath all faith healing and kindred phenomena there are three pretty clearly defined bases. First, the action or reaction of mind upon body; second, the control of mental attitudes by the complex of faith; and, as an interrelated third, the control of the lower nerve centers by suggestion.

The Bases of Faith and Mental Healing

There is an almost baffling interplay of what one may call these three controlling principles, and the exhaustive discussion of the whole subject demands the knowledge of the specialist. But we do know, to begin with, that just as there are demonstrated bodily

[1] " Three Thousand Years of Mental Healing."

approaches to both the mental and spiritual aspects of life, so there are equally undeniable mental and even spiritual approaches to physical conditions. We have here to fall back upon facts rather than upon a definite knowledge of what happens in the shadowy border-land across which the mind takes over and organizes and acts upon what is presented to it by the afferent nervous system. Nothing, for example, could be really more profound than the difference between waves of compression and rarefaction transmitted through the luminiferous ether and the translation of their impact into light. Somewhere between the retina of the eye, with its magic web of sensitive nerve ends, and the proper registering and transforming regions of the brain something happens about which Science can say no final word.

What happens in the case of light is equally true of sound and tactual sensation. That vivid and happy consciousness of well-being which we call health is just the translation of normal balances, pressures and functionings in the mechanism of the body into an entirely different order of phenomena. Health is a word of manifold meaning and if its foundations are established in the harmonious coöperation of physical processes, its superstructure rises through mental attitudes into what, for want of a more clearly defined word, we call spiritual states. Two orders meet and merge within us. Above a world of idea, insight, desire and subordination of means to ends, the whole driven by the will and saturated with emotion, a world which has its contacts with the unseen and eternal and derives its strength from the truly immaterial; below a world of material and forces in subjection to the laws of physics and chemistry and involved in the processes of the conservation and transformation of physical energy, and consciousness the clearing-house for the whole.

Cannon's Study of Emotional Reactions Upon Physical States

This interplay of body and mind has of late been made the subject of careful and long continued experimentation with a special reference to the reactions of strong emotion upon bodily states, particularly as registered in chemical changes. These experiments have been carried on with an almost incredible patience and attention to detail under the most difficult circumstances, and their conclusions seem final. Professor Walter B. Cannon of Harvard University has recently put the result of such investigation at our service in a most interesting way.[1] (It ought to be said, however, that a similar series of experiments repeated at the laboratories of the University of Chicago failed to produce the same results.)

Strong emotion affects almost every physical region, modifies almost every physical function. The normal secretion of digestive fluids is greatly increased by hunger (though here, of course, hunger itself may have a physical basis) and also by what the investi-

---

[1] "Bodily Changes in Pain, Hunger, Fear and Rage," quoted without page references.

gator calls sham feeding—food, that is, taken by an animal and so deflected as not to pass into the digestive tract at all stimulates the gastric flow quite as much as if it were actually received into the stomach. On the other hand unhappy emotional disturbance greatly retards the digestive processes. Pain, for example, results in pronounced inhibitions of the secretion of gastric juice while happy emotional states produce naturally the opposite effect. Pain is often accompanied by nausea, indeed the nausea of a sick headache may be only secondary, induced by a pain springing from quite another source than retarded digestion.

Professor Cannon's experiments are most interesting as he traces the variations of the flow of adrenal secretion induced by emotion and then retraces the effect of the chemical changes so produced upon bodily and mental states. The secretion of adrenin[1] is greatly increased by pain or excitement. The percentage of blood sugar is also greatly increased by the same causes. The heaviness of fatigue is due, as we know, to poisonous uneliminated by-products resulting from long continued or over-taxing exertion of any sort. Under the influence of fatigue the power of the muscles to respond to any kind of stimulus is greatly reduced. (It is interesting to note, however, that muscular fibre detached from the living organism and mechanically stretched and relaxed shows after a period the same decrease in contractability under stimulation.) On the other hand

[1] I follow Cannon in the form of this word.

any increase in adrenal secretion results in renewed sensitiveness to stimulation, that is by an increased power of the muscle to respond. Falling blood pressures diminish proportionately the power of muscular response. Rising blood pressure is effective " in largely restoring in fatigued structures their normal irritability " and an increase of adrenin seems to raise blood pressure by driving the blood from the interior regions of the body " into the skeleton muscles which have to meet, by extra action, the urgent demands of struggle or escape."

Adrenin is of real use in counteracting the effects of fatigue or in enabling the body to respond to some unusual call for effort. The coagulation of the blood is also affected by the same agent, that is, it coagulates very much more rapidly.[1] Coagulation is also hastened by heightened emotion; a wound does not bleed so freely when the wounded one is angry or excited. A soldier, then, in the stress of combat is not only rendered insensible to fatigue and capable of abnormal activity, but his wounds are really not so dangerous as they would otherwise be. There are here suggestions of elemental conditions having to do with struggle and survival, conditions which play their very great part in the contests of life.

Emotions set free, as has been said, larger percentages of sugar which are immediately utilized by the muscles in heightened or fatiguing effort. All these experiments point very clearly to reservoirs of power, both physical and mental, upon which we may draw

[1] Cannon thinks, however, that this effect is produced indirectly.

in times of stress and under emotional excitement.[1]
Such emotionally induced chemical actions and reactions as have been indicated release these stored
energies, render us for the time being unconscious of
fatigue and even guard us against the too rapid exhaustion of vital power. Whatever heightens emotion, therefore, modifies the very chemical structure
of the body.

The Two Doors

There are other changes as well. The breath is
quickened, the lungs are expanded, waste products are
very much more rapidly eliminated and so in answer
to summoning states of the soul the body as a whole
readjusts itself in marvellous subtle forms, mobilizing
all its forces for the contests which the emotion anticipates, or indeed which the emotion itself calls out.
And if all this seems unduly technical it is only to
bear out with something like a scientific accuracy the
statements made a little earlier that two orders meet
and merge within us and that the reactions of our
loves, our fears, or our longings upon our bodily
processes may be stated in terms of the test tube and
the chemist's scale.

Such changes as are thus registered react in turn

[1] Excessive emotional reactions upon bodily states may explain,
as Cannon suggests, the more obscure phenomena of religious
frenzy such as the ceremonial dances of savages, the " Danse
Macabre" of the Middle Ages, the feats of the whirling
dervishes, the jumping and shouting of revivalism; also, maybe,
the modern jazz.

upon mental attitudes. Fatigue produces mental depression. An accumulation of uneliminated waste darkens all our horizons; irritability of mind and soul attend physical irritability; any unhappy modification in the balance of the physical registers automatically an equally unhappy modification in the balance of the psychic. Most of us, as we come to know ourselves better, recognize marked alterations even in spiritual states which we are taught to refer to physical condition, but just as truly altered spiritual conditions produce altered physical states. There is an endless give and take and there are, therefore, two doors of approach to our pains, wearinesses and sicknesses.

The Challenge of Hypnotism

Medicine, surgery and hygiene as at present organized largely approach personal well-being from the physical side. They have for their support a body of fact and a record of accomplishment which cannot be put out of court without sheer intellectual stultification. Modern medicine has been so massively successful in dealing with disease on the basis of a philosophy which makes everything, or nearly everything, of the body and nothing or next to nothing of the mind, that medicine was in danger of becoming more sheerly materialistic than almost any other of our sciences; Physics and Chemistry had their backgrounds in which they recognized the interplay of realities too great for their formulæ and forces too subtle for their most sensitive instruments. But medicine was almost in the way of forgetting all this when it was compelled—and

that for its own good—to take account of an entirely
different set of forces.

This was, to begin with, as far as the modern
scientific approach is concerned, first made clearly apparent in Hypnotism. Hypnotism seems to be such a
modification of normal mental conditions under the
power of commanding suggestion as really for the
time being to focus consciousness and mental action
generally in one suggested line. A new set of inhibitions and permissions are thus imposed upon normal
consciousness. Attention is withdrawn from the usual
frontiers (if one may use the word) to which, consciously or subconsciously, it has always been directed
and centered upon one single thing.[1]

The hypnotized person becomes, therefore, uncon-

---

[1] Sidis defines Hypnosis as the disassociation of the superior and
inferior nerve centers. They commonly work in perfect harmony,
their blended unity forming one conscious personality. "In
hypnosis the two systems or nervous centers are disassociated, the
superior centers and the upper consciousness are inhibited or
better cut off, split off from the rest of the nervous system with
its organic consciousness, which is thus laid bare, open to the
influence of external stimuli or suggestions. . . . In hypnotic
trance . . . we have direct access to man's organic consciousness and through it to organic life itself." . . . If we broaden
this last sentence to include not only organic consciousness but the
deeper strata of personality in which not only individual but
perhaps racial experience is bedded, we have the key to a vast
range of obscure phenomena. Sidis believes that " strong permanent impressions or suggestions made on the reflex organic consciousness of the inferior centers may modify their functional
disposition, induce trophic changes, and even change organic
structure " and this in a sentence is probably what lies behind all
faith and mental healing.—" The Psychology of Suggestion," pp.
69 and 70.

scious of any reporting agencies outside the field of his abnormally focused attention. Normal conditions of pain or pleasure cease for the time to become real. Attention has been forced entirely out of normal channels and given a new direction. Then we discover, strangely enough, that though those messages of the afferent nerves cease to have any effect upon the subject, the imaginings of the subject carried back along outgoing lines produce the most unexpected results in physical states. If a postage stamp be placed upon the hand of the hypnotized subject and he be told that the stamp is a mustard plaster, the stamp reddens the skin and presently raises a blister. In other words, heightened and intensified expectant attention is able to produce the same results as an irritating agency.[1]

Changed Attention Affects Physical States

We are concerned here chiefly with the fact and it is a fact capable of far-reaching application. Of course the nature and extent of the changes thus produced are the battlegrounds of the two schools. Medical Science is quite willing to admit that while functional action may thus be modified no real organic changes can be produced. There is a border-land so much still in shadow that no final word can be said about the whole matter, but it is incontestably true that modifications of attention have a reflex in the modification of physical states.

[1] Experiments by Krafft-Ebing and Forel. To be taken with caution. See Jacoby, "Suggestion and Psycho-Therapy," p. 153.

A pain which is not registered does not, for the time being at least, exist, and if the attention can either through hypnotism or by a persistent mental discipline be withdrawn from disturbing physical reports, then the conditions which produce them will at least be left to correct themselves without interference from consciousness and since the whole tendency of disturbed physical organism is to correct itself, the whole process probably goes on more quickly as it certainly goes on with less discomfort if attention is withdrawn.[1] The assumption of health is a tremendous health-giving force and if the condition to be remedied is really due to a mental complex which needs only some strong exertion of the will or readjustment of attitude to change, then marvellous results may follow changed mental and spiritual states. The apparently dumb may speak, the apparently paralyzed rise from their beds, the shell-shocked pull themselves together and those under the bondage of their fears and their pains be set free. There are so many illustrations of all this that the fact itself is not in debate.

The Power of Faith to Change Mental Attitudes

Now since mental attitudes so react upon bodily states, whatever strongly controls mental attitudes be-

[1] Organic changes (the storm center of the controversy) may possibly be induced through a better general physical tone. Such changes would not be directly due to suggestion but to processes released by suggestion. Organic change may certainly be checked and the effect of it overcome by increased resistance. So much conservative physicians admit. How far reconstruction thus induced may go is a question for the specialist.

comes a very great factor in mental healing. There is a long line of testimony that what may be called the complex of faith does just this with unique power, for faith implies supernatural intervention. If there be anywhere an all-prevailing power whose word is law and we could really be persuaded that such a power had really intervened—even if it actually had not— on our behalf and brought its supernatural resource to bear upon our troubled case, then we should have a confidence more potent in the immediate transformation of mental attitudes than anything else we could possibly conceive. If we really believed such a power were ready to help us, if we as vividly expected its immediate help, then we might anticipate the utmost possible therapeutic reaction of mind upon body. A faith so called into action should produce arresting results, and this as a matter of investigation is true.

In following through the theories of faith healing we may take here either of two lines. The devout may assert a direct divine interposition. God is. He has the power and the will; all things are plastic to His touch; He asks only faith and, given faith enough, the thing is done and there is no explaining it. Those who believe this are not inclined to reason about it; in fact it is beyond reason save as reason posits a God who is equal to such a process and an order in which such results can be secured. This is rather an achievement of faith than reason but the Christian Church generally has held such a faith—a faith sustained by the testimony which favours it and unaffected by the testimony which challenges it. The scientific temper

which seeks economy in all its explanations and asks
only for a cause sufficient for the effect and which is,
moreover, constantly trying to relate the unknown to
the known, takes another line and finds in faith healing just one more illustration of the power of mind
over body. This does not exclude God but it discovers
Him in resident forces and finds in law the revelation
of His method. The conclusions, then, to which we
are generally coming may not only be reconciled with
a devout faith, they may, when followed through, en-
rich faith; but they do subdue the whole great matter
to a sequence of cause and effect and they are gradually finding a satisfactory explanation for what has
heretofore been deeply involved in mystery.

Just as Hypnotism, through the very dramatic abnormality of it, in altering the sensitiveness of those
physical tracts from which attention is withdrawn or
in producing physical effects through suggestive focus-
ing, has helped us to understand the part which attention plays in the flux of physical states, so our later
studies of the subconscious help us here. We do know
that a great deal may really take place in personality
of which consciousness takes no account. Consciousness in its most active phases is alert, purposeful and
preoccupied with the immediate concern of the moment. Consciousness heeds commands and takes account of such conditions as strongly assert themselves,
but does not in its full drive take much account of suggestion unless the suggestion possesses unusual force.
Suggestions usually need leisurely turning over in the
mind and the mind commonly refers them—often

without knowing it—to those regions of mental action which lie beneath the threshold of strongly focused consciousness.

But suggestion does not thereby cease to work. It starts processes all its own which go on till they are worked through. After a longer or shorter period of incubation the outcome of suggestion is lifted into the light of consciousness, often to produce results all the more striking because we cannot explain them to ourselves or any one else. All this does not withdraw such phenomena from the realm of law; it only clothes them with the mystery of the unknown and extends the fields in which they may operate. Proper suggestion let fall into these unknown depths or improper suggestion as well, becomes an incalculable force in shaping the ends of life. We have here, then, well attested truths or laws—it is difficult to know what to call them—which help us to understand the bases of faith healing or mental healing by suggestion. Now directly we turn to such records as remain to us we find that such forces as these have been in action from the very beginning. All disease was in early times referred generally to spirit possession. If only the evil spirit could be exorcised the patient would get well and the priest was, of course, the proper person to undertake this. Religion and medicine were, therefore, most intimately united to begin with and healing most intimately associated with magic. The first priests were doctors and the first doctors were priests and what they did as priests and what they did as doctors were alike unreasonable and capricious.

The priest and his church have very unwillingly surrendered the very great hold over the faithful which
this early association of medicine and religion made
possible. Any order or institution which can approach
or control humanity through the longing of the sick
for health, has an immense and unfailing empire.

Demon Possession the Earliest Explanation of Disease

There are, says Cutten, three fairly well defined
periods in the history of Medicine. The first, beginning as far back as anything human begins and coming down to the end of the second century; the second,
ending with the fifteenth or sixteenth centuries; and
the third from perhaps the sixteenth century on. The
second period, he adds, was by far the most sterile and
stationary of the three " largely due to the prohibitive
attitude of the Church. The science of Medicine, then,
is almost wholly the result of the investigations and
study of the last period. This means that medicine
is one of the youngest of the sciences, while from the
very nature of the case it is one of the oldest of the
arts."

Demon possession was, as has been said, the earliest
explanation of disease. This would naturally be true
of a time almost wholly wanting in any conception
either of law or any relation of cause and effect beyond the most limited regions of experience. Since
the only cause of which man had any real knowledge
was his own effort he peopled his world with forces
more or less like himself, except that they were in-

visible, who operated practically the whole of natural phenomena. There was a spirit for every place and every happening; spirits for fields and hearths, thresholds and springs. Some of them were friendly, some of them naturally unfriendly, but they were everywhere in existence, everywhere in action and naturally if they were unfriendly they would from time to time and in various most curious ways get into the body itself and there do any amount of mischief.

The priest-doctor's task, therefore, was to get them out. He might scare them out, or scold them out, or pray them out, or trick them out. He would use his medicine as much to make the place of their temporary abode uncomfortable for the demon as remedial for the patient and, indeed, the curious and loathsome things which have been used for medicines might well disgust even a malevolent demon. One thing stands out very clearly and that is that whatever the medicine did or left undone, it worked through its influence upon the mind of the patient and not through any real medicinal value.

The Beginnings of Scientific Medicine

Of course along with all this would go a kind of esoteric wisdom which was part of the stock in trade of the healer. There were charms, incantations and magic of every conceivable sort. The medicine man of uncivilized or even half-civilized peoples really makes medicine for the mind rather than the body. There were, however, gleams of scientific light through all this murky region. The Egyptians knew something of anatomy though they made a most capricious use of it and there must have been some knowledge of hygienic methods; the prohibitions of Leviticus, for example, and of the Jewish law generally for which the Jew must have been, as far as medical science is concerned, somewhat in debt to the Egyptian and the Chaldean, really have sound hygienic reasons behind them. The Greeks began with demons but they ended with something which approached true science.

The real contribution of Greece, however, seems to have been on the positive rather than the negative side. They made much of health as an end in itself, had gods and goddesses of physical well-being. The Greek had constantly held before him such an ideal of physical excellence as had never before been approached and has never since been equalled. He seems to have been abstemious in eating; he practiced the most strenuous physical exercises; he lived a wholesome outdoor life, and so created a civilization in which health very largely took care of itself. An examination of what records remain to us hardly sustains the accepted opinion that the Greeks had made substantial advances along purely scientific lines,[1] but at any rate as far as medicine goes, there is little to choose between the Greece of the fourth century before Christ and the Europe of the sixteenth century after, save that the life of the Greek was far more

[1] Probably too strong a statement. For an opposite view strongly supported by a scholar's research see Singer's article in "The Legacy of Greece" (Oxford Press), p. 201.

normal, temperate and hygienic and the mind of the Greek more open, sane and balanced.

Plato anticipated conclusions which we are just beginning to reach when he said, "the office of the physician extends equally to the purification of mind and body. To neglect the one is to expose the other to evident peril. It is not only the body which, by sound constitution, strengthens the soul, but the well regulated soul, by its authoritative power, maintains the body in perfect health." Whether the best classic civilization made, consciously, its own this very noble insight of Plato, the best classic civilization did secure the sound mind and the sound body to an extent which puts a far later and far more complex civilization to shame. Perhaps the greatest contribution of the Greek to this whole great subject was his passion for bodily well-being and his marvellous adaptation of his habits and type of life to that end.

He did, moreover, separate religion, magic and medicine to some appreciable extent and he gave us at least the beginnings of a medical profession, approaching medicine from the scientific rather than the religious or traditional point of view. Even though his science was a poor enough thing, his doctors were none the less doctors and the medical profession to-day is entirely within its right when it goes back to Hippocrates for the fathering of it.

The Attitude of the Early and Medieval Church

Christianity changed all this and on the whole for the worse. And yet that statement ought to be im-

mediately qualified, for Christianity did bring with it
a very great compassion for suffering, a very great
willingness to help the sick and the needy. The Gospels are inextricably interwoven with accounts of the
healing power of the founder of Christianity. All the
later attitude of Christianity toward disease must be
considered in the light of this fact. We owe to Christianity the first real hospitals, the first really compas-
sionate and unselfish care for the sick and impulses
which, as they have finally worked out, have had more
to do with giving quality and direction to medicine and
particularly in investing the whole practice of medicine
with its true atmosphere than any other single force.

And yet all this has been a long, long time coming
true and for almost 1,500 years the Church and its
authorities were a hindrance rather than a help and
that for two or three outstanding reasons. Christianity, to begin with, sadly underestimated physical
values in its overinsistence upon spiritual values. The
body was at best but the tabernacle of the soul and
the soul being the chief concern, whatever happened
to the body was of little importance. The body was
not only underestimated, it was scorned and abused,
starved and scourged; it was the seat of unholy influences and impulses; its natural longings were at the
best under suspicion, at the worst under absolute condemnation. Christianity, speaking through the
Church, took immense care for its spiritual hygiene,
though even here it went wrong because it forgot
Plato's noble word, but it failed utterly in physical
hygiene.

Then again sickness and suffering were for the Church but the manifest punishment of some sin known or concealed. To interfere, therefore, was in some way to defeat the justice of God. Pestilences were inscrutable providences; they were the wrath of God made manifest. In the face of so stupendous a calamity anything man might do was not only futile but impertinent.

By a strange contradiction early and medieval Christianity, while making little of the body, nevertheless strongly opposed any study of anatomy which depended upon post-mortems or dissection. This probably because of their belief in the resurrection of the body. Any mutilation of the body after death would be a real handicap in the day of resurrection. But behind all this, equally real though intangible, was the desire of the Church to have the whole of life under its own direct control. It instinctively feared methods of thought or processes of investigation not directly a part of its own imperial administration of life. Some subtle distrust of the human reason went along with all this. As a result the Church, in the main, threw herself against the more independent processes of scientific thought, sought to subdue all the facts of life to her creeds and understandings and so became a real hindrance to any pursuit of truth or any investigation of fact which lay outside the region of theological control. How largely all this retarded growth and knowledge and the extension of human well-being it is difficult to say, but the fact itself is well established.

12807

Saints and Shrines

For one thing early Christianity continued the belief in demoniac possession. By one of those accidents which greatly influence history the belief in demon possession was strongly held in Palestine in the time of Christ and the Gospel narratives reflect all this in ways upon which it is not necessary to enlarge. The Gospels themselves lent their mighty sanction to this persuasion and there was nothing in the temper of the Church for more than a thousand years afterward to greatly modify it. Indeed the temper of the Church rather strengthened it. Origen believed that demons produce famine, unfruitfulness, corruptions of the air and pestilences. They hover concealed in clouds in the lower atmosphere and are attracted by the blood and incense which the heathen offered them as gods.

According to St. Augustine all diseases of Christians are to be ascribed to these demons and the church fathers generally agreed with these two, the greatest of them all. It was, therefore, sinful to do anything but trust to the intercession of the saints. The objection of the Church to dissection which is, of course, the indispensable basis for any real knowledge of anatomy was very slowly worn down. The story of Andreas Vesalius whom Andrew White calls the founder of the modern science of anatomy is at once fascinating and illuminating. He pursued his studies under incredible difficulties and perhaps could never have carried them through without the protection of Charles V whose physician he was. He was finally

driven out, a wanderer in quest of truth, was shipwrecked on a pilgrimage to the Holy Land and in the
prime of his life and strength "he was lost to the
world." But he had, none the less, won his fight and
the opposition of the Church to the scientific study of
anatomy was gradually withdrawn. But every
marked advance in medical science had really to fight
the battle over again. The Sorbonne condemned inoculation, vaccination had slowly to fight its way and
even the discovery of anesthetic, perhaps the greatest
single blessing ever given surgery, met with no little
theological obstruction. It is only fair to say in this
connection that so stupid a conservatism has been by
no means the sole possession of the Church and the
clergy. Medicine has been upon occasion almost as
conservative and the difficulties which Sir Joseph
Lister encountered in his endeavour to win the London hospitals for asepsis and anti-sepsis were quite as
bitter. The difficulties were of a piece with the opposition of the Church to scientific advancement. After
all a conservatism of this sort is a matter of temperament rather than creed or class.

But if the Church was strangely slow to give place
to medicine and surgery, the Church sought, through
agencies and methods of its own, to cure disease. It
is impossible to follow through in detail the long story
though it all bears upon the line we are following
through its massive testimony to the power of mind
over body. Since the Church believed in demon possession it sought to cure by exorcism and there are in
the ritual of the Church, as the ritual has finally taken

form, offices growing out of this long, long battle against evil spirits which have now little suggestion of their original purpose. The sign of the Cross was supposed to have commanding power, the invocation of the triune deity had its own virtue, the very breathing of the priest was supposed to influence the evil spirit and he fled defeated from the touch of holy water.

The Church possessed, as was everywhere then believed, not only a prevailing power over demons, but a supernatural power all her own for the healing of disease. This power was associated with saints and relics and shrines. During the lifetime of the saint this power was exercised through direct saintly interposition. After the death of the saint it was continued in some relic which he left behind him, or some shrine with which he had been particularly associated. There grew up gradually a kind of "division of labour among the saints in the Middle Ages." Each saint had its own peculiar power over some bodily region or over some particular disease. And so the faithful were guarded by a legion of protecting influences against everything from coughs to sudden death. There is almost an unimaginable range of relics. Parts of the true Cross possessed supreme value. St. Louis of France was brought back almost from death to life by the touch of the sacred wood. The bones and hairs of saints, rings which they had worn and all such things as these had value and to prove that the value was not resident in the relic but in the faith with which the relic was approached we have reported bones of saints possessing well authenticated healing value, later proved to have been the bones not of men but of animals. There have been sacred springs and consecrated waters almost without number. They will still show you in Canterbury Cathedral stones worn by the feet of countless pilgrims seeking at the shrine of Thomas à Becket a healing to the reality of which those who wore away those stones bore testimony in a variety of gifts which made the shrine of à Becket at one time one of the treasure houses of Christendom.

"The two shrines at present best known are those of Lourdes in France and Ste. Anne de Beaupré in the Province of Quebec. Lourdes owes its reputed healing power to a belief in a vision of the Virgin received there during the last century. Over 300,000 persons visit there each year." Charcot, it is worth noting, had confidence enough not in the shrine but in the healing power of faith to send fifty or sixty patients to Lourdes every year. His patients were, of course, the mentally and nervously unbalanced. The French government supervises the sanitary conditions at Lourdes and a committee of doctors have undertaken some examination of the diseased who visit the shrine for the guidance of their profession. Ste. Anne de Beaupré owes its fame to certain wrist bones of the mother of Christ.

Magic, Charms, and the King's Touch: The Rise of the Faith Healer

Religious faith is not always necessary—any faith

will do. Charms, amulets, talismans have all played their part in this long compelling story. The various metals, gems, stones and curious and capricious combinations of pretty much every imaginable thing have all been so used. Birth girdles worn by women in childbirth eased their pain. A circular piece of copper guarded against cholera. A coral was a good guard against the evil eye and sail-cloth from a shipwrecked vessel tied to the right arm was a preventive as well as a cure for epilepsy. There is almost no end to such instances. The list of charms and incantations is quite as curious. There are forms of words which will cure insomnia and indeed, if one may trust current observation, forms of words not primarily so intended may still induce sleepfulness.

The history of the king's touch as particularly helpful in epilepsy and scrofula, though useful also for the healing of various diseases, is especially interesting. This practice apparently began with Edward the Confessor in England and St. Louis in France and was due to the faith of those who came to be touched and healed in the divine right and lonely power of the king. It is significant that the practice began with these two for they, more than any kings of their time or most kings since, were really men of rare and saintly character. Curiously but naturally enough the English have denied any real power in this region to French kings and the French have claimed a monopoly for their own sovereigns. The belief in the king's touch persisted long and seems toward the end to have had no connection with the character of the monarch, for Charles II did more in this line than any one who ever sat on an English throne. During the whole of his reign he touched upward of 100,000 people. Andrew White adds that " it is instructive to note, however, that while in no other reign were so many people touched for scrofula and so many cures vouched for, in no other reign did so many people die of the disease."

Along with the king's touch went the king's gift—a piece of gold—and the drain upon the royal treasury was so considerable that after the reign of Elizabeth the size of the coin was reduced. Special coins were minted for the king's use in that office and these touching pieces are still in existence. William III refused to take this particular power seriously. " God give you better health and more sense," he said as he once touched a patient. In this particular instance the honest skepticism of the king was outweighed by the faith of the suppliant. We are assured that the person was cured. The royal touch was discontinued after the death of Queen Anne.

The list of healers began early and is by no means ended now. The power of the healer was sometimes associated with his official station in the Church, sometimes due to his saintly character and often enough only to a personal influence, the fact of which is well enough established, though there can be in the nature of things no finality in the estimate of his real efficacy. George Fox performed some cures; John Wesley also. In the seventeenth century one Valentine Greatrakes seems to have been the center of such excitements and reported healings as Alexander Dowie and others in our own time and it is finally through the healer rather than the saint or the king or shrine or relic that we approach the renaissance of mental and faith healing in our own time.

IV

THE APPROACH TO CHRISTIAN SCIENCE
AND MARY BAKER EDDY

THERE is, however, another stage in this long
line of development which needs to be considered since it supplies a double point of departure; once for the most outstanding healing cult in
our time—Christian Science—and once for the greatly
enlarged use of suggestion in modern medical practice,
and that is mesmerism and " animal magnetism."

Mesmerism a Point of Departure for Modern Healing Cults

Paracelsus[1] may be taken as a starting point just
here. He is known in the history of medicine " for
the impetus he gave to the development of pharma-
ceutical chemistry, but he was also the author of a
visionary and theosophic system of philosophy." He
believed in the influence of the stars upon men, but he
enlarged upon the old astrologic faiths. " He believed
the human body was endowed with a double magnetism, one portion attracted to itself the planets and
was nourished by them, the result of which was the

[1] A German-Swiss physician and alchemist, b. 1493, d. 1541.
These quotations, partly from authorities on faith healing and
partly from the history of Spiritualism, illustrate the underground
connection in this whole region.

mental powers, the other portion attracted and disintegrated the elements, from which process resulted the body." His world, therefore, was a world of competitive attractions. He believed the well had an influence over the sick through magnetism and used the magnet in his practice.

" This dual theory of magnetic cures, that of the magnetic influence of men on men and of the magnet on man, was prevalent for over a century." " It is, then, upon these ideas—the radiation from all things, but especially the stars, magnets and human bodies, of a force which would act in all things else, and which was in each case directed by the indwelling spirit, together with the conception of a perpetual contact between reciprocal and opposing forces—that the mysticism of the seventeenth and eighteenth centuries mainly depends." [1]

These ideas were adopted by a group of men who are now only names for us. The phenomena of magnetism fascinated them and supplied them analogies. There is, they thought, an all-prevailing magnetic influence which binds together not only celestial and terrestrial bodies, but all living things. Life and death were for them simply the registry of the ebbing and flowing of these immaterial tides and they ended by conceiving a vital fluid which could be communicated from person to person and in the communication of which the sick could be healed—the driftwood of their

[1] Podmore, " Modern Spiritualism," Vol. I, p. 45. I am in debt also to Cutten for general information and some quoted paragraphs.

lore has come down to us on the tides of time; we still speak of magnetic personalities—and they sought in various ways to control and communicate these mysterious forces.

One of them invented steel plates which he applied to the body as a cure for disease. He taught his system to Mesmer who made, however, one marked advance upon the technique of his predecessors and gave his name to his methods; he produced his results through physical contacts and passes. But he shared with his predecessors and stated with that compact clearness of which the French language is so capable even when dealing with obscure matters, that there is a "fluid so universally diffused and connected as to leave nowhere any void, whose subtlety is beyond any comparison and which by its nature is capable of receiving, propagating and communicating all impressions of movement. . . . This reciprocal action is subject to mechanical laws at present unknown."[1] This fluid in its action governs the earth and stars and human action.

He originated the phrase "Animal Magnetism" and was, though he did not know it, the originator of hypnotism; until well within our own time mesmerism was the accepted name for this whole complex group of phenomena. The medical faculties examined his claims but were not willing to approve them, but this made no difference in Mesmer's popularity. He had so great a following as to be unable to deal with them

[1] Price's "Historique de facts relatifs du Magnétisme Animal," quoted by Podmore.

personally. He deputed his powers to assistants, arranged a most elaborate apparatus and surrounded his whole procedure with a dramatic setting of stained glass, mirrored and scented rooms and mysterious music. The result of it all naturally, as far as his patients were concerned, was marked excitements and hysterias. They had often to be put into padded rooms. And yet the result of all this murky confusion was said to be numbers of marked cures. He was investigated by the French government and two commissions presented their reports, neither of which was favourable. Imagination, not magnetism, they said, accounted for the results. His popularity wore away markedly when he undertook to explain his method and reveal his secrets. He left Paris in 1815 and lapsed into obscurity.

The Scientific Investigation of Mesmerism in France

As has been said, there are two lines of development growing out of Mesmer and his methods. Ten years after Mesmer left Paris Alexandre Bertrand pointed out that after the elimination of errors due to fraud or mal-observation, the results which Mesmer and his associates had produced were due not to animal magnetism, but to expectation induced by suggestion and intensified by the peculiar setting which Mesmer had contrived for his so-called treatments. The schools of medicine were slow to follow out Bertrand's discovery and it was not until something like twenty years later, through the studies of Braid, that hypnotism began to be taken seriously.

But once the matter was brought broadly before them, the doctors began to follow it through. Charcot, in the Salpêtriére, used hypnotic suggestion for the correction of abnormal mental and nervous states. The psychologists took up the matter and hypnotic suggestion has come to be not only a legitimate subject for the investigation of the student and an accepted method in correction of abnormal mental states, but as it were a window through which we are beginning to see deeply into unsuspected depths and intricacies of personality.

Modern faith healing cults, however, have not come to us down this line, though the studies of Bertrand, Braid, Charcot, Du Bois and their associates supply the interpretative principles for any real understanding of them. Mesmerism naturally appealed to the type of mind most easily attracted by the bizarre and the mysterious. There are always amongst us the credulous and curious who find little enough either to awe or inspire them in the broad sweep of law, or in such facts as lie open to the light of reason. Such as these are impatient of discipline, eager to free themselves from the sequence of cause and effect; they are impressed by the occult powers and seek short cuts to health, or goodness, or wisdom. They delight to build up, out of their own inner consciousness, systems which have little contact with reality and which, through their very tenuousness, are as incapable of disproof as through their disengagement from normal experience they are capable of verification. They are the people of what the alienist calls the " idée fixe."

Everything for them centers about one idea; they have one key and one only to the marvellous complexity of life. Such a temper as this naturally disassociates them from reality and makes them contemptuous of contradictory experiences.

Mesmerism is Carried to America; Phineas Quimby an Important Link in a Long Chain

America has been far too rich in such a temper as this and it was never more so than in the forties and the fifties of the last century. Mesmerism crossed the ocean and while Braid and later Bernheim and Charcot were following it through on sound, psychological lines and bringing to bear upon it great insight and scientific discipline, it fell here into the hands of charlatans and adventurers. Phineas Parkhurst Quimby, best known for his connection with Mary Baker Eddy, hardly deserves the name of charlatan, though he was dangerously near being just that. He belonged to the border-land regions in thought and propaganda and he did give to the whole complex movement which we have been considering a direction which has played a relatively great part in its later development. He had a shrewd mind which ranged over wide regions; he is a pretty typical example of the half-disciplined, forceful and original personality which has played so large a part in American life. The New England of his time—Quimby was born in New Hampshire and spent his life in Maine—was giving itself whole-heartedly to a mysticism bounded on the one side (its higher and more representative side) by Emerson and the transcendentalists and on the other by healers, prophets of strange creeds and dreamers of Utopias. Phrenology, mind reading, animal magnetism, clairvoyance, all had their prophets.

Quimby belongs to this succession. His education was meagre, he did not even know how to spell according to the dictionary or punctuate according to the grammar.[1] He had his own peculiar use of words —a use by which Mary Baker Eddy was doubtless greatly influenced. He had marked mechanical ability and a real passion for facts. He was an original thinker, little in debt to books for his ideas though he was undoubtedly influenced by the temper of his environment to which reference has already been made. He had a speculative, but not a trained interest in religion and dealt freely with the orthodoxy of his time constrained by no loyalty to the accepted faith and no critical knowledge of its content. "Truth" and "Science" were characteristic words for him and he shared his speculations and conclusions freely with his disciples.

Quimby is Led to Define Sickness as Wrong Belief

In his early thirties he was supposed to be dying of consumption and suffered much from excessive medication. He recovered through an emotional crisis but does not seem to have followed out the possible suggestion of his recovery. He turned instead to mesmerism and travelled about with one Lucius Burkmer

[1] What is here said of Quimby is condensed from Dresser's "The Quimby Manuscripts."

over whom he had strong hypnotic influence. When hypnotized Burkmer (or Burkman) claimed the power to look as through a window into the bodies of Quimby's patients and discover, often with illuminating detail, their condition; a good many reputed cures followed. The testimonials to these cures and to the strange powers of Burkmer are themselves an arresting testimony to the lengths people go in the face of what they do not understand. " I have good reason to believe that he can discern the internal structure of an animal body and if there be anything morbid or defective therein detect and explain it. . . . He can go from point to point without passing through intermediate space. He passes from Belfast [Maine] to Washington or from the earth to the moon . . . swifter than light, by a single act of volition." [1]

Quimby had too alert an intelligence to rest content with the merely occult. He came to believe that Burkmer only saw what the patient thought, could do no more than describe the patient's idea of his own state, or else report the " common allopathic belief about the disease in question," and the cure, he was persuaded, was not in the medicine prescribed but in " the confidence of the doctor or medium." (Note that Quimby here associates the cures produced by the medical faculty and his own cures in one sweeping generalization.) What he was really dealing with then was " belief." It might be the belief of the doctor or the patient or the belief of his friends—but sickness was only " belief." This also was a sweeping generaliza-

[1] " The Quimby Manuscripts," p. 38.

tion but it becomes intelligible as we follow the process by which Quimby reached his conclusions and it helps us to understand the significance of Belief as one of the key words of Christian Science. Quimby was led to identify sickness and wrong beliefs through this analysis of mesmeric diagnosis and health and right belief through his own experiences as a healer. He had no training to help him to an understanding of the real facts which lay behind the belief in sickness. He became a skillful diagnostician of states of mind and a healer of such diseases as could be so treated. But he knew, scientifically, no more of what lay behind it all than a ploughman may know of what lies beneath the furrows he turns.

Quimby Develops His Theories

Mrs. Eddy took over the catch-words of his system and its loose assumptions, and a reasonably careful comparison of the Quimby manuscripts and " Science and Health " shows not only Mrs. Eddy's fundamental and never honestly acknowledged and finally categorically denied indebtedness to Quimby, but the confusion which Quimby's rather striking and original philosophy suffered at her hands. Beginning with his persuasion that health and sickness are phases of belief Quimby discarded mesmerism altogether and addressed himself to the minds of his patients. He had doubtless a keen intuitive knowledge of human nature and its morbid fancies and he was dealing generally with neurotic temperaments over which he exercised a strong and helpful power of suggestion. His explanation of disease—that it is a wrong belief—becomes grotesque enough when he comes down to detail. This, for example, is his diagnosis of Bronchitis—"You listen or eat this belief or wisdom [evidently that Bronchitis is real] as you would eat your meals. It sets rather hard upon your stomach; this disturbs the error of your body and a cloud appears in the sky. . . . The elements of the body of your belief are shaken, earth is lit up by the fire of your error, the heat rises, the heaven or mind grows dark . . . the lightning of hot flashes shoot to all parts of the solar system of your belief. At last the winds or chills strike the earth or surface of the body, a cold clammy sensation passes over you. This changes the heat into a sort of watery substance which works its way into the channels and pores to the head and stomach."[1]

This is Quimby at his worst but beneath it is the germ of the method and philosophy which have attained so luxurious a growth—the explaining, that is, of disease in terms of wrong belief. Inevitably in the elaboration of all this Quimby reached out to include religion and theology and even created his own distinctive metaphysics. He distinguished between the mind and spirit; he must of course discover in personality a power superior to fluctuating mental attitudes. He called his system a science since he was trying to reduce it to a system and discover its laws. He found a parallel to what he was doing in the narratives of healing in the Christian Gospels and claimed Christ as the founder of his science.[2]

[1] "Quimby Manuscripts," p. 118.   [2] Ibid., p. 185.

All belief opposed to his was " error "; " Truth " was naturally opposed to error. He subordinates the testimony of the senses to the necessities of his system; he defines God variously as Wisdom, as Truth, possibly as Principle though his use of the word Principle is far more intelligible than Mrs. Eddy's.[1] He increasingly identifies his system and the teachings of Jesus and ends by calling it " Christian Science." [2]

In substance in the more than 400 closely printed pages of the Quimby manuscripts as now edited we discover either the substance or the suggestion of all that Mrs. Eddy later elaborated. Now all this, confused as it is, brings us to the threshold of a distinct advance in mental and faith healing.

Mary Baker Eddy Comes Under Quimby's Influence

Practically faith and mental healing had depended, till Quimby took it up, upon persons or objects. The saint or the healer worked through personal contact; the shrine must be visited, the relic be touched. Such a system was naturally dependent upon accidents of person or place; it would not be widely extended nor continued nor made the basis of self-treatment. But if what lay behind the whole complex group of phenomena could be systematized and given real power of popular appeal through its association with religion it would possess a kind of continuing independence, conditioned only by the willingness of people to be persuaded of the truth of its philosophy or to answer to its religious appeal. It would then become a mental

[1] "The Quimby Manuscripts," p. 309. [2] *Ibid.*, p. 388.

and spiritual discipline to be written into books and taught by the initiated. As far as it could be associated with religion it would become the basis of a cult and it would have an immense field.

All difficult or chronic or obscure illnesses would offer an opportunity to its propagandists, and the necessary obscurities and irrationalities of such a system would simply be, for the minds to which it would naturally appeal, added elements of power. Any system which has sickness for its field and credulity for its reinforcement and a specious show of half truth for its philosophic form and religion to give its sanction and authority is assured, to begin with, of a really great following. Its very weaknesses will be its strength. It will work best as it is neither clear nor simple— though it must make a show of being both. And if, in addition, there is somewhere at the heart of it force and truth enough to produce a certain number of cures it will go on. What it fails to do will be forgotten or ignored in the face of what it really does do.

Now Quimby, through his own native force and such a combination of circumstances as occurs only once in long periods of time, stood upon the threshold of just such a revolution in the history of faith and mental healing as this. He anticipated the method and supplied the material, but he either did not or could not popularize it. He was not selfish enough to monopolize it, not shrewd enough to commercialize it, and, maybe, not fanatic enough to make it a cult. He was more interested in his own speculations than in making converts and without one of those accidents which become turning points in a movement nothing would have probably come of his work save its somewhat vague and loose continuance in the thought and teaching of a small group. (It is doubtful if New Thought, which as we shall see grew out of his work through his association with the Dressers, would have come to much without the stimulus of Christian Science against which it reacted.) Some one was needed to give the whole nebulous system organization and driving force and above all to make a cult of it.

Outstanding Events of Her Life: Her Early Girlhood

Mary Baker Eddy did just this and Christian Science is the result. It is idle to calculate the vanished alternatives of life but in all probability she never would have done it without Quimby. She and her followers would do far better to honestly recognize this indebtedness. It would now make little difference with either the position of their leader or the force of their system but it would take a pretty keen weapon out of the hands of their critics and give them the added strength which thoroughgoing honesty always gives to any cause. There is, on the other hand, little likelihood that Quimby's persuasions would ever have carried beyond the man himself if he had not found in Mrs. Eddy so creative a disciple.

The outstanding facts of Mary Baker Eddy's life are too well known to need much retelling here. The story of her life and the history of Christian Science as told by Georgine Milmine in *McClure's Magazine* during the years of 1907-8 is final. It is based upon thorough investigation, original documents and an exhaustive analysis of facts. The facts brought out in the various litigations in which Mrs. Eddy and the church have been involved confirm both the statements and conclusions of this really distinctive work. The official life by Sibyl Wilbur (whose real name seems to be O'Brien) is so coloured as to be substantially undependable. It touches lightly or omits altogether those passages in Mrs. Eddy's life which do not fit in with the picture which Mrs. Eddy herself and the church desire to be perpetuated.

Mrs. Eddy was descended from a shrewd, industrious and strongly characterized New England stock. Her father was strongly set in his ways, narrow and intense in his religious faith. Mary Baker was a nervous, high-strung girl, unusually attractive in personal appearance, proud, precocious, self-conscious, masterful. She was subject to hysterical attacks which issued in states of almost suspended animation. Her family feared these attacks and to prevent them humoured her in every way. In due time she joined the Tilton Congregational Church. She says herself that she was twelve years old at the time, but the records of the church make her seventeen. The range of her education is debated. Mrs. Eddy herself claims a rather ambitious curriculum. " My father," she says, " was taught to believe that my brain was too large for my body and so kept me out of school, but I gained book knowledge with far less labour than is usually requisite. At ten years of age I was familiar with Lindley Murray's Grammar, as with the Westminster

Catechism and the latter I had to repeat every Sunday. My favourite studies were Natural Philosophy, logic and moral science. From my brother Albert I received lessons in the ancient tongues, Hebrew, Greek and Latin. After my discovery of Christian Science most of the knowledge I gleaned from school books vanished like a dream. Learning was so illumined that grammar was eclipsed. Etymology was divine history, voicing the idea of God in man's origin and signification. Syntax was spiritual order and unity. Prosody the song of angels and no earthly or inglorious theme." [1]

Her Education: Shaping Influences

It is not fair to apply critical methods to one who confesses that most of the knowledge she had gleaned from school books vanished like a dream, but there is much in Mrs. Eddy's writing to bear out her statement. Those who knew her as a girl report her as irregular in attendance upon school, inattentive during its sessions and far from knowing either Greek or Latin or Hebrew. " According to these schoolmates Mary Baker completed her education when she had finished Smith's Grammar and reached Long Division in Arithmetic." The official biography makes much of an intellectual friendship between the Rev. Enoch Corser, then pastor of the Tilton Congregational Church, and Mary Baker. " They discussed subjects too deep to be attractive to other members of the family. Walking up and down in the garden, this

[1] " Retrospection and Introspection," 1909.

fine old-school clergyman and the young poetess as she was coming to be called, threshed out the old philosophic speculations without rancour or irritation." [1]

There is little reason to doubt her real interest in the pretty rigid Calvinistic theology of her time. Indeed, we could not understand her final line of religious development without taking that into consideration. Milmine suggests other forces which would naturally have influenced a sensitive and curious girl; for example, the current interest in animal magnetism, a subject which dominated certain aspects of her thinking to the end. Milmine suggests also that she may have been considerably influenced by the peculiar beliefs of the Shakers who had a colony near Tilton. The Shakers regarded Ann Lee, their founder, as the female principle of God and greater than Christ. They prayed always to " Our Father and Mother which art in heaven." They called Ann Lee the woman of the Apocalypse, the God-anointed woman. For her followers she was Mother Ann, as Mary Baker was later Mother Eddy. Ann Lee declared that she had the gift of healing. The Shakers also made much of a spiritual illumination which had the right of way over the testimony of the senses. The Shakers called their establishment the Church of Christ and the original foundation the Mother Church. The Shakers forbade audible prayer and enjoined celibacy. There are parallels enough here to sustain

[1] " The Life of Mary Baker Eddy," Sibyl Wilbur, 4th edition. Christian Science Publishing Company.

Milmine's contention that Mary Baker was at least largely influenced by suggestions from her peculiar group of neighbours.

*Her Unhappy Fortunes. She is Cured by Quimby.
An Unacknowledged Debt*

Mary Baker married George Washington Glover at the age of twenty-two. She was soon left a widow and her only son was born after his father's death. The story of the years which follow is unhappy. She was poor, dependent upon relatives whose patience she tried and whose hospitality was from time to time exhausted. Her attacks of hysteria continued and grew more violent. Her father sometimes rocked her to sleep like a child. The Tiltons built a cradle for her which is one of the traditions of this unhappy period of her life. She tried mesmerism and clairvoyance and heard rappings at night.

She married again, this time a Dr. Daniel Patterson, a travelling dentist. He never made a success of anything. They were miserably poor and his marriage was no more successful than most of his other enterprises. He was captured, though as a civilian, during the Civil War and spent one or two years in a southern prison. Futile efforts were made at a reconciliation and in 1873 Mrs. Patterson obtained a divorce on the grounds of desertion. Meanwhile she had been separated from her son, of whom she afterward saw so little that he grew up, married and made his own way entirely apart from her mother.

In 1861 Mrs. Patterson's physical condition was so

desperate that she appealed to Quimby. Her husband
had had some interest in homeopathy and she was
doubtless influenced by the then peculiar theories of
the homeopathic school. (Indeed she claimed to be a
homeopathic practitioner without a diploma.) She
had had experience enough with drugs to make her
impatient and suspicious of current methods of orthodox medication. Under Quimby's treatment she was
physically reborn and apparently spiritually as well.
It is necessary to dwell upon all these well-known de-
tails to understand what follows and the directions
which her mind now took. Milmine's analysis is here
penetrating and conclusive. She had always been in
revolt against her environment. Her marriages had
been unhappy; motherhood had brought her nothing;
she had been poor and dependent; her strong will and
self-assertive personality had been turned back upon
herself.

She had found no satisfaction in the rigid theologies
of the time. She had sought help from accepted religion and religion had had nothing to give her. We
have to read between the lines and especially to evaluate all this period in the light of " Science and
Health " itself to reconstruct the movement of her
inner life, but beyond a doubt her thought had played
about the almost tragic discrepancy between her own
experiences and the love and goodness of God. She
had known pain and unhappiness in acute forms and
had found nothing in what she had been taught ample
enough to resolve her doubts or establish her faith.

She found in Quimby's philosophy a leading which

she eagerly followed. Now for the first time she is really set free from herself. A truer sense of dramatic values would have led Mrs. Eddy herself to have made more of the unhappy period which began to come to an end with her visit to Quimby and would lead her disciples now to acknowledge it more honestly. It is a strong background against which to set what follows and give colour by contrast to her later life. The twice-born from Saul of Tarsus to John Bunyan have dwelt much upon their sins and sorrows, seeking thereby more greatly to exalt the grace of God by which they had been saved. Mary Baker Eddy came strongly to be persuaded that she had saved herself and consequently not only greatly underestimated her debt to Quimby, but emptied her own experiences of dramatic contrasts to make them, as she supposed, more consistent, and her disciples have followed her.

As a matter of fact, though her life as a whole is not an outstanding asset for Christian Science and is likely to grow less so, one must recognize the force of a conviction which changed the neurotic Mrs. Patterson of the fifties and sixties into the masterful and successful woman of the eighties and nineties. She belongs also to the fellowship of the twice-born and instead of minimizing the change those who seek to understand her, as well as those who seek to exalt her, would do well to make more of it. She did that herself to begin with. No master ever had for a time a more grateful disciple. She haunted Quimby's house, read his manuscripts, wrote letters for the paper, " dropped into verse " and through her extravagance " brought ridicule upon Quimby and herself."

Quimby died in 1866, accompanied to his last resting place by a tribute in verse from his grateful pupil. Mrs. Eddy had at the time apparently no thought of continuing his work except in a most modest way. She wrote Julius Dresser who had come under Quimby's influence, suggesting that he would step forward into the place vacated. " I believe you would do a vast amount of good and are more capable of occupying his place than any other I know of." [1] She asked Dresser's help in recovering from a fall which she had just had on the ice and which had so injured her, as she supposed, to make her the helpless cripple that she was before she met Quimby. This fall is worth dwelling upon for a bit, for it really marks a turning place in Mrs. Eddy's life. In her letter to Dresser she says that the physician attending " said I have taken the last step I ever should, but in two days I got out of my bed alone and will walk." [2] Sometime later in a letter to the *Boston Post* Mrs. Eddy said, "We recovered in a moment of time from a severe accident considered fatal by the regular physicians." There is a considerable difference between two days and a moment of time and the expression of a determination to walk in the Dresser letter and the testimony to an instantaneous cure in the *Boston Post* letter. Dr. Cushing, the physician who attended Mrs.

[1] "A History of the New Thought Movement," Dresser, p. 110.
[2] *Ibid.*

Eddy at the time, gives still a third account. He treated her, he says, over a period of almost two weeks and left her practically recovered. He also attended her in a professional capacity still later and offers all this in a sworn statement on the basis of his record books. There is a very considerable advantage in a philosophy which makes thought the only reality, for, given changing thought and a complacent recollection, facts may easily become either plastic or wholly negligible.

She Develops Quimby's Teachings Along Lines of Her Own

The real significance of this much debated but otherwise unimportant episode is that it seems to have thrown Mrs. Eddy upon her own resources, for now that Quimby was dead she begins to develop what she had received from him through both experience and teaching along lines of her own. She had found a formula for the resolution of problems, both physical and mental, which had hag-ridden her for years. She had a natural mental keenness, a speculative mind, a practical shrewdness (the gift of her New England ancestors) and an ample field. The theology, the medical science and indeed the philosophy or psychology of the New England of the sixties contributed strongly, through their limitations, to the growth of bizarre systems which had in them elements of truth. We shall need to come back to this again in any evaluation of Christian Science as a whole, but we cannot understand the rapid development of the movement of which Christian Science was just one aspect without taking all this into consideration.

Medicine itself has been greatly revolutionized within the last fifty years. While Mary Baker Glover Patterson Eddy was finding her unhappy way through border-land regions into a cloudy light, Louis Pasteur, sitting, in the phrase of Huxley, " as humbly as a little child before the facts of life," was making those investigations in bacteriology which were to be, in some ways, the greatest contribution of the nineteenth century to the well-being of humanity. He was following patiently the action of microscopic organisms, especially in their relation to health, discovering the secret of contagion and infection, outlining methods of defense against the attacks of these invisible armies, finding the true basis for inoculation, extending its operation, robbing hospitals of their terrors and surrounding surgery with safeguards heretofore undreamt of, literally performing miracles (in his control of swine plague and the like), and for the want of another subject preparing to experiment upon himself for the prevention of hydrophobia, and in doing it all in the most simple and humble way, naively unconscious of his own fame and living from first to last in a noble and comparative poverty which contrasts dramatically with the material well-being for which Mrs. Eddy was so eager. Nothing of this had ever come into Mrs. Eddy's field or those whom she addressed. With all the aid which the modern physician has at his control, diagnosis is still a difficult matter, physicians confess it themselves. There is still, with all the resource of modern medical science, a residuum of hopeless and obscure cases which baffle the physician. That residuum was very much larger fifty years ago than it is now.

She Begins to Teach and to Heal

The typical Protestant religious experience, as we have seen, was not great enough to contain all the facts of life. The molten passion of an earlier Calvinism had hardened down into rigidities which exalted the power of God at the cost of human helplessness. There was no adequate recognition among the devout of the sweep of law. Everything that happened was a special Providence and it was hard enough to fit the trying facts of life into an understanding of Divine Love when there was apparently so much in life in opposition to Divine Love.

A very great deal of the ferment of the time was just the endeavour to find some way out of all this and the group of which Mrs. Eddy was a part were really the first to try to find their way out except as roads of escape which were, on the whole, not ample enough had been sought by the theological liberalism of the time of which Unitarianism was the most respectable and accepted form. There are, as has been said, curious underground connections through all this region. We find homeopathy, spiritualism, transcendentalism, theological liberalism and faith healing all tied up in one bundle.

The line which Mrs. Eddy now came to follow is, on the whole, clear enough. She becomes in her turn teacher and healer, giving her own impress and colour to what she called the science she taught, claiming it more and more as her own and not only forgetting, but denying as she went on, her indebtedness to any one else. The whole thing gradually became in her mind a distinct revelation for which the ages had been waiting and this revelation theory is really the key to the contradictions and positive dishonesties which underlie the authorized account of the genesis of Christian Science. She associated herself with one of the more promising of her pupils who announced himself as Dr. Kennedy, with Mrs. Eddy somewhat in the background. Kennedy was the agent, Mrs. Eddy supplied him with the material of what was a mixed method of teaching and healing. She had always been desperately poor; now for the first time she had a respectable bank account.

There were corresponding changes in her personality and even her physique. She began to give lessons, safeguarding her instructions from the very first in such ways as to make them uncommonly profitable. Her pupils paid $100 for the course and agreed also to give her a percentage of the income from their practice. In the course of litigation which afterward follows, the courts pronounced that they did not find in her course of instruction anything which could be " in any way of value in fitting the defendant as a competent and successful practitioner of any intelligible art or method of healing the sick." The court, therefore, was of the opinion that " consideration for the agreement had wholly failed." In a sense the court was mistaken. Mrs. Eddy was giving her disciples something which, whether it fitted them to be competent and successful practitioners of any intelligible art or method of healing the sick, or no, was of great financial advantage both to them and to their teacher. She afterward raised her tuition fee to $300 and stated that God had shown her in multitudinous ways the wisdom of this decision.

Early Phases of Christian Science

Everything was, to begin with, a matter of personal relationship between Mrs. Eddy and her students. They constitute a closely related group, the pupils themselves extravagant in their gratitude to their teacher. There were, of course, schisms, jealousies, recriminations, litigation, but none the less, the movement went on. The first attempt at organization was made at Lynn in 1875. A hall was rented, meetings were held in the evening, the society was known as the " Christian Scientists " and as an organization Christian Science came into the world. The first edition of " Science and Health " was also published in 1875. There was difficulty in finding a publisher; those who assisted Mrs. Eddy financially were losers in the enterprise. They were never reimbursed, though " Science and Health " afterward became the most remunerative single publication in the world. Two years later Mrs. Glover (for after her divorce from Patterson she had taken her earlier married name) married Gilbert Eddy and so took the name by which she is best known to the world.

There is much in this period of Mrs. Eddy's life to indicate that she had not yet reached an inner serenity of faith. She was never able to free herself from a perverted belief in animal magnetism or mesmerism which showed itself in fear rather than faith. She believed herself persecuted and if she did not believe in witchcraft she believed in something curiously like it. Indeed, to Mrs. Eddy belonged the rather curious distinction of having instigated the last trial for witchcraft in the United States and with a fitting sense of historic propriety she staged it at Salem. The judge dismissed the case, saying that it was not within the power of the Court to control the defendant's mind. The case was appealed, the appeal waived and the whole matter rests as a curious instance in the records of the Salem court.

Mrs. Eddy does not appear as the plaintiff in the case. The complainant is one of her students, but Mrs. Eddy was behind the complaint, the real reason for which is apparently that the defendant had refused to pay tuition and royalty on his practice and was interfering with the work of the group of which Mrs. Eddy was leader. The incident has value only as showing the lengths to which the mind may be led once it has detached itself from the steadying influences of experience-tested reality. It is interesting also to note that in one way and another Mrs. Eddy and her church have been involved in more litigation than any other religious teacher or religious movement of the time.

She Writes " Science and Health" and Completes the Organization of Her Church

Nothing apparently came of the first tentative organization in 1875. The first incorporated Church of Christ Scientist was chartered in 1879 with twenty-six charter members and Boston as its seat. Meetings of this church were held, to begin with, in Lynn and Boston, but Lynn was not friendly to the new enterprise and the Boston group became the center of further growth. Mrs. Eddy left Lynn finally in 1882 and during all the next period the history of Christian Science is the history of the Mother Church in Boston and of the Massachusetts Metaphysical College. Mrs. Eddy suffered no dissent, her pupils either followed or left her. She was the controlling force in the whole movement. She began to surround herself with a certain mystery and delighted in theatrical effects. She had written and rewritten " Science and Health" until it began to take final form. The *Journal of Christian Science* became the official organ of Mrs. Eddy's movement as " Science and Health " was its gospel.

The movement reached beyond Boston and New England and invaded the West. It was now so outstanding as to create general public interest. The churches began to take notice of it and indeed, whatever has been for the last twenty years characteristic of Christian Science was then actively in action. What follows is the familiar story of Mrs. Eddy's own personal movements, her withdrawal to Concord, her growing detachment from the movement which she nevertheless ruled with an iron hand, the final organization of the church itself along lines wholly dictated by its leader, the deepening of public interest in the movement itself, Mrs. Eddy's removal from Concord to Newton and her death. She left behind her the strongest and most driving organization built up by any religious leader of her time. Of all those, who since the Wesleys have inaugurated and carried through a distinct religious movement, only Alexander Campbell is in the same class with Mrs. Eddy and Campbell had behind him the traditional force of the Protestantism to which he gave only a slightly new direction and colouring. Mrs. Eddy's contributions are far more distinct and radical.

We need, then, to turn from her life, upon whose lights and shadows, inconsistencies and intricacies, we have touched all too lightly, to seek in " Science and Health " and the later development of Christian Science at once the secret of the power of the movement and its significance for our time.

V

CHRISTIAN SCIENCE AS A PHILOSOPHY

CHRISTIAN SCIENCE has a considerable group of authorized publications and a well-conducted department of publicity. Its public propaganda is carried on by means of occasional lectures, always extremely well advertised and through its reading rooms and periodicals. Its unadvertised propaganda is carried on, naturally, by its adherents. Every instance of obscure or protracted illness offers it an opportunity and such opportunities are by no means neglected. But the supreme authority in Christian Science is Mary Baker Eddy's work " Science and Health." This is read at every Sunday service and is the basis of all lectures and explanatory advertisements. In general its exponents do not substantially depart from the teachings of its book, nor, such is the discipline of the cult, do they dare to. There are doubtless such modifications of its more extreme and impossible contentions as every religion of authority experiences. Christian Science cannot remain unaffected by discussion and the larger movements of thought. But it has not as yet markedly departed from the doctrines of its founder and must thereby be judged.

The book in its final form represents a considerable evolution. The comparison of successive editions reveals an astonishing amount of matter which has been discarded, although there has been no real modification of its fundamental principles. References to malicious animal magnetism which fill a large place in the earlier editions, are almost wholly wanting in the last, and there has been a decided progress toward a relative simplicity of statements. The book is doubtless much in debt to Mrs. Eddy's literary adviser, Mr. Wiggins, who brought to the revision of Mrs. Eddy's writings a conscientious fidelity. One needs to stand a good ways back from the book itself in order at all to get any balanced view of its philosophy but, so seen, its fundamentals are almost unexpectedly simple.

Christian Science a Philosophy, a Theology, a Religion and a System of Healing; General Conditions Which Have Lent it Power

Christian Science is offered as a philosophy, a theology, a religion and a method for the practical conduct of life and it needs to be considered under each of these four heads. It demands also for any proper understanding of it the backgrounds of Mrs. Eddy's peculiar temperament and checkered history. It is a growth. For her fundamentals Mrs. Eddy is, beyond reasonable debate, in debt to Quimby and in some ways Quimby's original insights have suffered at her hands. None the less, in its final form " Science and Health " is what Mrs. Eddy has made it and it is what it is because she was what she was. She shared with her own generation an absorbing interest in fundamental theological problems. She inherited a religion which has reduced the whole of life to rigid and on the whole too narrow theological formulæ. She was not able to fit her experience into the formula which her faith supplied and yet, on the other hand, her faith exercised a controlling influence over her life. She was in a small and pathetic way a kind of nineteenth century Job grappling with the old, old question given sin and, above all, pain and suffering to find God. She could not adjust either Divine love or a just Divine sovereignty to what she herself had been called upon to bear. A natural tendency toward the occult and the desperate willingness of the hopelessly sick to try anything which promises a cure, led her in many directions. So much her biography explains.

Quimby was the first teacher she found whose system seemed to offer any key at all to the intellectual and spiritual puzzle in which she found herself and when his system seemed to be proved for her by her recovery from a chronic abnormal state, she thereafter followed and elaborated what he suggested. Here a certain natural shrewdness and ingenuity of mind stood her in good stead. She was helped by her own ignorances and limitations. If she had been a trained thinker, familiar with a wide range of philosophic speculation, she would never have dared write so dogmatically; if she had been a great philosopher with the philosopher's inclusive vision, she would never have dared build so much on foundations so narrow.

Mrs. Eddy was, unconsciously to herself, a type. She thought and felt for multitudes of perplexed people unable to reconcile the more trying experiences of life with what faith they had in the love and goodness of God, unable on the other side to find the love and goodness of God in the wide sweep of law and the orderly sequence of cause and effect, and incapable under any circumstances of the patient analysis needed to trace to all their sources the threads of their strangely mingled webs of life; impressionable folk under the spell of words; speculative; at once credulous and skeptical; intellectually alert enough to want to do their own thinking and not intellectually disciplined enough to do it well; persuaded that the Bible has both a message and authority and unable to find in their traditional interpretation of it either a satisfying message or an adequately directing authority; impatient of discipline and pathetically eager for some short cut to happiness and well-being. In a very signal way Mrs. Eddy has spoken and written for this type particularly in American life. Her very style a liability as it is, when tested by either logic or the accepted standards of good writing, has, nevertheless, been an asset with those who have made her their prophetess.

The secret of Mrs. Eddy's power and the power of her system after her is most largely in her essential intellectual and spiritual kinship with such a temper and intellectual status as this, but she possessed also a real measure of creative capacity, a marked reach of speculative power, rare shrewdness and a masterful temper. Mrs. Eddy believed herself to have found her system in the Old and New Testaments—but she

did not. She gradually built it up out of the suggestions which had been given her to begin with; she
gave it colour and direction from her own experiences;
she proved it to her own satisfaction in the healings
which seemed to result from it, then fitted it all as
best she could into the framework of her inherited
Christian faith and read its meanings back into the
Scriptures. It is a pseudo-philosophy pseudo-Chris-
tianized (if one may use the word) by a curious combination of ingenuity, devotion, main strength and
even awkwardness. And though Christian Science is
carrying on to-day as a religion rather than as either
a philosophy or a system of healing, it will stand or
fall on the intellectual side as a philosophy and not as
a religion.

The Philosophic Bases of Christian Science

It is professedly an idealistic monism based on carefully selected facts and depending for its proof upon
certain results in the experience of those who accept
it. An idealism because there is for Mrs. Eddy no
reality save in mind, a monism because there is for
Mrs. Eddy only one reality and that is God. For a
definition of God she offers only synonyms and affirmations though here perhaps she follows only the
usual procedure of theology. God is divine Principle,
Life, Truth, Love, Soul, Spirit, Mind—and all these
capitalized, for it makes a vast difference in the philosophy of Christian Science whether such familiar
words as these are spelled with a capital letter or not.
It would be possible from Mrs. Eddy's own words to

pretty effectually prove what has been more than once claimed: that Christian Science does not offer a personal God, but all our terminology in this region is necessarily somewhat loose, though hers is excessively so. Some of her definitions of God are as personal as the Westminster Catechism or the Thirty-nine Articles. The writer believes, however, after such dispassionate consideration of the philosophy of Christian Science as he is able to give, that it would make absolutely no difference in its philosophic basis whether God were conceived as a person or not. If the God of Christian Science be taken merely as the exaltation of an abstract idealism or a philosophic Absolute everything would be secured which is otherwise secured.

Up to a certain point Christian Science marches with other idealistic systems. From Plato down we have had philosophers a plenty, who have sought to build for us a universe whose only realities are mind and its attributes, or perhaps more technically, consciousness and its content. It is truly a difficult enough matter to relate the world without and the world within, once we begin thinking about it (though happily and in the practical conduct of life this is not so hard as the philosophers make out, otherwise we should be in a hopeless state), and it is natural enough for one type of mind to simplify the problem by making the world within the only world. Nor have there been wanting those who have sought to reduce everything to a single reality whether matter or mind, and ever since we have had theology at all a perplexed humanity has been seeking to reconcile the goodness and the power of God with the sin and sorrow of our troubled world.

But Christian Science parts company soon enough with this great fellowship of dreamers and philosophers and takes its own line. It affirms consciousness and its content to be the only reality; it affirms the divine Mind to be the ultimate and all-conditioning reality; it affirms love and goodness to be the ultimate qualities of the divine Mind, but it meets the problem of sin and evil by denying them any reality at all. (Here it is in more or less accord with certain forms of mysticism.) But even as Christian Science cuts this Gordian knot it creates for itself another set of difficulties and involves itself in those contradictions which will eventually be the undoing of it as a philosophy.

It Undertakes to Solve the Problem of Evil. Contrasted Solutions

What Christian Science is seeking is an ideal order with a content of unqualified good and it secures this by denying the reality of every aspect of experience which either challenges or contradicts its own idealism. What is distinctive, then, in Christian Science is not its affirmations but its denials. All systems of philosophic idealism face practically the same problem and offer various solutions. They most commonly resolve evil of every sort—and evil is here used in so wide a way as to include sin and pain and sorrow—into an ultimate good.

Evil is thus an " unripe good," one stage in a process

of evolution which, when it has had its perfect and all-transforming way, will reveal both moral and physical evil to have been no evil at all but simply aspects of life, trying enough at the time and puzzling enough when taken by themselves, but having their own distinct and contributory value when considered in their relation to the final whole. Such an approach as this does not in any wise diminish for the individual either the reality of pain or the unhappy consequences of sin, but it does ask him to judge the wisdom and love of God not by their passing phases but by their outcome in the wealth and worth of character.

Robert Browning sang this sturdily through a long generation riding down its difficulties by the sheer force of an unconquerable optimism and subduing argument to lyric passion.

> " The evil is null, is naught, is silence implying
>   sound;
> What was good shall be good, with, for evil, so much
>   good more;
>   On the earth the broken arcs; in the heaven a per-
>   fect round.
>
> " And what is our failure here but a triumph's evidence
>   For the fullness of the days? Have we withered or
>   agonized?
>   Why else was the pause prolonged but that singing
>   might issue thence?
>   Why rushed the discords in, but that harmony should
>   be prized? "

Others affirm the self-limitation of God.[1] In His

[1] Walker, for example, in his extremely suggestive Spiritual Monism and Christian Theism.

respect for that human freedom which is the basis of self-regulated personal action and therefore an essential condition of character, He arrests Himself, as it were, upon the threshold of human personality and commits His children to a moral struggle justifying the inevitable incidents of moral defeat by the greatness of the ends to be attained. A vast deal of what we call evil—broadening evil to include not only moral defeat but also pain—is either a consequence or a by-product of what Henry Churchill King calls the fight for character. Such a solution as this is consistent with the love of God and the moral order; whether it is consistent with a thoroughgoing monism or not is another question. William James doubted it and so frankly adopted Pluralism—which is perhaps just a way of saying that we cannot reconcile the contending forces in our world order with one over-all-controlling power—as his solution of the problem.

Josiah Royce has valiantly maintained, through long and subtle argument, the goodness of the whole despite the evil of the incidental. " All finite life is a struggle with evil. Yet from the final point of view the Whole is good. The Temporal Order contains at no one moment anything that can satisfy. Yet the Eternal Order is perfect. We have all sinned, and come short of the glory of God. Yet in just our life, viewed in its entirety, the glory of God is completely manifest. These hard sayings are the deepest expressions of the essence of true religion." [1] He finds the root of evil

[1] "The World and the Individual," Royce, Vol. II, Chap. 9—passim.

in the dissatisfaction of the finite will—a dissatisfaction which on the other hand is the secret of the eventual triumph of good.

We suffer also through our involution with " the interests and ideals of vast realms of other conscious and finite lives whose dissatisfactions become part of each individual man's life when the man concerned cannot at present see how or why his own ideals are such as to make these dissatisfactions his fate." We suffer also through our associations with nature, none the less " this very presence of evil in the temporal order is the condition of the perfection of the eternal order." He dismisses definitely, in an argument still to be quoted, the conclusion of the mystic that an " experience of evil is an experience of unreality . . . an illusion, a dream, a deceit " and concludes: " In brief, then, nowhere in Time is perfection to be found. Our comfort lies in the knowledge of the Eternal. Strengthened by that knowledge, we can win the most enduring of temporal joys, the consciousness that makes us delight to share the world's grave glories and to take part in its divine sorrows,—sure that these sorrows are the means of the eternal triumph, and that these glories are the treasures of the house of God. When once this comfort comes home to us, we can run and not be weary, and walk and not faint. For our temporal life is the very expression of the eternal triumph."

One may gravely question whether philosophy has ever so completely made out its case as Professor Royce thinks. He is affirming as the reasoned conclusion of philosophy what is rather a faith than a demonstration, but none the less, all honest thinking has hitherto been brave enough to recognize the reality of evil and to test the power of God and His love and goodness not by the actuality of present pain, or the confusion of present sin, but rather by the power which He offers us of growing through pain to health or else so bearing pain as to make it a real contribution to character and of so rising above sin as to make penitence and confession and the struggle for good and the achievement of it also a contribution to character. So St. Paul assures us that all things work together for good for those that love God. "The willingness," says Hocking, "to confront every evil, in ourselves and outside ourselves, with the blunt, factual conscience of Science; willingness to pay the full causal price for the removal of the blemish; this kind of integrity can never be dispensed with in any optimistic program." [1]

Sir Henry Jones takes the same line. "The first requisite for the solution of the contradiction between the demand of religion for the perfection of God, and therefore the final and complete victory of the good in the other, is the honest admission that the contradiction is there, and inevitable; though possibly, like other contradictions, it is there only to be solved." [2]

The Divine Mind and Mortal Mind

Christian Science solves this problem, as has been

---

[1] "The Meaning of God in Human Experience," p. 175.
[2] "A Faith that Enquires," p. 45.

said, by denying the reality of evil, but since we have an abundance of testimony to pain and sickness, Mrs. Eddy goes a step farther. She denies the reality of the testimony of the senses wherever pain and sickness are concerned.[1] (Mrs. Eddy's denial of the reality of sin is hardly parallel to her denial of the reality of physical ills.) And here the word comes in which is made to carry a heavier load than any one poor word was ever burdened with before. All that is involved in the recognition of physical ills and indeed all that is involved in the recognition of the material side of existence is error. (Once fairly on her road Mrs. Eddy makes a clean sweep of whatever stands in her way.) What one may call the whole shadowed side of experience is not only ignored, it is denied and yet before it can be explained away it has to be explained. It is, in brief, for Mrs. Eddy and her followers the creation of mortal mind. Mortal mind, she says, " is nothing claiming to be something; mythology; error creating other errors; a suppositional material sense; . . . that which neither exists in science nor can be recognized by the spiritual sense; sin; sickness; death." [2]

Mortal mind is that side of us which accepts our entanglement in the facts and forces of the world order and upon mortal mind so vaguely conceived Mrs. Eddy throws the whole burden of responsibility for all the unhappy aspects of experience and conditioning circumstances. She gives it a surprising range of

[1] " Science and Health," last edition, pp. 108, 120, 293, 488.
[2] *Ibid.*, p. 591.

creative power. It has created everything Mrs. Eddy does not like or believe in. In other words, there is not one reality but two, one the reality of well-being, the other the reality of unhappiness and suffering, but according to Mrs. Eddy the first reality is the only real reality, the second is an unreal reality which we ourselves create through false beliefs and which we may escape at any moment by simply shifting the center of our creative idealism. Mrs. Eddy makes what she means by mortal mind reasonably clear through endless repetition and some analysis, but she never for a moment accounts for its existence. It is no creation of what she calls the divine Mind; indeed she says in substance that God is not conscious of it at all; it lies entirely outside the range of His knowledge. (Page 243.)

God is Good. Since He is good He cannot have created nor be responsible for, nor even recognize pain, sorrow or suffering. " The Divine Mind cannot suffer " (page 108, also page 335), " is not responsible for physical and moral disasters " (page 119). God did not create matter (the Father mind is not the father of matter) (page 257), for matter means pain and death, nor do such things as these belong in any way to the order of the Divine Mind. They have no admitted reality in Mrs. Eddy's scheme of a true idealism. Man is " God's spiritual idea " and since he belongs by right to an order in which there is neither sin nor sorrow nor death, such things as these have no reality for him save as he admits them. What really admits them is mortal mind, the agent of another system of Belief in which humanity has in some way, which is never really explained, become entangled, and we may apparently escape from the one order to the other simply by a change in our beliefs. For all the shadowed side of life has reality only as we accept or believe in it; directly we cease to believe in it or deny it it ceases to be.

It is, as near as one can make out, a myth, an illusion, whose beginnings are lost in obscurity and which, for the want of the revelation vouchsafed through her, has been continued from age to age by the untaught or the misled. For example, Arsenic is not a poison, so we are told again and again. It is only a poison because people think it is;[1] it began to be a poison only because people thought it was, it continues to be a poison only because the majority of people think it is now and, such is the subtle and far-reaching influence of mind upon mind, it will continue to be a poison as long as any one continues to believe it to be. Directly we all believe that Arsenic is not a poison it will be no poison. Poisons, that is, are the creation of mortal mind. Pain is pain only through the same mistaken belief in the reality of it. " By universal consent mortal belief has constituted itself a law to bind mortals to sickness, sin and death." And so on at great length and almost endless repetition.

The Essential Limitations of Mrs. Eddy's System

Since matter conditions us who were born to be unconditioned and since matter is apparently the root of

[1] Page 178.

so many ills, the seat of so many pains, matter goes
with the rest. Mrs. Eddy is not always consistent in
her consideration of matter; sometimes she confines
herself to saying that there is neither sensation nor life
in matter—which may be true enough save as matter
both affords the material for sensation and conditions
its forms, which is an immense qualification,—but
again and again she calls matter an illusion. Consistently the laws of physics and chemistry should disappear with the laws of hygiene and medicine, but
Mrs. Eddy does not go so far as that though it would
be difficult to find a logical stopping place once you
have taken this line. Mortal mind is apparently the
source of all these illusions.

Mrs. Eddy's disposal of matter, along with her constant return to its misleading mastery in experience
is an outstanding aspect of her book. The writer is
inclined to believe that Mrs. Eddy's formula: " There
is . . . no matter in life and no life in matter,"
is an echo of Tyndall's famous utterance—made about
the time she was working with her system—that he
found " in matter the promise and potency of all life."
There is surprisingly little reference in " Science and
Health " to philosophic or scientific sources. Cutter's
physiology is quoted in some editions—an old text-
book which the writer remembers to have found
among his mother's school books. There are a few
references to popular astronomy, but in general for
Mrs. Eddy modern science does not exist except in
the most general way as the erroneous expression of
error and always with a small s as against the capital

S of her own system. Nor does she show any knowledge of other philosophic idealisms nor any acquaint-
ance with any solution of the problems she was facing
save the commonplaces of evangelical orthodoxy.
" Science and Health " knows nothing also of any
medical science save the empirical methods of the
medical science of 1860 and 1870.

But she cannot have been wholly influenced—being
a woman of an alert mind—by the controversy which,
in the seventies and eighties, was raging about a
pretty crass and literal materialism, and her writings
probably reflect—with a good deal of indirection
—that controversy. Here is a possible key to a good
many things which are otherwise puzzling enough.
She is, in her own fashion, the defender of an idealistic
interpretation of reality and experience. Now all
idealistic systems have had to dispose of matter in
some way. In general idealists find in matter only the
reflection in consciousness of the material which sense
experience supplies, and since the raw material is in
every way so different from the mental reflection, the
idealist may defend his position plausibly in assuming
matter to be, in its phenomenal aspects, really the
creation of thought. But he must account for the
persistency of it and the consistency of experience so
conditioned. He does this by assuming the whole
interrelated order to be held, as it were, in solution,
in some larger system of thought which really supplies for us our environment and if he be both devout
and consistent he calls this the thought God.[1] In this

[1] So Royce in " The World and the Individual."

way he solves his problem—at least to his own satisfaction—and even supplies a basis for Theistic faith. But he does not deny the working reality of his so-called material experiences nor does he, like Mrs. Eddy, accept one aspect of this experience and deny the other. This is philosophically impossible.

A thoroughgoing theistic monism must find in matter some aspect or other of the self-revelation of God. It may be hard pressed to discover just how the psychical is " stepped down " to the physical. (That is the essential difficulty in all Creationism.) But something must be assumed to get a going concern in any department of thought and there is much in that resolution of matter into force and force into always more tenuous and imponderable forms—which is the tendency of modern science—to render this assumption less difficult to the rational imagination than perhaps any other we are asked to make. When the final elements in matter have become electrons and the electron is conceived as a strain in a magnetic field and thus the

> " Cloud-capped towers, the gorgeous palaces,
> The solemn temples, the great globe itself,
> Yea, all which is inherent,"

become the projection into sensibly apprehended form of the flux of an infinite and eternal energy, it is not hard to define that energy in terms of a divine will. Indeed it is hard not to do just that. But there is no place in such a resolution as this for the conclusions of " Science and Health."

Or we may accept in one form or another a dualism

in which the practical mind is generally content to rest. According to this point of view we have to do with a reality which may be known under two aspects. It is the chemical action and interaction of elements—and the mind which measures and combines them; it is the physical action and interaction of force—and the mind which directs the process. Biologically " the living creature gives an account of itself in two ways. It can know itself as something extended and intricately built up, burning away, moving, throbbing; it can also know itself as the seat of sensation, perceptions, feelings, wishes, thoughts. But there is not one process, thinking, and another process, cerebral metabolism (vital processes in nerve-cells); there is a psycho-physical life—a reality which we know under two aspects. Cerebral control and mental activity are, on this view, different aspects of one natural occurrence. What we have to do with is the unified life of a psycho-physical being, a body-mind or mind-body." [1] In short there is no philosophy or science outside the covers of her own book to which Mrs. Eddy may turn for support and though this does not prove the case against her—she might be right and the whole disciplined thought of her time be wrong—this latter supposition is so improbable as to rule it out of court.

The materialism against which she contends has ceased to exist. The matter which she denies does not exist in the sense of her denial. There was, even when she was writing, a line of which she was apparently wholly ignorant which has since been im-

[1] J. A. Thomson, " The Outline of Science," p. 548.

mensely developed, and of all this there is naturally no reflection at all in her work. It is more hopelessly out of touch with the laborious and strongly established conclusions of modern thought in every field than the first chapters of Genesis for there one may, at least, substitute the science of to-day for the science of 3,000 years ago and still retain the enduring insights of the faith then voiced, but there is no possible accommodation of " Science and Health " to either the science or the philosophy of the twentieth century. It must be left to a consistent Christian Scientist to reconcile his gospel with the freer movements of the world of which he is still a citizen—though perhaps this also might be urged against a deal of contemporaneous Christian faith—but it is all an arresting testimony to the power of the human mind to organize itself in compartments between which there is no communication.

Experience and Life

Beyond all this is the fact of which " Science and Health " takes no account—the conditioning of conscious life and working experience by its material environment however conceived. This is true of every phase of life and all our later emphasis upon the power of the mind in one direction and another to escape this conditioning scarcely affects the massive reality of it. Christian Science makes no attempt at all to escape this—save in the region of physical health—or else it provides an alibi in the phrase, " I have not demonstrated in that region yet." But it does not thus escape

the limitation imposed upon us all and if we may dare
for a moment to be dogmatic, it never will.   At the
best we live in a give and take and if, through discipline and widening knowledge, we may push back a
little the frontiers which limit us, and assert the supremacy of soul over the material with which it is so
intimately associated, we do even this slowly and at
great cost and always in conformity with the laws of
the matter we master.

There is a body of evidence here which can no more
be ignored than gravitation, and we best dispose of
association of personality with the material fabric of
the body and the world of which it is a part, not by
denying their mutual interdependence but by discovering therein the laws and methods of an infinite wisdom.
Here are ministries through which we come to consciousness of ourselves, here are materials upon which
we exercise our power, here are realities which hold
us fast to normal and intelligible lives, here are masters
whose rule is kind and servants whose obediences em-
power us.   They condition our happinesses as well as
our unhappinesses and supply for us the strings of that
harp of the senses upon which the music of life is
played.   Life really gains its spiritual content through
the action and interaction of the aspiring self upon
its environment—whether that environment be intimate
as the protest of a disturbed bodily cell or remote as
Orion and the Pleiades.[1]   The very words which Mrs.

[1] "And I am inclined to think that the error of forgetting that
spirit in order to be real or that principles, whether of morality,
religion or knowledge, must be exemplified in temporal facts, is

Eddy uses would be idle if this were not so and though a thoroughgoing defender of her system may read into its lines a permission for all this, the fundamentals of her system deny it.

Christian Science breaks down both philosophically and practically just here. It is none the less a dualism because it denies that it is. It confronts not one but two ranges of reality; it gains nothing by making mortal mind the villain in the play. It is compelled to admit the existence of the reality which it denies, even in the fact of denying it. What we deny exists for us—we could not otherwise deny it. Royce has put all this clearly, strongly, finally. " The mystic first denies that evil is real. He is asked why, then, evil seems to exist. He replies that this is our finite error. The finite error itself hereupon becomes, as the source of all our woes, an evil. But no evil is real, hence no error can be real, hence we do not really err even if we suppose that evil is real. Here we return to our starting point and could only hope to escape by asserting that it is an error to assert that we really err or that we really believe error to be real, and with a process thus begun there is indeed no end, nor at any stage in this process is there consistency." [1] All this is subtle

a no less disastrous error than that of the sciences which have not learned that the natural, when all the meaning of it is set free, blossoms into the spiritual like the tree into flower. Religion and philosophy and science also have yet to learn more fully that all which can possibly concern man, occupy his intelligence or engage his will, lies at the point of intersection of the natural and spiritual."—"A Faith that Enquires," p. 27.

[1] " The World and the Individual," Vol. II, p. 394.

enough, but if we are to make our world by thinking and unthinking it, all this is unescapably true.

When, moreover, you have reduced one range of experience to illusion there is absolutely nothing to save the rest. If evil is error and error evil and the belief that evil is an illusion is itself an illusion what is there to guarantee the reality of good? The sword with which Mrs. Eddy cut the knot of the problem of evil is two-edged. If the optimist denies evil for the sake of good and points for proof to the solid coherency of the happier side of life, the pessimist may as justly deny good for the sake of evil and point for proof to the solid coherency of the sadder side of life; he will have no trouble in finding his facts. If sickness is a dream then health is a dream as well. Once we have taken illusion for a guide there is no stopping until everything is illusion. The Eastern mystic who went this road long before Mrs. Eddy and who thought it through with a searching subtleness of which she was incapable, reached the only logical conclusion. All experience is illusion, entire detachment from action is the only wisdom, and absorption in an unconscious something which only escapes being nothing is our appointed destiny:

> " We are such stuff
> As dreams are made of,
> And our little life
> Is rounded with a sleep."

Sense-Testimony Cannot Be Accepted for Health and Denied for Sickness

Christian Science, then, is not monism, it is rather

a dualism; it confronts not one but two ranges of reality and it is compelled to admit the existence of the reality which it denies, even the fact of denying it, for it is a philosophical axiom that what we deny exists for us—we could not otherwise deny it. Denial is the recognition of reality just as much as affirmation. To repeat, it is this continuous interwoven process of trying to reconcile the one-sided idealism of Christian Science with the necessity of its argument and the facts of life which gives to " Science and Health " what one may call its strangely bifocal character, though indeed this is a somewhat misleading figure. One has the same experience in reading the book that one has in trying to read through glasses which are out of focus; you are always just seeing and just missing because Mrs. Eddy herself is always just seeing and just missing a really great truth.

This fundamental inconsistency penetrates the whole system even down to its practical applications. Christian Science denies the testimony of the senses as to sickness and yet accepts them as to health. It goes further than this, it accepts the testimony of the senses of other people—physicians, for example, in accepting their diagnosis. The edition of " Science and Health " published in 1918 offers in chapter eighteen a hundred pages of testimonials sent in by those who have in various ways been helped by their faith. These letters are shot through and through with a recognition of the testimony of the senses which no explanation can possibly explain away. " I was afflicted with a fibroid tumour which weighed not less than fifty pounds, attended by a continuous hemorrhage for eleven years." If the senses have any language at all, this is their language. A growth cannot be known as a fibroid tumour without sense testimony, nor its weight estimated without sense testimony, nor a continuous hemorrhage be recorded, or its cessation known without sense testimony, nor can epilepsy be diagnosed, nor bilious attacks recognized without sense testimony. On page 606 a grateful disciple bears witness to the healing of a broken arm, testimony to said healing being demonstrated by a visit to a physician's office " where they were experimenting with an X-ray machine. The doctor pointed out the place as being slightly thicker at that part, like a piece of steel that had been welded." In other words, Christian Science cannot make out its case without the recognition of the veracity of a sense testimony, whose truth its philosophy denies.

Mrs. Eddy seems to dismiss all this in one brief paragraph. " Is a man sick if the material senses indicate that he is in good health? No, for matter can make no conditions for man. And is he well if the senses say he is sick? Yes, he is well in Science, in which health is normal and disease is abnormal." [1]

---

[1] Page 120. It is only fair to say that Mrs. Eddy is hampered by her own want of clear statement. The phrase (so often used in " Science and Health ") " in Science " is probably in her mind equivalent to " in the ideal order " and if Mrs. Eddy had clearly seen and clearly stated what she is groping for : that the whole shadowed side of life belongs to our present world of divided powers and warring forces and unfinished enterprises, that God has something better for His children toward which we are being

If Mrs. Eddy and her followers believe so specious a statement as that, to set them free from an inconsistency which is central in their whole contention, they are welcome to their belief, but the inconsistency still remains.   You can go far by using words in a Pickwickian sense but there is a limit.   A consistent idealism is philosophically possible, but it must be a far more inclusive and deeply reasoned idealism than Christian Science.   The most thoroughgoing idealisms have accepted the testimony of the senses as a part of the necessary conduct of life as now conditioned. Anything else would reduce us to unspeakable confusion, empty experience of its content, dissolve all the contacts of life and halt us in our tracks for we cannot take a step safely without the testimony of the senses and any scheme of things which seeks to distinguish between the varying validities of sense testimony, accepting only the evidence of the senses for health and well-being and denying the dependability of whatever else they register, is simply an immense caprice which breaks down under any examination.

The Inescapable Reality of Shadowed Experience

Evil does not cease to be because it is denied.   The acceptance of sense testimony is just as necessary in the region of pain and sickness as in driving a motor-

led through the discipline of experience and that we may therefore seek to conceive and affirm this ideal order and become its citizens in body, mind and soul, she would have escaped a perfect web of contradiction and been in line not only with the great philosophies but with historic Christian faith.   But then Christian Science would not be Christian Science.

car down a crowded street and the hypothesis of a misleading mortal mind, instead of explaining everything, demands itself an explanation. What Mrs. Eddy calls mortal mind is only the registry of the dearly bought experience of the race. We began only with the power to feel, to struggle, to will and to think. We have been blind enough and stupid enough but we are, after all, not unteachable and out of our experience and our reflections we have created the whole splendid and dependable body of human knowledge. What we know about pain is itself the outcome of all the suffering of our kind. We began with no developed philosophy nor any presuppositions about anything. Experience reflects encompassing realities which we are able to escape only as we make their laws our ministers. We did not give fire the power to burn, we discovered that only in the school of the touch of flame. We did not give edged steel the power to cut, we found that out through death and bleeding wounds. We did not give to poisons their deadly power, our attitude toward them is simply the outcome of our experience with them.

Conditioned as we are by those laws and forces with which this present existence of ours is in innumerable ways inextricably interwoven, our tested and sifted beliefs are only the outcome of an action and interaction of recipient or creative personality upon its environment old as human consciousness, and if in all this we have become persuaded of pain and suffering and shadowed experience, it is only because these are as real as any elements in experience can possibly be. To attempt to write them out or deny them out or juggle them out in any kind of way save in bravely meeting them and humbly being taught by them and in the full resource of disciplined power getting free from them by removing the causes which create them, is to cheat ourselves with words, lose ourselves in shadows which we mistake for light and even if in some regions we seem to succeed it is only at the cost of what is more bitter than pain and more deadly than wounds—the loss of mental and spiritual integrity. This is a price too great to pay for any mere healing.

VI

CHRISTIAN SCIENCE AS A THEOLOGY

"SCIENCE AND HEALTH" is offered, among other things, as a key to the Scriptures, and along with her interpretation of both the Old and the New Testaments in terms of her peculiar philosophy Mrs. Eddy rewrites the great articles of the Christian creeds. A careful student of Mrs. Eddy's mental processes is able in this region to understand them better than she understood them herself. She had, to begin with, an inherited reverence for the Bible as an authority for life and she shared with multitudes of others a difficulty to which reference has already been more than once made. For what one may call the typical Protestant consciousness the Bible is the final revelation of God, governing, if only we can come to understand it, both our faith and our conduct of life, but the want of a true understanding of it and, above all, the burdening of it with an inherited tradition has clouded its light for multitudes of devout souls.

Science and Health Offered as a Key to the Scriptures

Such as these have been almost pathetically eager to accept any interpretation, no matter how capricious, which seemed to read an intelligible meaning into its difficult passages, or reconcile its contradictions, or make it a more practical guide in the conduct of life. Any cult or theory, therefore, which can seem to secure for itself the authority of the Bible has obtained directly an immense reinforcement in its appeal to the devout and the perplexed, and Mrs. Eddy has taken full advantage of this. Her book is veined with Scripture references; two of her chapters are expositions of Biblical books (Genesis and Revelation) ; and other chapters deal with great doctrines of the Church.

It Ignores All Recognized Canons of Biblical Interpretation. Illustrations

Mrs. Eddy naturally sought the authority for her philosophy between the covers of the Scriptures. Beyond debate her teachings have carried much farther than they otherwise would, in that she claims for them a Scriptural basis, and they must be examined in that light. Now there are certain sound and universally recognized rules governing the scholarly approach to the Old and New Testaments. Words must be taken in their plain sense; they must be understood in their relation to their context. A book is to be studied also in the light of its history; the time and place and purpose of its composition, as far as these are known, must be considered; no changes made in the text save through critical emendation, nor any translations offered not supported by accepted texts, nor any liberties be taken with grammatical constructions. By such plain tests as these Mrs. Eddy's use of the Scriptures will not bear examination. She violates all recognized canons of Biblical interpretation on almost every page.[1]

Her method is wholly allegorical and the results achieved are conditioned only by the ingenuity of the commentator. It would require a body of citation from the pages of " Science and Health," not possible here, to follow through Mrs. Eddy's peculiar exegesis. One needs only to open the book at random for outstanding illustrations. For example, Genesis 1: 6, " And God said, let there be a firmament in the midst of the waters and let it divide the waters from the waters." The word " firmament " has its own well established connotation gathered from a careful study of all its uses. We can no more understand the earlier chapters of Genesis without an understanding of Hebrew cosmogony than we can understand Dante without a knowledge of medieval cosmogony. But, given this knowledge which is the common possession of all sound scholarship, we can at least understand what the passage means, even though we have long left behind us the naïve conception of the vaulted skies to which it refers.

[1] This is a brief—and a Christian Scientist may protest—a summary dismissal of the claim of " Science and Health " to be a "key to the Scriptures." But nothing is gained—save of the unnecessary lengthening of this chapter—in going into a detailed examination of her method and conclusions. She has insight, imagination, boundless allegorical resource, but the whole Bible beneath her touch becomes a plastic material to be subdued to her peculiar purpose by omissions, read-in meanings and the substantial and constant disregard of plain meanings. To the student the whole matter is important only as revealing the confusion of the popular mind which receives such a method as authoritative.

All this is a commonplace not worth repeating at the cost of the white paper upon which it is printed, save as the ignoring of it leads to such an interpretation of the passage as that which Mrs. Eddy offers: " spiritual understanding by which human conception material mind is separated from Truth is the firmament. The Divine Mind, not matter, creates all identities and they are forms of Mind, the ideas of Spirit apparent only as Mind, never as mindless matter nor the so-called material senses " (page 505). Comment is not only difficult but impossible in the face of a method like this. If such an interpretation were an exception it might seem the unfair use of a hypercritical temper to quote this particular expression of Mrs. Eddy's mind. But her whole treatment of Scripture suffers from the same method.

Everything means something else. The Ark is " the idea, or reflection of truth, proved to be as immortal as its Principle." Babel is " self-destroying error "; baptism is " submergence in Spirit "; Canaan is " a sensuous belief "; Dan (Jacob's son) is " animal magnetism "; the dove is " a symbol of divine Science "; the earth is " a type of eternity and immortality "; the river Euphrates is " divine Science encompassing the universe and man "; evening " the mistiness of mortal thought "; flesh " an error, a physical belief "; Ham (Noah's son) is " corporeal belief "; Jerusalem " mortal belief and knowledge obtained from the five corporeal senses "; night, " darkness; doubt; fear "; a Pharisee, " corporeal and sensuous belief "; river is " a channel of thought "; a rock is " a spiritual foundation "; sheep are " innocence "; a sword " the idea of Truth." [1]

Mrs. Eddy does not hesitate to make such textual modifications of passages as suit her purpose and even when she is not dealing with her texts in such ways as these, she is constantly citing for her proofs passages which cannot by any recognized canon of interpretation possibly be made to mean what she says they mean. Beneath her touch simple things become vague, the Psalms lose their haunting beauty, even the Lord's Prayer takes a form which we may reverently believe the author of it would not recognize.

" Our Father: Mother God, all harmonious, Adorable One, Thy kingdom is come; Thou art ever present. Enable us to know—as in heaven, so on earth—God is omnipotent, supreme. Give us grace for to-day; feed the famished affections; and love is reflected in love; and God leadeth us not into temptation, but delivereth us from sin, disease and death. For God is Infinite, all Power, all Life, Truth, Love, over all and All."

Its Conception of God

It was quite as inevitable that she should undertake to fit her speculations into the fabric of the theology in which she and most of her followers had been trained, as that she should try to secure for her speculation the weight of the authority of the Bible. She would have to take for her point of departure the centrality of Christ, the outstanding Christian doctrines, markedly the Incarnation and the Atonement and she would need somehow to dispose of the Sacra-

[1] Glossary, p. 579—passim.

ments. All this is inevitably implied in the persistent designation of her whole system as a Christian system.

The chapter headings in " Science and Health " and the sequence of chapters are the key to the movement of her mind; they are determined by her association of interests. Marriage is on the same level with Prayer, Atonement and the Eucharist, and Animal Magnetism with Science, Theology and Medicine. It is hard to know where to begin in so confused a region. She is handicapped, to begin with, by the rigidity of her idealism and actually by her limitation both of the power and personality of God. This statement would probably be as sharply contradicted by Mrs. Eddy's apologists as anything in this study, but it is not hastily made. Philosophically He is for Mrs. Eddy only an exalted ideality into relation with which we may think ourselves by a change in our system of belief. Actually, as we shall see, this conception yields to emotional and devotional needs—it is bound to— but in theory it is unyielding.

Now the accepted Christian conception of God is entirely different. Both the Old and New Testaments conceive a God who is lovingly and justly conscious of all our need, who is constantly drawing near to us in manifold appeals and approaches and who has, above all, in the Incarnation made a supreme and saving approach to humanity. He is no more rigid than love is rigid; His attitude toward us, His children, changes as the attitude of a father toward the changing tempers of a child. Now all this may be true or it may be only the dream of our strangely sensitive personalities, but whether it be true or not, it is the Christian conception and any denial of this or any radically different substitution for it cannot call itself Christian save as it writes into the word Christian connotations to which it has heretofore been utterly strange.

Mrs. Eddy's Interpretation of Jesus Christ

Mrs. Eddy begins, therefore, with the handicap of a philosophy which can be adjusted to Christian theology only through fundamental modifications of that theology. It is hard to systematize the result. Mrs. Eddy distinguishes between Jesus and Christ. Her conception of Jesus is reasonably clear whether it be historically true or not, but her conception of the Christ is vague and fluctuating. Jesus was apparently the first Christian Scientist, anticipating, though not completely, its philosophy and demonstrating its practices. His teachings are so interpreted as to be made to yield a Christian Science content. When He urged the commandment: " Thou shalt have no other gods before me " what He really meant was, " Thou shalt have no belief of Life as mortal; thou shalt not know evil, for there is one Life." [1] " He proved by His deeds that Christian Science destroys sickness, sin and death. Our Master taught no mere theory, doctrine or belief; it was the divine Principle of all real being which He taught and practiced." [2] " He taught His followers the healing power of Truth and Love " [3] and " the proofs

---

[1] Page 19. All citations from last edition.
[2] Page 26.   [3] Page 31.

of Truth, Life and Love which Jesus gave by casting out error and healing the sick, completed His earthly mission." [1] "The truth taught by Jesus the elders scoffed at because it demanded more than they were willing to practice." [2]   They, therefore, crucified Him and He seemed to die, but He did not.   Apparently He was not dead when He was entombed and His three days in the tomb gave Him " a refuge from His foes, a place in which to solve the great problem of being."   In other words He demonstrated His own healing in the tomb.   " He met and mastered, on the basis of Christian Science, the power of mind over matter, all the claims of medicine, surgery and hygiene. He took no drugs to allay inflammation; He did not depend upon food or pure air to resuscitate wasted energies; He did not require the skill of a surgeon to heal the torn palms and bind up the wounded side and lacerated feet, that He might use those hands to remove the napkin and winding sheet and that He might employ His feet as before." [3]

" His disciples believed Jesus to be dead while He was hidden in the sepulchre, whereas He was alive, demonstrating within the narrow tomb the power of the spirit to overrule mortal, material sense."   His ascension was a final demonstration in which He " rose above the physical knowledge of His disciples and the material senses saw Him no more."   He attained this perfection of demonstration only gradually and He left behind Him an incomplete revelation which was to wait for its full illumination for the coming of Mrs.

[1] Page 41.   [2] Page 41.   [3] Page 44.

Eddy and Christian Science. Perhaps more justly He left behind Him, according to Mrs. Eddy and her followers, a body of teaching which could not be clearly understood until she came to complete the revelation. At any rate, Christian Science is really His second coming.

Christian Science His Second Coming

In an advertisement printed in the New York *Tribune* on January 23, 1921, Augusta E. Stetson says: " Christ in Christian Science is come to the understanding of those who looked for His reappearing." And if certain sentences which follow mean anything, they mean that, in the thought of Mrs. Eddy's followers, she completes what Jesus began and fulfills the prophecy of His reappearing. " Her earthly experience runs parallel with that of her Master; understood in a small degree only by the few who faintly see and accept the truth, she stood during her earthly mission and now stands on the mount of spiritual illumination toward whose heights no feet but those of the blessed Master have so directly toiled, first in agony and finally, like Jesus Christ the masculine representative of the Fatherhood of God, she as the feminine representative of the motherhood of God, will appear in triumphant demonstration of divine power and glory as the combined ideal man in God's image and likeness."

And, indeed, there are not wanting intimations in " Science and Health " which give to Mrs. Eddy a certainty in this region which Jesus Himself did not

possess. He falters where she firmly trod. No need
to dwell upon the significant omissions which such an
interpretation of the historic Jesus as this demands.
The immensely laborious and painstaking scholarship
which has sought, perplexedly enough it must be confessed, to discover behind the Gospel narratives the
fundamental facts and realities of His life, is entirely
ignored. Mrs. Eddy has no place for the social aspects of the teachings of Christ, indeed His whole
system of ethic could be "blacked out"; as far as her
teaching is concerned it would make absolutely no
difference.

Mrs. Eddy distinguishes, in theory at least though
there is no consistency in her use of terms, between
Jesus and the Christ. "Jesus is the human man, and
Christ is the divine idea; hence the duality of Jesus,
the Christ" (page 473). "Jesus is the name of the
man who, more than all other men, has presented
Christ, the true idea of God, healing the sick and the
sinning and destroying the power of death" (page
473). "In an age of ecclesiastical despotism, Jesus
introduced the teaching and practice of Christianity
. . . but to reach His example and test its unerring
Science according to His rule, . . . a better understanding of God as divine Principle, Love, rather
than personality or the man Jesus, is required" (page
473).

It is difficult enough to know just what this means,
but as one stands far enough back from it all it seems
to reduce Jesus historically to the first outstanding
Christian Science teacher and healer. "Jesus estab-

lished what He said by demonstration, thus making His acts of higher importance than His words. He proved what He taught. This is the Science of Christianity. Jesus *proved* the Principle, which heals the sick and casts out error, to be divine " (page 473). He is, therefore, historically of chiefest value as the demonstrator of Christian Science, the full philosophy of which apparently awaited a later revelation.

" Christ is the ideal Truth, that comes to heal sickness and sin through Christian Science, and attributes all power to God " (page 473). " He unveiled the Christ, the spiritual idea of divine Love " (page 38). The Christ of Christian Science, then, is an ideal Truth, a spiritual idea, apparently an abstraction. But Mrs. Eddy is not consistent in her use of these two names. On one page Christ is " the spiritual idea of divine Love "; on the next page " we need Christ and Him crucified " (page 39), though how an ideal truth or a spiritual idea could possibly be crucified we are not told. In many of her passages Mrs. Eddy uses the familiar phrase, Jesus Christ, in apparently its ordinary connotations.

The Incarnation: Christian Theology and Christian Science Belong Really to Different Regions

The Incarnation is disposed of in the same vague way. " Those instructed in Christian Science have reached the glorious perception that God is the only author of man. The virgin mother conceived this idea of God and gave to her ideal the name of Jesus." [1]

[1] Page 29.

" The illumination of Mary's spiritual sense put to si-
lence material law and its order of generation, and
brought forth her child by the revelation of Truth.
The Holy Ghost, or divine Spirit, overshadowed the
pure sense of the Virgin-mother with the full recognition that being is Spirit." [1]   " Jesus was the offspring
of Mary's self-conscious communion with God." [2]
Now all this is neither honest supernaturalism nor the
honest acceptance of the normal methods of birth.   It
is certainly not the equivalent of the Gospel account
whether the Gospel account be accepted or rejected.
To use a phrase which has come into use since " Science and Health " was written, this is a " smoke
screen " under cover of which Mrs. Eddy escapes the
necessity of either accepting or denying the testimony
of the Gospels.

Something of this, one must confess, one may find
in not a little religious teaching old and new, but it
is doubtful if there is anywhere so outstanding an
instance of what one may call the smoke screen method
in the consideration of the Incarnation, as in the passages just quoted.   As a matter of fact all this is
simply the attempt to fit the idealistic dualism, which
is the real philosophic basis of Christian Science and
which, in so far as it is capable of explanation at all,
can be as easily explained in two pages as two hundred, into the theology in which Mrs. Eddy was nurtured and which was a background common to both
herself and her disciples.   Christian Science would
carry far less weight in the race it is running if it

[1] Page 29.   [2] Page 30.

frankly cut itself clear of a theology with which it has fundamentally no affinity. This indoctrination of an idealistic dualism with a content of Christian theology probably heightens the appeal of the system to those who are most at home in a new faith as they discover there the familiar phrases of their older faith, but it weakens the fundamental Christian Science apologetic. I think, however, we ought justly to recognize this as simply an inevitable aspect in the transition of Christian Science from the orthodox faith and experience of historic Christianity to a faith and experience of its own.

Seen as a curious half-truth development made possible by a whole group of forces in action at the end of the nineteenth century, Christian Science is reasonably intelligible, but as a system of doctrine built upon the hitherto accepted bases of Christian fact and teaching, it is not intelligible at all and the long controversy between the Christian theologian and the Christian Science lecturer would best be ended by recognizing that they have so little in common as to make attack and counter-attack a movement in two different dimensions. The one thing which they have in common is a certain set of words and phrases, but these words and phrases have such entirely different meanings on the one side and the other as to make the use of them hopelessly misleading.

The Atonement. The Cross of Christian Science and the Cross of Theology

There are passing references to the Cross in

" Science and Health," but the word is used generally in a figurative and sentimental way. Mrs. Eddy's cross is simply the pain of being misunderstood and criticised in the preaching and practice of Christian Science, though indeed the Cross of Jesus was also the outcome of hostilities and misunderstandings and a final and terribly fierce method of criticism. One feels that mainly she is thinking of her own cross as a misunderstood and abused woman and for such suggestion she prefers the Cup as a figure to the Cross. As for the Atonement " every pang of repentance and suffering, every effort for reform, every good thought and deed will help us to understand Jesus' Atonement for sin and aid its efficacy." [1] " Wisdom and Love require many sacrifices of self to save us from sin." All this seems to be in line with the moral theory of the atonement until we see that in such a line as this there is no recognition of the fact that again and again we suffer and that largely for others, and when she adds that " Its [the atonement] scientific explanation is that suffering is an error of sinful sense which Truth destroys, and that eventually both sin and suffering will fall at the feet of everlasting love " (page 23), those passages cancel one another, for if suffering be " an error of sinful sense " it is hard to see how any pang of it can help us to understand Jesus' atonement unless His suffering be also " an error of sinful sense," and this is to reduce the atonement to a like error.

In another connection Mrs. Eddy finds the efficacy of the Crucifixion " in the practical affection and good-

[1] Page 19.

ness it demonstrated for mankind." But this turns out to be nothing more than that the Crucifixion offers Christ a needed opportunity for the instruction of His disciples to triumph over the grave. But since in another connection we are told He never died at all (chapter Atonement and Eucharist, paragraph " Jesus in the tomb ") even this dissolves into unreality. Moreover the " eternal Christ in His spiritual selfhood never suffered." [1] Whichever road she takes here Mrs. Eddy reaches an impasse. It ought to be said, in justice to Mrs. Eddy, that her treatment of the atonement reflects the difficulty she found in the theology in which she had been trained as a girl and that there are many true insights in her contentions. She was at least seeking a vital and constructive interpretation and doubtless her observations, confused as they are, have been for her followers a real way out of a real difficulty. Here, as in so many other regions, " Science and Health " is best understood by its backgrounds.

As a matter of fact there is in Christian Science absolutely no soil in which to plant the Cross as the Cross is understood in Christian theology. There is no place in Christian Science for vicarious atonement, whether by God or man; there is little place in Christian Science for redemptive suffering; there is a rather narrow region in which suffering may be considered as instructive, a guide, perhaps, to lead us out of unhappy or shadowed regions into the regions of physical

[1] A curious and far-off echo of early Docetism which also in its own way reduced Christ's suffering to a simple seeming to suffer.

and, maybe, spiritual and moral well-being, and to quench the love of sin.[1] Mrs. Eddy sometimes speaks of Christ as the Saviour but if her system be pressed to a logical conclusion she must empty the word of all the associations which it has hitherto had and make it simply the equivalent of a teacher or demonstrator.

Sin an Error of Mortal Mind

Sin along with sickness and death are the projections of mortal error, the creations of mortal mind; sin, sickness and death are to be classified as effects of error. Christ came " to destroy the belief of sin." All this is to root sin simply in the mind. No intimation at all here of the part which a perverted will may play in the entanglements of life; no intimation of the immense force of the emotional side of life; no intimation here of the immense part which sheer selfishness plays. Mrs. Eddy's sin is far too simple. There is, once more, a sound reason for that. Mrs. Eddy is twice-born, if you will, but the struggle from which she finally emerged with whatever measure of victory she attained was not fought out with conscience as the field of battle, or in the final reconciliation of a divided self finding unity and peace on some high level.

If Mrs. Eddy's true struggle was of the soul and not of complaining nerves she has left no record of it anywhere. It was rather the reaction of a speculative

---

[1] Page 36. But this is to recognize the reality of suffering. Mrs. Eddy is here on the threshold of a great truth—that suffering is an aspect of education—but she goes no further.

mind against the New England theology. Her experience is strangely remote from the experience of Saul of Tarsus, or Augustine, or John Bunyan. This is not to deny that in the practical outcome of Christian Science as evidenced in the life of its adherents there is not a very real power of helpful moral adjustment, but the secret of that must be sought in something else than either its philosophy or its theology. Christian theologians themselves have been by no means agreed as to what sin really is. Under their touch it became too often a theological abstraction rather than entanglement of personality caught in manifold urgencies and pulled this way and that by competing forces battling in the will and flaming in passion and desire. But a sin which has no reality save through a mistaken belief in its existence is certainly as far from the fact of a world like ours as is a sin which is only one factor in a scheme of redemption.

But at any rate, if sin have no reality except our mistaken persuasion that it be true and if we are delivered from it directly we cease to believe in it and affirm in the stead of it the reality of love and goodness, then while there may be in such a faith as this both the need and possibility of the recasting of our personal lives, there is in it neither need nor possibility of the Christian doctrine of the atonement. Naturally since man is incapable of sin, sickness and death, he is unfallen, nor is "his capacity or freedom to sin any part of the divine plan." "A mortal sinner is not God's man. Mortals are the counterfeits of immortals; they are the children of the wicked one, or the one evil which declares that man begins in dust or as a material embryo " (page 475).

Here also is an echo from an early time and a far-off land. It is not likely that Mrs. Eddy ever heard of Mani or Manicheeism, or knew to what a travail of soul St. Augustine was reduced when he fought his way through just a kindred line of teaching which, to save God from any contact with or responsibility for evil, affirmed our dual genesis and made us on one side children of darkness and on the other the children of light, without ever really trying to achieve in a single personality any reconciliation of two natures drawn from two entirely different sources. Nor does Mrs. Eddy know that one Eusebius, finding much evidence of this faith in the Christianity of the fourth century, dismissed it briefly enough as "an insane heresy." Heresy it certainly was for all those who were fighting their way out of their paganism into an ordered Christian faith and whether it be insane or no, it is of all the explanations which have been offered for the presence of evil in a world supposedly ruled by the love and goodness of God, the one which will least bear examination. It has been dead and buried these thousand years.

We may deny, if we are so minded, any freedom of the will at all, so involving ourselves in an inevitable sequence of cause and effect as to make us also simply weather-vanes driven east or west by winds of inheritance and environment which we have no power to deflect and to which we can only choose to respond. But to deny us the freedom to sin and so to shut us up to a determinism of goodness is no more in accord with the facts than to deny us the power to be good and shut us up to a determinism of sin. If we are free at all we are free in all directions.

The Sacraments Disappear. Mrs. Eddy's Theology a Reaction from the Rigid Evangelicism of Her Youth

" Science and Health " deals in the same radical way with the sacraments. Nothing at all, apparently, is made of baptism save that Mrs. Eddy says our baptism is a purification from all error. In her account of the Last Supper the cup is mostly dwelt upon and that only as showing forth the bitter experience of Jesus. The bread " is the great truth of spiritual being, healing the sick " and the breaking of it the " explaining " it to others. More is made of what is called the last spiritual breakfast with the Disciples by Lake Galilee than of the Last Supper in the upper room. " This spiritual meeting with our Lord in the dawn of a new light is the morning meal which Christian Scientists commemorate " (page 35). " Our bread," she says, " which cometh down from heaven, is Truth; our wine, the inspiration of Love " (page 35). All this is of a piece with the general allegorical use of the Old and New Testaments in " Science and Health," but it is a marked departure from the sacrament of the Lord's Supper even in the simple memorial way in which it is kept by non-liturgical churches.

Mrs. Eddy's theology, then, is in part a reaction from the hard phrasing of the evangelical doctrines in which she was trained and it is indeed in part a reaching out toward the interpretation of these doctrines in terms of life and experience, but as a theology it is extraordinarily loose and even though the familiar phrases of Protestant and Catholic faiths are employed, what is left is wholly out of the current of the main movement of Christian theology heretofore. The central articles of the historic creeds practically disappear under Mrs. Eddy's treatment.

Here, then, is a philosophy which will not bear examination, a use of Scripture which can possibly have no standing in any scholarly fellowship, and a theology which empties the central Christian doctrines of the great meanings which have heretofore been associated with them. And yet in spite of all this, Christian Science gets on and commends itself to so considerable a number of really sincere people as to make it evident enough that it must have some kind of appealing and sustaining power. Where, then, is the hiding of its power? Partly, of course, in its spaciousness. There are times when a half-truth has a power which the whole truth does not seem to possess. Half truths can be accepted unqualifiedly; they are capable of a more direct appeal and if they be skillfully directed toward needs and perplexities they are always sure of an acceptance; they make things too simple, that is one secret of their hold upon us. This, of course, is more largely true among the spiritually undisciplined and the mentally untrained, but even the wisest folk find it easier upon occasion to accept a half truth which promises an easy satisfaction or deliverance than a whole truth which needs to be wrestled with and may be agonized over before it brings us into some better estate.

The Real Power of Christian Science is in Neither Its Philosophy Nor Its Theology

We have already seen what predisposing influences there were in the breaking down of what we have called the accepted validations of historic Christianity —due, as we have seen also, to many contributing causes—to offer unusual opportunity to any new movement which promised deliverance. But one must seek the conditions which have made possible so many strange cults and movements in America, not only in the breakdown of the historic faiths, but also in the state of popular education. Democracy tends, among other things, to lead us to value a movement by the number of people whom it is able to attract. We are, somehow, persuaded that once a majority has accepted anything, what they have accepted must be true and right. Even a strong minority always commands respect. Any movement, therefore, which succeeds in attracting a considerable number of followers is bound to attract others also, just because it has already attracted so many. One has only to listen to the current comment on Christian Science to feel that this is a real factor in its growth.

Democracy believes in education, but has not commonly the patience to make education thoroughgoing. Its education is very much more likely to be a practical or propaganda education than such training as creates the analytical temper and supplies those massive backgrounds by which the departures of a day are always to be tested. In America particularly there is an outstanding want of background. It needs history, philosophy, economic understanding and a wealth of racial experience to give to any people either the power to quickly discriminate between the truth and the half-truth, or to carry itself with poise through a transitional period. But one may not dispose of the distinct hold of Christian Science upon its followers by such generalizations. The real inwardness of no religion can ever be known from its theology. A sincere devotion may attend a most deficient theology and we need to be charitable in judging the forms which other people's faith takes. What seems unreasonable to one may seem quite right to another and whatever carries a sincere faith deepening into a positive spiritual experience accomplishes for the moment its purpose. These studies of Christian Science are severe—for one must deal with it as honestly as he knows how—but the writer does not mean that they should fail in a due recognition of the spiritual sincerity of Christian Scientists. We must therefore go in to what is most nearly vitally central in the system to find the real secret of its powers. It continues and grows as a system of healing and a religion.

VII

CHRISTIAN SCIENCE AS A SYSTEM OF HEALING AND A RELIGION

CHRISTIAN SCIENCE practice is the application of its philosophy and theology to bodily healing. This is really the end toward which the whole system is directed. " Science and Health " is an exposition of Mrs. Eddy's system as a healing force. Her philosophy and theology are incidental, or—if that is not a fair statement—they both condition and are conditioned by her system of healing. There is hardly a page in her book without its reference to sickness and health. Her statements are consequently always involved and one needs to stand quite back from them to follow their outline. Here, as elsewhere, one may read deeply and indirectly between the lines attitudes and beliefs against which she is reacting. Her reactions against the environment of her girlhood and early womanhood affect her point of view so distinctly that without the recognition of this a good deal of what she says is a puzzle without a key.

Christian Science the Application of Philosophy and Theology to Bodily Healing

She had been taught, among other things, that sickness is a punishment for sin. One may safely assume this for the theology of her formative period fell back upon this general statement in its attempt to reconcile individual suffering and special providence. One ought not justly to say that Mrs. Eddy ever categoric- ally affirms that she had been taught this, or as cate- gorically denies the truth of it, but there are state- ments—as for example page 366—which seem to im- ply that she is arguing against this and directing her practitioners how to meet and overcome it. This per- haps accounts for the rather difficult and wavering treatment of sin and sickness in a connection where logically sickness alone should be considered.

Mrs. Eddy would not naturally have thus asso- ciated sin and sickness had they not been associated for her in earlier teaching and yet, as has been said, all this is implicit rather than explicit. The key to a great deal in " Science and Health " is not in what the author says, but in the reader's power to discover behind her statements what she is " writing down." Her system is both denial and affirmation. In the popular interpretation of it quite as much is made of denial and the recognition of error as of its more posi- tive aspects, but in the book there is a pretty constant interweaving of both the denial of evil and the affirma- tion of well-being.

There is a sound element of wisdom in many of her injunctions, but more needed perhaps fifty years ago than now. We must remember constantly that Mrs. Eddy is writing against the backgrounds of a somber theology, a medical practice which relied very greatly on the use of drugs which was at the same time lim-

ited in its materia medica and too largely experimental
in its practice. She was writing before the day of the
trained nurse with her efficient poise. The atmosphere
of a sick room is not naturally cheerful and generally
both the medical procedure and the spiritual comfort of
the sick room of the fifties and sixties did very little to
lighten depression. When, therefore, Mrs. Eddy
urges, as she does, an atmosphere of confidence and
sympathy she is directly in the right direction.

Looseness of Christian Science Diagnosis

As we pass beyond these things which are now commonplace, what she says is not so simple. It is difficult to say how far the healing which attends upon
Christian Science is in her thought the result of Divine Power immediately in exercise, and how far it
is the outcome of disciplines due to the acceptance of
her theology and philosophy. It is hard also to distinguish between the part the healer plays and the
contribution of the subject. There is no logical place
in Christian Science practice for physical diagnosis.
" Physicians examine the pulse, tongue, lungs, to discover the condition of matter, when in fact all is Mind.
The body is the substratum of mortal mind, and this
so-called mind must finally yield to the mandate of
immortal Mind " (page 370).

The result of this in practice is that the Christian
Science healer accepts either the diagnosis of the
medical schools, reported second-hand or else the patient's own statement of his condition. Needless to
say there is room for very great looseness of diagnosis

in such a practice as this. The actuality of sickness must be recognized neither directly nor indirectly. The sickness must not be thought or talked. Here also, as far as the patient is concerned, is a procedure of undebated value. It all comes back, as we shall see presently, to suggestion, but any procedure which frees the patient from depressing suggestion and substitutes therefor an encouraging suggestion is in the right direction. At the same time those who are not Christian Scientists would rather stubbornly believe that somebody must recognize the fact of sickness or else we cannot begin to set in action the machinery for curing it, even if that machinery be Christian Science itself, and we do not change this rather stubborn fact by covering sickness with the blank designation Error. Even the error is real for the time being.[1]

The results of fear are constantly dwelt upon and this too is in the right direction. Much is made of the creative power of mind in that it imparts purity, health and beauty (page 371). When Mrs. Eddy says on page 373 that disease is expressed not so much by the lips as in the functions of the body she is making one of those concessions to common sense which she makes

[1] The writer once received an unexpected sidelight on the practice of the Christian Science healer in this connection. He once enjoyed the friendship of a Christian Science healer with whom he often played golf. He called this healer up one morning to make an appointment. His voice was not recognized over the telephone and he was mistaken for a patient. The reply came back in professional tones—"And what error are you suffering from this morning?" When he answered that his own particular error was his persuasion that he could play golf the telephone atmosphere was immediately changed.

over and over again, but when she attempts to explain how erroneous or—as one may venture to call it—diseased belief expresses itself in bodily function one is reminded of Quimby. Temperature, for example, is wholly mental. Mrs. Eddy's reason for believing this is apparently because " the body when bereft of mortal mind at first cools and afterward it is resolved into its primitive mortal elements." " Mortal Mind produces animal heat and then expels it through the abandonment of a belief or increases it to the point of self-destruction " (page 374). Fever is a mental state. Destroy fear and you end fever.

In all this there is a profound ignorance of the real causes of fever which helps us to understand the marked deficiencies of the whole system. There is nowhere any recognition of the body as an instrument for the transformation and conservation and release of energy real as a dynamo. There is nowhere any recognition of the commonplaces of modern medical science in the tracing of germ infections. True enough, medical science had hardly more than begun when " Science and Health " was first written to redefine fevers in terms of germ infection and the consequent disorganization of the balance of physical functionings, and the oxidation of waste materials real as fire on a hearth, but that is no reason why such ignorance should be continued from generation to generation.

The Power of Mental Environment

In general, Christian Science practice as indicated in

"Science and Health" is a strange mingling of the true, the assumed and the false; its assumptions are backed up by selected illustrations and all that challenges it is ignored. Disease is unreal because Mind is not sick and matter cannot be (page 393). But Mind is "the only I, or Us, divine Principle, . . . Life, Truth, Love; Deity, which outlines but is not outlined" (page 591). In other words Mind is an ideal affirmation which Mrs. Eddy assumes to underlie human experience and possibly to reveal itself through human experience, and it certainly does not follow that while an ideal affirmation is not sick, a human being involved in the necessary relationships of our present material existence may not be. Mrs. Eddy never clearly distinguishes between what a speculative mind may affirm and actual experience report. Her dialectic is a constant wrestling with reality in a range of statement which involves her in many contradictions. She recognizes what she denies and denies what she recognizes and, in a lawyer's phrase, constantly changes the venue.

But through and behind it all is an intelligible method. Confidence is to be reëstablished, fear is allayed, the sufferer from error led to commit himself to healing forces. These healing forces are not consistently defined. Sometimes they are the "power of the mind to sustain the body" (page 417); sometimes "the power of Christian Science" (page 412), or "the power of Truth" (page 420) or divine Spirit, or her book itself. "Continue to read and the book will become the physician, allaying the tremor which

Truth often brings to error when destroying it " (page 422).

Mrs. Eddy sometimes anticipates in a vague way the reaction of thought and emotion upon physiological function to which Cannon has given such careful attention, but her definite statements are strangely inadequate. " What I term *chemicalization* is the upheaval produced when immortal Truth is destroying erroneous mortal belief. Mental chemicalization brings sin and sickness to the surface, forcing impurities to pass away, as is the case with a fermenting fluid " (page 401).[1] She recognizes the limits of Christian Science practice when she advises her followers to leave surgery and the adjustment of broken bones and dislocations to the fingers of a surgeon until the advancing age admits the efficacy and supremacy of mind (page 401).

Great care is to be taken as to the patient's mental environment. Mrs. Eddy's constant emphasis upon this explains the excessive separatist nature of Christian Science. More than almost any other of its cults it separates its followers from those who do not belong to the cult. They cannot, naturally, attend churches in which the reality of disease is recognized; they must have their own nurses as well as their own healers; in certain regions they must confine their reading to their own literature; their children must be educated, on their religious side, in their own cult schools and they cannot consistently associate themselves with remedial movements which assume another

[1] Compare " The Quimby Manuscripts," p. 118.

philosophy as their basis. It is difficult for a detached observer to see how a consistent Christian Scientist reconciles the general conclusions of a modern scientific education with the presuppositions of his cult. That he does this is one more testimony to a power which indeed is exercised in many other fields than the field of Christian Science to keep in the practical conduct of life many of our governing conceptions in different and apparently water-tight compartments.

Christian Science Defines Disease as a Belief Which if Treated as an Error Will Disappear

The answer to such a line of criticism is, of course, in the familiar Christian Science phrase that perfect demonstration has not yet been achieved in the regions in which the Christian Scientist appears to be inconsistent. But beyond this is the rather stubborn fact that in some of these regions demonstration never will be realized; Christian Science is confined to the field in which suggestion may operate. Mrs. Eddy is most specific about diseases, concerning which the medical practice of her time was most concerned and in the light of later medical science most ignorant—fever, inflammation, indigestion, scrofula, consumption and the like. These are all beliefs and if treated as error they will disappear. Even death is a dream which mind can master, though this doubtless is only Mrs. Eddy's way of affirming immortality. She hardly means to say that death is not a fact which practically has to be reckoned with in ways more final and unescapable than any other fact in life. As Dr. Campbell Morgan once said: "If you have the misfortune to imagine that you are dead, they will bury you."

Mrs. Eddy concludes her chapter on Christian Science Practice with an allegory which she calls a mental court case, the suggestion of which is to be found in one of the Quimby manuscripts.[1] Since this manuscript is dated 1862 it anticipates Mrs. Eddy by almost thirteen years. The setting is like the trial of Faithful and Christian in the town of Vanity Fair as recorded in Bunyan's "Pilgrim Progress." Doubtless memories of Mrs. Eddy's reading of that deathless allegory are reproduced in this particular passage which the author is inclined to believe she wrote with more pleasure than anything else ever turned out by her too facile pen. Personal Sense is the plaintiff, Mortal Man the defendant, False Belief the attorney for Personal Sense, Mortal Minds, Materia Medica, Anatomy, Physiology, Hypnotism, Envy, Greed and Ingratitude constitute the Jury. The court room is filled with interested spectators and Judge Medicine is on the bench. The case is going strongly against the prisoner and he is likely to expire on the spot when Christian Science is allowed to speak as counsel for the defense. He appeals in the name of the plaintiff to the Supreme Court of Spirit, secures from the jury of the spiritual senses a verdict of "Not Guilty" and with the dismissal of the case the chapter on Christian Science Practice ends.

Christian Science Has a Rich Field to Work

Now what can finally be said of the whole matter?

[1] "The Quimby Manuscripts," p. 172.

In general, two things. Recognizing the force and reality of psycho-therapy Christian Science gets its power as a healing system from the great number of people who are open to its appeal and the shrewd combination of elements in the appeal itself. In spite of our great advance in medical knowledge and practice and in spite of the results of an improved hygiene there remains in society at large a very great deposit of physical ill-being sometimes acute, sometimes chronic, sometimes clearly defined, sometimes vague, badly treated cases, hopeless cases and a great reach of cases which are due rather to disturbed mental and moral states than to ascertainable physical causes. Illness has its border-land region as well as thought and the border-land faiths make their foremost appeal to those who, for one reason or another, live in border-land physical states.

And, to repeat, the number of those who belong to this group is unexpectedly large. Naturally such as these grasp at anything which offers help; they supply to the manufacturer of cure-all drugs their clientele; they fill printed pages with testimonials of marvellous cures achieved where the regular medical faculty had been helpless; they crowd about every faith healer; they are the comrades of the pilgrims to Lourdes and Ste. Anne de Beaupré; they belong to the fellowship of those who, in the Middle Ages, haunted shrines and sought out relics and asked to be touched by kings. We discover their forebears in the pages of the Gospels and as far back as any records go we see this long, pathetic procession of the hopeless or the handicapped seeking help. And again and again they get it, for we have also seen that, given faith enough either in a saint or a shrine or a system, psycho-therapy with certain subjects and in certain cases does heal. But this type of healing depends upon no one philosophy or no single force except indeed those obscure forces which are released by suggestion.

While this was being written certain evangelistic faith healers in the city of Detroit were sending out broadsides of testimonials to their healings, as definite in detail as the testimonials in " Science and Health," or the *Christian Science Journal,* and yet the basal principles by which these men have claimed to work are as different from the basal principles of Christian Science as east is from west. While this is being re-vised Coué, the apostle of suggestion according to the Nancy school, is besieged in New York by those who have been led to hope for healing through the success of his method. Whether the relic be true or false does not matter if only the relic be believed in.

One of the Most Strongly-Drawn Systems of Psycho-therapy Ever Offered

Now Christian Science is one of the most strongly drawn psycho-therapeutic agencies ever offered. Most faith healing systems heretofore have depended upon some place, some thing, some healer. Here is a system capable of the widest dissemination and de-pendent only upon a book and its interpreters. It uni-versalizes what has heretofore, for one reason or an-other, been localized. It is shrewdly organized, as far as propaganda goes, and effectively directed. It is widely advertised by its friends—and its critics. Its temples, for beauty and dignity, put to shame most Protestant churches. Its rituals combine in an unusual way the simple and the dramatic. It is so fortunately situated as to be able to keep finance—which is a trying element in Protestant Church life—in the background. Its followers have that apostolic fervour which attaches to movements sure of their divine commission and not yet much worn by time. It possesses distinctly one of Sir Henry Jones' hall-marks of religion. "It impassions the spirit of its disciples and adds consequence to the things it sanctions or condemns."

It draws upon deeply established Christian reverences and faiths. It secures for its authority the persistent but perplexed faith in the Bible which the average Protestant inherits and for those who believe in it the force of this authority is no wise weakened by the fact that by every sound canon of Biblical interpretation it is illicit. Its very dogmatism is an asset. It could not do its work if it were less sure. The confusions of the systems which try the critically minded are a contribution to the devout who find in them an added opportunity for faith. Its experience meetings create enthusiasm and confidence. It is, in short, more than any one of the movements we are here considering, a clearly defined cult whose intensities, limitations and mystic assurances all combine to produce among its disciples the temper most favourable to suggestion and it locks up on its force as a system of healing.

An accurate analysis of what it actually accomplishes would require an immense and probably impossible labour—a knowledge of each case, an accurate diagnosis when even for the trained diagnostician the thing is difficult enough, and the following up of all reported cases. The medical faculty would probably have done better to have taken such movements as these more seriously and to have brought to them a trained investigation which, except in the case of Lourdes, has never even been attempted. Doubtless there is looseness and inconsistency in the whole system. Almost any one who has had a practical observation of the working of Christian Science has knowledge enough not only of looseness and inconsistency but of what seems to the non-Christian Science mind positive untruth. Something, however, must always be allowed here for the way in which the mind acts under excitement and for the way in which delusion deludes. All this combines to make any final judgment in this region difficult, but there still remains, after all qualification, an arresting solidity of achievement. Christian Science does work, especially with the self-absorbed, the neurotic and those who have needed, above all, for their physical deliverance, a new access to faith and courage. Christian Science practitioners have also an unusual opportunity in what may be called moral rehabilitation with physical consequences. The physician has a better chance with the bodies of his patients than with their souls; the minister a better chance with the spiritual needs of his parishioners than with their bodies and habits; the Christian Science practitioner to an unusual extent has the whole of life under his control and it ought in all fairness to be conceded that this power is helpfully employed.

The very discipline of Christian Science is itself a therapeutic. There are really a good many things which become non-existent directly you begin to act as if they did not exist. An atmosphere in which no one refers to his ailment and every one to his well-being is a therapeutic atmosphere. Psychologists have taught us that if we go through the motions of being happy we are likely to have an access of happiness; if we go through the motions of being unhappy we have an access of misery. If we go through the motions of being well, very often we achieve a sound measure of health.

But it is Fundamentally a System of Suggestion

All this has been so strongly dwelt upon of late as to make any extended consideration of it unnecessary here, as indeed any extended consideration is impossible for any one save a specialist. What we are more concerned with is the way in which the discipline and philosophy of Christian Science produce their results. The answer to this question is as plain as anything can be in our present state of knowledge, for essentially, as a healing force, Christian Science stands or falls with the therapeutic power of suggestion. It is a strongly drawn system of psycho-therapy because it is a strongly drawn system of suggestion. Its suggestion involves assumptions which are sometimes philosophy, sometimes theology, and more commonly a baffling interplay of the two.

But the outcome of it all is the practical persuasion on the part of the patient that he is not sick and does not need so much to get well as to demonstrate that he is well, and that in this demonstration he has an absolute force on his side. To this end the whole body of affirmation, persuasion, assumption, suggestion and technique of Christian Science is directed. As one tries to analyze these separate elements they are, taken singly, inconsistent, often unverifiable and often enough, by any tests at all save the tests of Christian Science, positively untrue. But as Mrs. Eddy has combined them and as they are applied in practice they do possess an undeniable power. They are not dependent, as has been said, fundamentally upon persons or things or places. Here is a coherent system, the force of which may be felt when it is not understood and it bears upon the perplexed or the impressionable with very great power. It would be appreciably weakened if any one of its constituent elements were taken out of it. But fundamentally it can do no more than any other system of suggestion, unquestionably accepted, can do.

It is Bound to be Affected by Our Growing Understanding of the Ranges of Suggestion

A deal of water has gone under the bridge since Mary Baker Eddy began her work. What was then almost wholly involved in mystery is now beginning to be reduced to law. The psychology of suggestion is by no means clear as yet, nor are the students of it agreed in their conclusions, but we do know enough about the complex character of consciousness, the actuality of the subconscious and the reaction of strongly held attitudes upon bodily states to be in the way, generally, of freeing this whole great matter from the priest, the healer, the charlatan or the prophet of strange cults and referring it hereafter for direction and employment to its proper agents—the physician, the expert in disordered mental conditions and the instructed spiritual adviser.

It is now generally agreed that suggestion, however induced, may positively affect bodily function. If it is a wrong suggestion its effects are hurtful, right suggestion its effects are helpful. Now since a vast range of physical maladjustments—and this may be broadened to include nervous maladjustments as well—is functional, suggestive therapeutics have a far-reaching and distinct field. When Christian Science or any other healing cult reports cures in this field, those cures, if verified by sufficient testimony, may be accepted as accomplished. Those who have accomplished them may take what credit they will for their own agency in the matter, but for all that the cure is no testimony at all to the truth or falsity of their system. It proves only that those helped have believed it.

The matter of organic healing is more difficult. Medical Science does not generally admit the possibility of organic change through suggestion. There may be, however, a real difference of opinion as to whether a particular trouble is functional or organic.

Here is a border-land not so much of fact as of
diagnosis. A cure may be reported as of an organic
trouble when the basal diagnosis was wrong and it
was only functional, but the body possesses undoubtedly the power of correcting or at least of limiting
organic disease. Tuberculosis is an organic disease
but it is again and again limited and finally overcome
without the knowledge of the subject. Post-mortem
examinations may reveal scars in the lungs and so
reflect processes only thus brought to light.

Whatever serves general physical well-being may
greatly help the body in eliminating disease and se-
curing a going measure of physical health. In such
indirect ways as these suggestion may, therefore,
while not acting directly upon diseased organism, contribute most distinctly to arrest organic disease.
Thoughtful physicians are ready to concede this and
thus open a door for a measure of organic healing
which technically their science denies. A very revealing light has been let in upon this whole region
by hypnotism. Some of the students of hypnotism are
inclined to go as far as to admit organic change under
hypnotic suggestion. " Strong, persistent impressions
or suggestions made on the reflex organic consciousness of the inferior centers may modify their functional disposition, induce trophic changes, and even
change organic structures."[1]

Christian Science, then, as a healing agency has a
great field for there are always folk enough to heal.
It has a method, a discipline highly effective in produc-

[1] Sidis, " The Psychology of Suggestion," p. 70.

ing changed mental and spiritual states and, strangely enough, it is all the more effective because it is so narrowly true. Those to whom it makes its appeal are, for the most part, not capable of analyzing through to their sources its fundamental inveracities, nor would they be inclined to do that if they were able. Its vagueness and its spacious rhetoric really give it power. It does produce results and probably one case of physical betterment has a prevailing power which a chapter of criticisms cannot overcome and, more than that, one case of physical betterment may screen a dozen in which nothing happened at all.

For Christian Science has in this region two alibis which can always be brought into action, the most perfect ever devised. If it fails to cure it is either because the one who was not cured lacked faith, or because of the erroneous belief of some one else. A system which believes that the toxic effect of poisons depends upon the vote of the majority in that arsenic will cease to be a poison when everybody ceases to think of it as a poison and will be a poison as long as anybody believes it is, is perfectly safe even if it should fail to cure a case of arsenical poison, for until facts and experience cease to weigh at all there will always be some one somewhere believing that arsenic is a poison and that one will be the scapegoat for the system.

As a Religion it is Strongest in Teaching That God Has Meaning for the Whole of Life

Christian Science is, however, more than a system of

mental therapeutics, it is also a religion and due allowance must be made in any just appraisal of it for the way in which it has made religion real to many for whom religion had ceased to have a working reality. It needs to be said on one side that a good deal of Christian Science religion is really taking the Ark of God to battle, using religion, that is, for comfort, material prosperity, health and just such tangible things. But Christian Science meets a demand of the time also just here. Our own age, deeply entangled in material satisfactions, has no mind to postpone the satisfactions of religion to a future life. The monk and, indeed, the generality of the devout in the medieval Church sought in self-limited earthly joy a proper discipline for the soul and a state in contrast to which the felicities for which they paid so great a price should be the more welcome. The devout of Mary Baker Eddy's time, though inclined to find in material well-being a plain mark of divine favour, none the less accepted sickness and sorrow as from the hand of God and prayed that with a meek and lowly heart they might endure this fatherly correction and, having learned obedience by the things they suffered, have a place amongst those who, through faith and patience, inherit His presence.

But our own time is not so eager to inherit promises as to enter into possession. A religion which does not demonstrate itself in actual well-being is under suspicion. The social passion now much in evidence among the churches grows out of this as well as the many cults which seek the proof of the love of God in health, happiness and prosperity. And indeed all this is natural and right enough. If religion be real the fruits of it should be manifest, though whether these are the more significant and enduring fruits of the spirit may be questioned. A religion which demonstrates itself in motor-cars and generous incomes and more than comfortable raiment may be real enough to those who profess it, but its reality is not quite the reality of the religion of the Sermon on the Mount.

Christian Science is in line with a distinct contemporaneous demand to demonstrate God's love in about the terms of Jacob's famous vow at Bethel—" If God will be with me and will keep me in this way that I go, and will give me bread to eat and raiment to put on so that I come again to my father's house in peace, then shall the Lord be my God." This is a far cry from the noble protestation of Job which sounds still across the years: " Though he slay me, still will I trust in him."

And yet the more sensitive and richly endowed among the followers of Mary Baker Eddy have found in Christian Science other values than these. They have passed, by a sort of saving instinct, beyond its contradictions and half-truths to what is centrally best in the whole system. God, that is, has a meaning for life not hereafter but now, not in creeds but in experience, not alone in hard disciplinary ways, but in loving and intimate and helpful ways. True enough, this is no monopoly of Christian Science; Christianity holds this truth in fee simple. But unfortunately, in ways which it is perfectly possible to trace, the great emphases of Christianity have in the past been too largely shifted from this.

There has been and still is in most Protestant churches too much reticence about the meaning of God for the individual life and maybe too great hesitation in really using to the full the proffer of divine power. The accepted understandings of the place of pain and suffering in life have been, as it were, a barrier between the perplexed and their God; His love has not, somehow, seemed sufficiently at the service of men, and though Christian Science secures the unchallenged supremacy of the love of God by emptying it of great ranges of moral meaning and shutting away therefrom all the shadowed side of life, it has probably justified the love of God to multitudes who have, for one reason and another, heretofore questioned it and they have discovered in this new-found sense of God's love and presence, a reality and wealth of religious experience which they had never known before.

It Exalts the Power of Mind But Ignores Too Largely the Processes by Which Mind Realizes Its Ideals

There is also in Christian Science practice and philosophy the apprehension of a real truth which New Thought formulates much more clearly. Mind is creative. (Not alone mind with a capital " M " but our own every-day, human, small " m " mind.) The trouble is that Christian Science hopelessly short-circuits the creative process. Our human world is finally what we make it through our insight, our understanding and above all by our sense of values, but the actual achievement of changed purposes in a changed world is a process whose immensity is not even so much as hinted at in " Science and Health." Christian Science too largely ignores and seems commonly to deny the whole disciplinary side of life with its inevitable accompaniment of failure, fault and pain. Pain is no delusion; pain is the sign of something gone wrong in the great business of normal physical life. Nor is sin only an unreality which " seems real to human erring belief "; sin is a sign that something has gone wrong in the struggle for a normal, disciplined, moral life. Nor is the whole body of evil simply a shadow to be dismissed as easily as one turns one's back upon some darkness and faces toward the light; evil is the sign of something gone wrong, or something not yet attained in the massive progress of a humanity which combines in itself so many discordant elements, which has so long a way to go and so much to learn and so many things to conquer as it struggles upward toward a happier state.

Christian Science cannot in the end be true to the great facts of experience, which have a power beyond the force of any assertion to countervail, unless it is false to Mary Baker Eddy's philosophy, nor can it be true to its philosophy without impoverishing moral and spiritual endeavour. It is hard to find a place in the system—taken rigidly—for sympathy or tenderness or the richest of human qualities, or for those elements of wealth in character contributed by pain bravely borne or sorrow uncomplainingly accepted.

There is little place in Christian Science for the Beatitudes and less still for that fine courage which is itself the one assured victory which the hard beset may win on any field of battle. The writer believes that while this severe judgment is justified by " Science and Health," it is not justified by the practical outcome of the cult in the lives of many of its disciples. They are in devotion and kindness the equal of many in the Church and superior to some. Their loyalty to their Church rebukes a good deal of orthodox easy-going. All of which proves at least that life is bigger than our theories about it and in the end subdues those who would make the best of it, to communities of experience and understanding in which we are all strangely kin. For, after all, unpleasant things cannot be thought out; they must be fought out and dug out and lived out. The whole redemptive force of society in thoroughgoing and far-reaching ways must be brought to bear upon the very sources of all the evil side of life, and the bare philosophy of Christian Science is not equal to this task.

Is Not Big Enough for the Whole of Experience

It is doubtful if Christian Science has ever made an appreciable change in the mortality statistics of any city and yet if the Public Health Department were to permit for forty-eight hours the milk or water supply of a city to be polluted, statistics would disclose that within ten days. This is only an illustration but it does illustrate. We must work if we are to dig up the roots of evil things and get a better growth in their stead and anything which attempts to substitute for this a denial of the reality of the evil, a mystical religious attitude and a mere formula of faith, no matter how oft repeated or how sincerely accepted, or indeed no matter how efficacious in certain selected regions among certain selected groups, is on the whole not a contribution to human well-being.

Very likely Mrs. Eddy's followers in the practical conduct of their lives are already recognizing this and gradually, and maybe unconsciously, adapting themselves to it. There are already signs of certain processes of conformity to the necessities of experience; these are likely to go farther. If Christian Science follows the history of such movements in the past, it will, after having made its own distinct assertion of whatever measure of truth it contains, be gradually swept back into the main current of religion and practice. It will maintain a nominal distinctness, but in the general conduct of life it will lose its more outstanding characteristics and become largely a distinction without a difference. Milmine, in her thoughtful criticism of Christian Science at the end of her history says that the future of Christian Science stands or falls with psycho-therapy.

That is true only on the one side. As far as Christian Science has true religious insights and approaches it will go on in spite of what happens to psycho-therapy, though there is enough in psycho-therapy to assure its future within well-defined regions if that were all. Something bigger than psycho-therapy will finally judge and dismiss Christian Science to its own place

—life and experience will do that—and it is safe to say that in the end Christian Science will have to come to terms with a truth bigger than its own, with a body of experience which cannot be dealt with on the selective process of taking what you want and denying the rest, and more than that, it will have to come to terms with the whole great matter of an intellectual, moral and spiritual struggle governed by law and conditioned by the vaster world of which we are a part. This is not to deny that Christian Science and allied teachings have made contributions of real value to our common problem. It is only to affirm that here is something not big enough for the whole either of truth or experience.

VIII

NEW THOUGHT

NEW THOUGHT has been defined as "an attitude of mind, not a cult." It is really both. It is necessary to include it in this study because it is a cult; it is hard justly to appraise it because it is an attitude of mind. Attitudes of mind are as elusive as the play of light on running water. We can estimate their force and direction only as we have an understanding of the main currents of thought by which they are carried along and as far as New Thought goes these main currents are far older than the cult itself.

New Thought Difficult to Define; " An Attitude of Mind, Not a Cult "

New Thought has never had an apostolic succession or a rigid discipline or a centralized organic form. This has given to it a baffling looseness in every direction, but has, on the other hand, given it a pervasive quality which Christian Science does not possess. It has a vast and diffuse literature and so merges into the general movement of contemporaneous thought as to make it difficult to find anywhere a distinct demarcation of channels.

New Thought is either a theology with a philosophic

basis or a philosophy with a theological bias. It is centrally and quite distinctly an attempt to give a religious content to the present trend of science and philosophy, a reaction against old theologies and perhaps a kind of nebula out of which future theologies will be organized. For a great theology is always the systematic organization of a complex of forces, a massive structure wrought through the years by manifold builders subduing a rich variety of material to their purposes.

The teaching of the Scriptures, old traditions, the needs of worship and organization, political and social circumstances, changing moral ideals, the trend of philosophies and sciences, the challenge of schisms and heresies, the sanctifying power of blind custom and the mystical authority of the Church itself all combine to make a theology. Once a great theology is so constituted it possesses an immense power over life. It shapes character and ideals and gives direction to faith, orders effort and so becomes, as it were, a mould into which souls and societies are cast.

Theologies may be changed, in fact they are always in the way of being changed, but they yield slowly to transforming forces. Nothing is so persistent as organized faith and yet the very strength of a great theology is always its weakness. It is never really anything else than a crystallization of past forces. The experiences which voice themselves in theology have cooled and hardened down; the philosophy which is implicit in theology is past philosophy; the science implicit in theology is senescent science.

There is always in evidence, then, in the regions of theology a disturbing pressure occasioned by the reaction of contemporaneous movements in science and philosophy and understandings of life generally upon these old and solidly established inherited forms. Currents of thought are always, as it were, running past the great formulæ since thought is free and formulæ are rigid, and then returning upon them. From time to time this movement gathers great force. The old has been rigid so long, the new is so insistent that the conflict between them fills an age with its clamour, stresses souls to its travail, breaks down ancient forms without immediately building up their equivalent, and contributes uncertainties and restlessnesses everywhere in evidence.

Now this is exactly what has been happening in the region of religion in the last thirty years. An inherited order, strongly fashioned and organized and long essentially unchanged, has been compelled to take account of the forces about it. Certainly theology is not so static as an earlier paragraph would seem to indicate, none the less the great theological centralities do possess an immense power of resistance. We have already seen how little Protestantism had changed since the Reformation until it met the full impact of modern science and philosophy. We have had really until our own time and still largely continue a theology with the Creation story of the ancient Hebrews, the outlook upon life of the age of the Apostles, the philosophy of the Greek fathers, St. Augustine's conception of human nature and the expectation of the end

of the world and the issues of history of the Jewish
apocalypse given a Christian interpretation.

True enough, there are in all this precious and timeless qualities but there is also through all the fabric
of our formulated faith the interweaving of such understandings as those who shaped our creeds had, of
law and history and truth. Any far-reaching change,
then, in philosophy or science was bound to profoundly
affect religion and even forty years ago far-reaching
modifications of the old order were overdue.

New Thought is just one outcome of the tremendous impact of contemporaneous thought upon our inherited theology; a detached fragment or rather group
of fragments, for even as a cult New Thought, as has
been said, is loosely organized and its varying parts
have in common only a common drift. Yet that drift
is significant for it has beneath it the immense force
of a philosophy which has been gathering head for
more than a century. It is to this, therefore, that we
ought to address ourselves for any understanding of
the changed outlook upon life which is carried, as it
were, from the surface of profounder tides.

" The Rediscovery of the Inner Life "

Josiah Royce dismisses the whole of philosophy
from Spinoza to Kant in one single pregnant phrase.
He calls it " the rediscovery of the inner life." It is
along this line that modern philosophy and religion
approach each other. Religion has always been the
setting forth of the inner life in terms of its relationship to God and the proofs of the reality of religion

have always been found in the experiences of the soul.
The mystic particularly made everything of the inner
life; he lived only in its realities. For the sake of its
enrichment and its empowerment he subjected himself
to rigorous disciplines. Its revelations were to him
all sufficient, for having found God therein he asked
for nothing beside.

Wherein, then, is this new mysticism, or better, this
new cult of the inner life different from the old? It
is not easy to answer that question in a paragraph,
though it is easy to feel the answer in any comparison
of the great classics of mysticism—which are mostly
spiritual autobiographies—and New Thought literature. To turn from St. Augustine to Dresser, or from
St. Theresa to Trine is to change spiritual and intellectual climates. There is in the modern literature
little reflection of such spiritual struggle as fills the
great Confessions with the agony of embattled souls,
nor any resolution of such struggle into the peace of a
soul " fully awake as regards God but wholly asleep
as regards things of this world and in respect of herself." This testimony of St. Theresa is illuminating
as a contrasting background for New Thought. There
the soul is very much awake, both as regards things of
this world and in respect of herself.

These new cults of the inner life are far more self-
conscious than the old and far more self-analytical.
They seek to discern the laws in answer to which they
act and utilize those laws in the practical conduct of
life. They are always either appealing to underlying
philosophies or else trying to make a philosophy of

their own. Mysticism made everything of God and nothing of itself. It plotted its mystic way but knew nothing of psychology. New Thought seeks to discover in psychology a road to God. The centers of mysticism were emotional; the centers of New Thought are intellectual. All these cults are far more akin to Gnosticism than mysticism, though they are saved, yet not wholly, from the lawlessness of Gnosticism by a pretty constant return to the outstanding conclusions of science and philosophy.

Spinoza's Quest

Now if we seek to discover the real genesis of the movement and trace its development we would better begin, so deep are the roots of things, with Spinoza rather than Quimby. Here the deeper currents, upon the surface of which New Thought moves, take their rise and here also we return to Royce's phrase—" the rediscovery of the inner life "—and the philosopher who inaugurated the philosophic quest for just this discovery.

Spinoza was one of the last of the mystics and the first of the modern philosophers. He shared with the mystics of an earlier time a consuming sense of the futility of life save as life perfected itself in contemplations of an eternal excellency and communion with something far greater than itself. " After experience had taught me," he says (and this is quoted from Royce's " Spirit of Modern Philosophy "), " that all the usual surroundings of social life are vain and futile, seeing that none of the objects of my fears contained in themselves anything either good or bad except in so far as the mind is affected by them, I finally resolved to inquire whether there might be some real good which would affect the mind singly, to the exclusion of all else, whether there might be anything of which the discovery and attainment would enable me to enjoy continuous, supreme and unending happiness."

Now there is in all this a strangely modern note— dissatisfaction with what is offered by the commonplace and the accepted, a great emphasis upon the mind as the key to the readjustments of life, a quest for some single formula which would offer " continuous, supreme and unending happiness." This is exactly what Mary Baker Eddy and all the other perplexed and bodily broken " seekers " who gathered about Quimby were really wanting and this is what, for one reason or another, the proffered religious experiences of their time failed to secure them. " This was, then," to quote Royce, " the beginning of Spinoza's Pilgrim's Progress." (As indeed it is the beginning of every Pilgrim's Progress.) " But now, for what distinguishes him from other mystics and makes him a philosopher and not a mere exhorter, he has his religious passion, he must reflect upon it . . . the philosopher must justify his faith."

We have no need here to follow Spinoza along all the way, difficult and misty enough, by which he sought to justify his faith. The outstanding fact is enough. He is a mystic who reasons his way through where the elder mystic has felt his way through, and the goal which he finally reaches, though it be the goal which the earlier mystics had found by other roads,— the loss of self in God—is none the less such an achievement of reason as Spinoza was able to compass.

Kant Reaffirms the Creative Power of Mind

So this polisher of lenses bequeathed to the century which followed him its greatest inheritance and set for it its greatest task: the inner life as the supreme concern of the philosopher and the discovery of its laws and the interpretations of its realities the supreme task of philosophy. Those who continued his work began far enough, apparently, from the point where he left off and went a road strangely remote from his. Having taken the inner life for their study they sought to lay bare its very foundations. Nowadays, if we are so minded, we dictate to machines which write our words curiously enough in shallow lines upon wax cylinders and when the cylinders are full shave off the fragile record and begin again.

This is what the eighteenth century did for the mind. It reduced it to a virgin surface, it affirmed the reality of nothing except the impressions thereupon registered by what sense supplied. We owe to experience and to experience only " all that vast store which the busy and boundless fancy of man has painted on it [the white paper of the mind] with an almost endless variety." We have nothing with which to begin but sensation; we have nothing to go on with but reflection. " These two, namely external, material things as the objects of sensation, and the operations of our own minds within as the objects of reflection, are the only originals from whence all our ideas take their beginnings." [1] Such things as these are perhaps enough to begin with, but they are not enough to go on with as our thinkers soon enough discover. Some way must be found to relate the material thus supplied and to build it up into a glowing, continuous, reasonable and conscious inner life.

So in turn the philosophers laboured at their problem. They made much not only of reflection but of association; they found a place for memory and imagination; they discovered that we may as truly define experience in terms of ideas as of sensation; they discovered finally that by no possible process even of the most ingenious reasoning can you get the full wealth of life out of a mind which was nothing more to begin with than a piece of white paper, any more than you can get Hamlet (if we may suppose Shakespeare to have used a dictaphone) out of a wax cylinder, a needle and a diaphragm.

So Kant ended what Spinoza began, by reaffirming the creative power of the mind itself. It does far more than passively receive, it interprets, organizes, contributes, creates. True enough, it is not an unconditioned creator, it has laws of its own in obedience to which it finds both its freedom and its power. It must take the material which experience supplies and yet, in its higher ranges, in the regions of conduct and faith, that is, where conscience has become the guide and the necessities of the soul the law, we do

[1] Locke, "Essay Concerning the Human Understanding."

possess the power in enfranchising obediences and splendid adventures of faith to make a world rich in goodness, power and peace. And here, once more, there is a strangely modern note. Life is a pilgrim's progress. We are set out to discover " whether there might be some real good, the discovery and attainment of which would enable us to enjoy continuous, supreme and unending happiness." And we do possess the power within ourselves, if only we may discover the controlling laws and release effective forces, to come at least a stage nearer our goal. All this makes for that exaltation of the creative self which is so marked a characteristic of present-day attitudes and which is perhaps the distinctive affirmation of New Thought.

Utilitarianism, Deism and Individualism the Practical Outcome of a Great Movement

But it needed time for all this to work itself out. The philosophic basis for it had been supplied but it is a far cry from philosophy to the practical conduct of life. Kant's transcendental philosophy needed a deal of working over before it became practicable for the man in the street. And to begin with what was deepest in the philosophy of the Enlightenment led in unexpected directions. " While the practical tendencies of all speculative thought inevitably appear in the opinions and customs of a general public far removed from their sources, it is particularly true of the philosophy of the Enlightenment, that its influences had no small part in shaping the popular point of view concerning the moral, religious and political convictions of that age." [1] Utilitarianism, Deism and Individualism were, says Hibben, the popular and practical outcome of the whole movement,—Utilitarianism in Ethics, Deism in Religion, Individualism in Politics. These three growths—and they have borne a deal of bitter fruit in the last one hundred years—grow out of one soil. In general they are due to Locke's sensationalism, Hume's skepticism, a new emphasis upon reason as opposed to revelation and the self-sufficiency of the individual. If conscious life is nothing but sensation worked over and built up, then pleasurable sensations are the best we can aspire to, happiness is the end of the quest. So Utilitarianism defined goodness in terms of happiness and gave to conduct generally a grasping, greedy quality for which we have paid over and over again in the disappointments and disillusionments of an age, which, supposing itself to have discovered the true secret of well-being, found too much of its seeming happiness only Dead Sea fruit.

They Bear a Bitter Fruit: the Reactions Against Them

Deism in its reaction against Religion as merely revelation and in its endeavour to find a rational basis for faith set God apart from His world, detached, unheeding and offering no real recourse to a travailing humanity between whom and Himself it built a rigid fabric of impersonal law. The Individualism of the

[1] Hibben, " The Philosophy of the Enlightenment," p. 253.

eighteenth century was partly a reaction against old despotisms of Church and State—and a Declaration of Independence. It was in part a pride of accomplishment and a new affirmation of the self-sufficiency of the questing reason. There was in it also a sound recognition of the worth of personality of which the world then stood in need and which has since supplied a foundation for a saving passion for education and human well-being. But Individualism as practically applied by the first three-quarters of the nineteenth century—unexpectedly reinforced as it was by aspects of Darwinism—stressed the right of the strong and the doom of the weak. It made competition the law of economic development, the survival of the fittest the goal of a life of struggle.

Consciously or unconsciously the politics, industry and religion of the nineteenth century were greatly influenced by these outstanding conceptions. No need to say how utterly they have broken down. They have made for the deepening strife of classes and of nations, they have essentially defeated the bright promise of a time which seemed to have more to hope for than almost any other great period of history.

And yet they were never unchallenged. They were challenged by the essential spirit of Christianity; they were challenged by the poets who found that they could shape no songs out of such stuff as this; they were challenged by philosophers who sought to build for themselves and for us a world more free and true; they were challenged by a group of great novelists who created out of the wealth of their imagination characters and situations in which love and human worth had their way in spite of a thousand obstacles. They were challenged by prophets of a better world, the Ruskins and Carlyles who soundly rated the ethics of selfishness and the political economies of competition and the politics of self-assertion and who stirred deeply the more sensitive of their time. And finally they were challenged, and here we begin to approach again the genesis of New Thought, by a philosophic movement which found its point of departure in certain great aspects of earlier thinking which had been much obscured by the difficult forms in which it had been stated: the supremacy, that is, of the soul over all its surroundings.

Now this return to what we may call the creative and controlling power of spiritual forces is the key to the modern approach to life. We do not understand, it may be, the meaning of our own terms. Spirit is a vague enough word but we do know that the initiative is with desire and purpose and understanding. These are positive and masterful; they are by no means free; they are conditioned by the vaster order of which they are a part, none the less our human world is plastic to their touch and our material world as well. Carlyle has chanted all this gustily enough but there is kindling truth in his stormy music. " Thus, like some wild flaming, wild thundering train of heaven's artillery does this mysterious mankind thunder and flame in long-drawn, quick succeeding grandeur through the unknown deep. Earth's mountains are levelled and her seas filled up in our passage. Can the earth which is but dead in a vision resist spirits which have reality and are alive?"

New England Transcendentalism. Quimby Again and the Dressers

Curiously enough this quotation from a book which nowadays nobody likely reads save perhaps in some college course on early Victorian literature, brings us within sight of the beginnings of New Thought. A little group of English and American thinkers, part philosophers, part poets, part rebels against the established order, anticipated trained students in their return upon the higher and more positive side of an older philosophy. They made much of the inner life, its powers and its possibilities; they affirmed the creative power of the soul; they conceived life to lie plastic to the touch of vision and desire; they thought themselves to be standing upon the threshold of a new world. They were impatient of discipline; they dreamed impossible things and gave their dreams the authority of reality. They were hard enough to understand and they sorely tried practical plodding folk, but they kindled their time and released forces which are yet in action.

New England, through a group of adventurous thinkers of whom Emerson was the most distinguished, responded strongly to Transcendentalism. Another group, as has been said, responded strongly to mesmerism and spiritism, which were also a part of the ferment of the time in which Christian Science and New Thought (I use New Thought here in the technical sense) find their source. And finally, Quimby, who is a rather unexpectedly important link in a long chain,—important, that is, to the student of modern cults—reacted against mesmerism, felt and thought his way toward some understanding of the force of suggestion in abnormal states, applied his conclusion to faith and mental healing and gathered about him—as has been said before—a little group of disciples who have between them released far-reaching movements.

Mrs. Eddy and the Dressers were the outstanding members of this little group of disciples. Mrs. Eddy soon dissociated herself from the others and she supplied in " Science and Health " a distinctive philosophy to her movement. She organized it into a church; she imposed upon it a distinctive discipline. No little of the power of Christian Science is due to this narrow rigidity which is itself the projection of the personality of Mary Baker Eddy. But Christian Science did not carry with it the whole of the group which had come under Quimby's influence, nor indeed all of those who came under Mary Baker Eddy's influence. There was during all the formative period of these modern cults a perpetual process of schism.

We have as a result, then, two divergent movements related in underground ways, though as marked in difference as in resemblance, both of them beginning about the same time, both of them reactions against accepted religious forces and validations, both of them with a marked therapeutic content, both of them adventures in the conduct of life.

In the summary which follows I am in debt to

Dresser's recent "History of the New Thought Movement." The name New Thought was chosen as the title of a little magazine devoted to mental healing, published in 1894 in Melrose, Mass. "The term became current in Boston through the organization of the Metaphysical Club in 1895. About the same time it was used by Mr. C. P. Patterson in his magazine *Mind* and in the title of two of his books." Other names were suggested—in England, Higher Thought; in Boston, Higher Life; in New York the little group was for a time known as the Circle of Divine Ministry; in the west the movement was known as Divine Science or Practical Christianity. There were groups also which called themselves the Home of Truth or the Society of Silent Unity.

New Thought Takes Form

New Thought, as has been said, lacks the definite direction which Christian Science has always had. Its organizations have grown up quietly, more or less irregularly and have had always a shifting character. "The first New Thought Society with a regular leader and organization in Boston was the Church of the Higher Life established in 1894."[1] The Metaphysical Club was an outgrowth of the New Thought group in Boston. Dresser gives a list of the original members, chiefly significant through the presence among them of some of Quimby's disciples and others whose books have since held a high place in New Thought

[1] All citations in this section are from Dresser's "History of New Thought," unless otherwise indicated.

literature. There were manifest connections between the movement and liberal (particularly Unitarian) theology.

The first New Thought convention was held in Boston in 1899 (there had been earlier conventions of the Disciples of Divine Science—a related movement —in western cities) and the second in New York City in 1900. The New York convention was the first to make any general statement of the " purposes " of the League. We find on the New York program one Swami Abhedananda, lecturer on the Vedanta philosophy. Here is an early indication of the return of Eastern religions upon the West which is also one of the marked characteristics of the religious development of our time. We do not need to follow through in detail the list of successive conventions with their topics and their speakers. The group is not so large but that the same names reappear. There are marked attempts in the earlier conventions to associate leaders in recognized schools of philosophy and theology with the movement. One does not discover this tendency in the later convention lists.

The local groups throughout the country have had varying fortunes. They have from time to time changed their names and naturally their leaders. The west has responded perhaps more strongly than the Atlantic seaboard. The movement is particularly strong on the Pacific Coast. There are no available statistics and generalizations are of doubtful value. The Cincinnati and Kansas City groups are offered by Dresser as typical organizations, but they seem on the whole to be exceptional rather than typical. The strength of the New Thought movement is not in its organization but in its influence. " In England as in America interest was aroused by Christian Science, then came a gradual reaction and the establishment of independent branches of the movement." " It is difficult," says Dresser, " to obtain information pertaining to the influence of New Thought literature in foreign languages." The more significant New Thought books, however, have been variously translated and widely sold. New Thought leaders sometimes advise their disciples to retain their old church associations and the movement has naturally tended to merge in religious liberalism generally and to become only an aspect of the manifold religious gropings of a troubled time.

In the Constitution and By-Laws of the New Thought Alliance, published in 1916, the purposes of the society are " to teach the infinitude of the Supreme One, Divinity of Man and his Infinite possibilities through the creative power of constructive thinking and obedience to the voice of the Indwelling Presence which is our source of Inspiration, Power, Health and Prosperity." We discover here the same tendency toward the deification of capital letters which we have already noted in Christian Science.

Its Creeds

In 1917 the International New Thought Alliance went further than at any other time before in the direction of a creed and set forth the following series of affirmations: " We affirm the freedom of each soul as to choice and as to belief, and would not, by the adoption of any declaration of principles, limit such freedom. The essence of the New Thought is Truth, and each individual must be loyal to the Truth he sees. The windows of his soul must be kept open at each moment for the higher light, and his mind must be always hospitable to each new inspiration.

" We affirm the Good. This is supreme, universal and everlasting. Man is made in the image of the Good, and evil and pain are but the tests and correctives that appear when his thought does not reflect the full glory of this image.

" We affirm health, which is man's divine inheritance. Man's body is his holy temple. Every function of it, every cell of it, is intelligent, and is shaped, ruled, repaired, and controlled by mind. He whose body is full of light is full of health. Spiritual healing has existed among all races in all times. It has now become a part of the higher science and art of living the life more abundant.

" We affirm the divine supply. He who serves God and man in the full understanding of the law of compensation shall not lack. Within us are unused resources of energy and power. He who lives with his whole being, and thus expresses fullness, shall reap fullness in return. He who gives himself, he who knows, and acts in his highest knowledge, he who trusts in the divine return, has learned the law of success.

" We affirm the teaching of Christ that the Kingdom of Heaven is within us, that we are one with the Father, that we should judge not, that we should love one another, that we should heal the sick, that we should return good for evil, that we should minister to others, and that we should be perfect even as our Father in Heaven is perfect. These are not only ideals, but practical, every-day working principles.

"We affirm the new thought of God as Universal Love, Life, Truth, and Joy, in whom we live, move and have our being, and by whom we are held together; that His mind is our mind now, that realizing our oneness with Him means love, truth, peace, health and plenty, not only in our own lives but in the giving out of these fruits of the Spirit to others.

"We affirm these things, not as a profession, but practice, not in one day of the week, but in every hour and minute of every day, sleeping and waking, not in the ministry of the few, but in a service that includes the democracy of all, not in words alone, but in the innermost thoughts of the heart expressed in living the life. 'By their fruits ye shall know them.'

"We affirm Heaven here and now, the life everlasting that becomes conscious immortality, the communion of mind with mind throughout the universe of thought, the nothingness of all error and negation, including death, the variety of unity that produces the individual expressions of the One-Life, and the quickened realization of the indwelling God in each soul that is making a new heaven and a new earth."

We discover in this creed a more distinct recognition of ideals and truths which inherited Christianity supplied than in the earlier statements of purpose. In the annual address of the President there is distinct reference to the relation of the New Thought gospel to the churches. " I am asked often: What is the relation of this movement to the Church? This is not a new religion. It is not an institution seeking to build itself up for the mere sake of the institution. We do not ask anybody to leave the church. We ask them to become better members of their churches than before. New Thought is designed to make people better and more efficient in whatever relation of life they may find themselves. In other words: ' New Thought teaches men and women only the old common-sense doctrine of self-reliance and belief in the integrity of the universe and of one's own soul. It dignifies and ennobles manhood and womanhood.' The main idea on which Christianity is founded is that of communion with God, that of worshipping God in spirit and in truth. This is the very corner-stone of those modern movements that recognize men and women as the living temples of the God within. . . . I predict that this new interpretation and new understanding will become universal in the new age which is now dawning."

A further paragraph, however, reveals the synthetic character of the movement. " It is the realization in practical affairs of the teachings not only of the Nazarene, but of every other great religious teacher since the world began; for in their essence these teachings are fundamentally alike; and the New Thought and other new spiritual movements are but the efforts to apply, in our relations one with another, these simple and sublime truths."

The Range of the Movement

I have quoted at length from these programs, affirmations and this one address to indicate the range of the movement as it has found official expression. We must look, however, to the literature of the movement as a whole for a full understanding of its reach and influence. The literature in general falls into three classes: (1) books concerned mostly about healing; (2) books which instruct as to character, spiritual states and fullness of life; (3) what one may call success books which apply New Thought to business and the practical conduct of life. The lines of demarcation between these three types of books is, of course, not clear and there is a material which is common to all of them, but the distinction thus suggested is real.

As a principle of healing New Thought differs from Christian Science in almost the whole range of its assumptions. It does not deny the reality of matter, not the reality of suffering, nor does it distinguish, as does Christian Science, between the Divine Mind and the mortal mind. There are, according to New Thought, healing forces which may be trusted to do their remedial work in us, if only we surrender ourselves to them and let them have their way. There is nothing in New Thought which quite corresponds to the "demonstration" of Christian Science. It would seem to an impartial observer that Christian Science asks of its disciples an intensity of positive effort which New Thought does not demand. Dresser, for example, believes all suffering to be the result of struggle. Directly we cease to struggle we cease to suffer, provided, of course, that our cessation is in the direction of relaxation and a trust in a higher power. In some regions, however, Christian Science and New Thought as thereapeutic agents work along the same line, but where Christian Science denies New Thought ignores. Here New Thought makes more use of psychological laws; it follows James generally in its psychology, as it follows Emerson in its thought of the over-soul, though in this region Emerson's detached serenity of faith is given body in an insistence upon the divine immanence for which New Thought is in debt to the suggestions and analogies of modern science.

New Thought makes much of the shifting of attention and its disciplines are rather the disciplines of the mystic than the disciplines of the Christian Scientist. It seeks in substance to ascertain the laws of mind in action and then, through the utilization of this knowledge, to secure health, happiness and prosperity. It makes much, of course, of the centrality of mind both in well-being and pain. It hardly goes so far as to say that pain is an error in belief, but it does say that pain is a matter of consciousness and that as we are masters of consciousness we are masters of pain. It believes in thought transference and absent treatment, but it is perhaps more conservative in the cases which it is willing to undertake than Christian Science and recognizes the limitations of the healer.

The Key-Words of New Thought

Its key-words are Harmony, Realization, Affirmation and Poise. Just here New Thought is a strangely interwoven web. It makes much of " vibration " and " friction." It is evidently under the spell of the wave theory of light and heat. It is most dependable in its analysis and application of laws of mental action, most undependable in trying to account for the relation of mind to body and in its explanation of the physical phenomena of disease. Fatigue, for example, " is evidently due to the calling of power into a new direction. It [evidently the power] comes into contact with dense matter, with an uncultivated portion of the being, physical as well as mental, and meeting with resistance friction of some sort is the natural result." One has only to compare a statement like that with Cannon's careful study of bodily changes under emotional states, to see the difference between speculation controlled by analogy and the illuminating experimental methods of modern science.

When Dresser adds that " we shall eliminate disease not by fighting it, not by studying its causes, or doctoring its physical effects, but by seeing the wisdom of the better way," he is on dangerous ground, for if we are not to study the causes of disease but to take as our guide the serene generalizations of a speculative mind we are shutting in our faces one of the doors by which we enter into that knowledge of the mind of God, of which New Thought makes so much. How shall we know the mind of God except as we ask endless patient and careful questions of every revelation of the divine method, whether in sickness or health?

New Thought, however, takes a far more constructive view of suffering than Christian Science. For New Thought suffering is at least disciplinary and instructive: it compels reflection: it brings us to a knowledge of the law. It is certainly, therefore, just and it may be kind. Indeed, New Thought occasionally goes so far as to say that suffering is also a revelation of love and must be so accepted and entertained. Its general conclusions in this region are far more safe than its insistence upon vibration and friction and its spacious technicalities.

When Dresser says that there is a difference " between ignoring a trouble, between neglecting to take proper care of ourselves and that wise direction of thought which in no way hinders while it most surely helps to remedy our ills," he is on perfectly safe ground. When he adds that there is a strong reason for believing that " there is a simple, natural way out of every trouble, that kind nature, which is another name for an omniscient God, is ever ready to do her utmost for us " he is speaking with a wise and direct helpfulness, though here as generally New Thought errs on the side of too great a simplification. There is a way out of every trouble but it is not always simple, it is often laborious and challenging. We have accomplished marvels in the matter of tropical sanitation but the way out has been anything but simple. It has involved experimentations which cost the lives of physicians who offered themselves for humanity as nobly as any soldier on any battlefield; it involved the sweat of hard driven labour digging drainage ditches, the rebuilding of the foundations of cities and a thousand cares and safeguards. If New Thought wishes to dismiss such a process as this with the single adjective " simple " it may do as it pleases, but this is not simplicity as the dictionary defines it.

Its Field of Real Usefulness

All that way of thinking of which New Thought is just one aspect is fatally open to criticism just here. It ignores the immense travail of humanity in its laborious pilgrimage toward better things and it is far too ready to proclaim short-cuts to great goals when there never have been and never will be any short-cuts in life. None the less, trust and quietness of mind and soul and utter openness to healing, saving forces are immense healing agents and in its emphasis thereupon New Thought has recalled us to that which in the very intensity of life's battles we are in the way of forgetting. And beyond doubt, in that obscure range of diseases which are due to the want of balanced life—to worry, fear, self-absorption and over-strain—the methods of New Thought have a distinct value.

In general, as one follows the history and literature of New Thought one finds that, though it began with a group more interested in healing than anything else, healing has come to play a progressively less important part in the development of the movement and the larger part of its literature deals with what one might call perhaps the laws of mental and spiritual hygiene. The principles implicit in New Thought as a healing cult carry of their own weight into other regions. It is important enough to get well—that goes without saying—but it is more important to keep well. Good health on the whole is a kind of by-product. We suffer as distinctly from spiritual and mental mal-adjustments as from physical. We suffer also from the sense of inadequacy, the sense, that is, of a burdening disproportion between our own powers and the challenge of life. New Thought has addressed itself increasingly to such states and prob-lems as this. Here it ceases to be a cult or a method of healing and has become a most considerable influ-ence and here also it in general takes the direction of and is identified with what is truest in the Christian religion, what is sanest and most clear visioned in present-day thinking. The typical books just here are Trine's " In Tune with the Infinite" and a similar literature.

Its Gospel of Getting On

Another application of New Thought is in the direc-tion of personal efficiency. There is a considerable literature in this region. It does not specifically call itself New Thought but it is saturated with the New Thought fundamentals and has distinctly the New Thought outlook. Marden is the most popular and prolific writer in this connection and the titles of his books are suggestive—" Keeping Fit," " Selling Things," " The Victorious Attitude," " Training for

Efficiency," "Getting On," "Self-Investment," "Be
Good to Yourself," "He Can Who Thinks He Can,"
"Character," "Opportunity," "An Iron Will."
Something like this has, of course, been done before
but the modern efficiency literature moves along a
wider front than earlier books and makes a fuller use
of the new psychology. All this literature dwells
strongly upon the driving power of a self-assertive
personality strongly controlled by will, single visioned
and master of its own powers. It suggests lines of
approach by which other people's wills can be overcome, their interest aroused or their coöperation
secured.

Quotation is almost impossible—there is such an
abundance of material and much of it is commonplace.
It takes a deal of padding to make shelves of books
out of the familiar and generally accepted truisms
which are the "Sermon on the Mount" and the
"Beatitudes" of this gospel of personal efficiency.
Keep fit, keep at it, assert yourself, never admit the
possibility of failure, study your own strength and
weakness and the strength and weakness of your competitor and success is yours. Look persistently on the
bright side of every situation, refuse to dwell on the
dark side, recognize no realities but harmony, health,
beauty and success.

It is only just to say that success is generously defined and the disciples of this New Thought are asked
also to live in the finer senses—the recognition of
beauty and friendship and goodness, that is—but on
the whole the ideal character so defined is a buoyant

optimist who sells his goods, succeeds in his plans and has his own way with the world. It is the apotheosis of what James called " The Religion of Healthy-Mindedness "; it all fits easily into the dominant temper of our time and seems to reconcile that serving of two masters, God and Getting On, which a lonely teacher long ago thought quite impossible.

Naturally such a movement has a great following of disciples who doubtless " have their reward." So alluring a gospel is sure to have its own border-land prophets and one only has to study the advertisements in the more generally read magazines to see to what an extent all sorts of short-cuts to success of every sort are being offered, and how generally all these advertisements lock up upon two or three principles which revolve around self-assertion as a center and getting-on as a creed. It would be idle to under-estimate the influence of all this or, indeed, to cry down the usefulness of it. There is doubtless a tonic quality in these applications of New Thought principles of which despondent, hesitating and wrongly self-conscious people stand greatly in need.

The Limitations and Dangers of Its Positions

But there is very great danger in it all of minimizing the difficulties which really lie in the way of the successful conduct of life, difficulties which are not eliminated because they are denied. And there is above all the very great danger of making far too little of that patient and laborious discipline which is the only sound foundation upon which real power can possibly be established. There is everywhere here an invitation to the superficial and, above all, there is everywhere here a tendency toward the creation of a type of character by no means so admirable in the actual outcome of it as it seems to be in the glowing pages of these prophets of success. Self-assertion is after all a very debatable creed, for self-assertion is all too likely to bring us into rather violent collisions with the self-assertions of others and to give us, after all, a world of egoists whose egotism is none the less mischievous, though it wear the garment of sunny cheerfulness and proclaim an unconquerable optimism.

But at any rate New Thought, in one form or another, has penetrated deeply the whole fabric of the modern outlook upon life. A just appraisal of it is not easy and requires a careful analysis and balancing of tendencies and forces. We recognize at once an immense divergence from our inherited forms of religious faith. New Thought is an interweaving of such psychological tendencies as we have already traced with the implications and analogies of modern science. The God of New Thought is an immanent God, never clearly defined; indeed it is possible to argue from many representative utterances that the God of New Thought is not personal at all but rather an all-pervading force, a driving energy which we may discover both in ourselves and in the world about us and to which conforming we are, with little effort on our own part, carried as upon some strong, compelling tide.

The main business of life, therefore, is to discover the direction of these forces and the laws of their operation, and as far as possible to conform both character and conduct, through obedience to such laws, into a triumphant partnership with such a master force—a kind of conquering self-surrender to a power not ourselves and yet which we may not know apart from ourselves, which makes not supremely for righteousness (righteousness is a word not often discovered in New Thought literature) but for harmony, happiness and success.

It Greatly Modifies Orthodox Theology

Such a general statement as this must, of course, be qualified. Even the most devout whose faith and character have alike been fashioned by an inherited religion in which the personality of God is centrally affirmed, find their own thought about God fluctuating. So great a thing as faith in God must always have its lights and shadows and its changing moods. In our moments of deeper devotion and surer insight the sense of a supreme personal reality and a vital communion therewith is most clear and strong; then there is some ebbing of our own powers of apprehension and we seem to be in the grip of impersonal law and at the mercy of forces which have no concern for our own personal values. New Thought naturally reflects all this and adds thereto uncertainties of its own. There are passages enough in New Thought literature which recognize the personality of God just as there are passages enough which seem to reduce Him to power and principle and the secret of such discrepancies is not perhaps in the creeds of New Thought, but in the varying attitudes of its priests and prophets. One may say, then, that the God of New Thought is always immanent, always force and law and sometimes intimate and personal. However this force may be defined, it carries those who commit themselves to it toward definite goals of well-being. The New Thought of to-day reflects the optimistic note of the scientific evolution of a generation ago. It is not exactly " God's in His heaven, all's right with the world," but it is the affirmation of streams of tendency whose unfailing direction is toward happiness and success.

If an element of struggle be implied in the particular sort of salvation which New Thought preaches, it is not at least clearly brought out. There has been amongst us of late a new and a very dearly bought recognition of the element of struggle which seems to be implicit in all life. The optimistic evolutionary philosophy in which New Thought roots itself is on the whole justified neither by history nor the insight of those who have been most rich in spiritual understanding, nor, indeed, by the outcome of that philosophy in our own time. The happy confidence that we do not need to struggle, but rather to commit ourselves to forces which make automatically for happiness and well-being, has only involved us more deeply in a struggle where in some ways the smug happiness and well-being of representative New Thought literature seem more remote than ever.

This elimination of the element of moral struggle and the need for deliverance which has so greatly coloured the older theologies gives a distinct character to New Thought theology. There is no place in it for a scheme of redemption; there is no place in it for atonement, save as atonement may be conceived as a vicarious sharing of suffering incident to all struggle for better things; there is no place in it for the old anthropologies of Christian theology. It has on the whole little to say about sin. Says Allen, in a very thoughtful short article on New Thought in Hastings' " Encyclopedia of Religion and Ethics," " New Thought excludes such doctrines as the duality of man and God, miracles in the accepted sense, the forgiveness of sins and priestly mediation. It seeks to interpret the world and nature as science has recorded them, but also to convey their finer and esoteric meanings to the human understanding. The fundamental purpose of religion and science is the same—namely, the discovery of truth." " New Thought does not teach the moral depravity of man. Such thoughts demoralize and weaken the individual. Miracles, in the accepted sense, New Thought does not conceive as possible in a universe of law. The only miracles are phenomena not understood, but nevertheless the result of law. It applies the pragmatic test to every religion and philosophy. Are you true? What do you give to a man to carry to his daily task? " " New Thought recognizes no authority save the voice of the soul speaking to each individual. Every soul can interpret aright the oracles of truth."

Tends to Become a Universal and Loosely-Defined Religion

Worship becomes, therefore, contemplation rather than adoration, and a vast deal of the liturgical material which Christianity specifically has heretofore supplied becomes useless for this cult. Christian hymnology would need much editing before it would serve New Thought purposes; the whole conception of prayer would need to be altered. Naturally, then, on its more distinctly religious side New Thought is at once fluctuating and incomplete. It is the proclamation, to quote one of its spokesmen, of a robust individualism and, in the individual, mind is supreme. Right thinking is the key to right living. New Thought affirms the limitless possibilities of the individual. Here perhaps it is more loose in its thinking than in any other region. It makes free use of the word "infinite" and surrounds itself with an atmosphere of boundless hope as alluring as it is vague.

The interest of New Thought is most largely in the present tenses of life; its future in an eternal progress which should, of course, imply immortality. New Thought is hospitable to truth from whatever source derived. It is particularly hospitable to the suggestions of oriental religions and, as far as it has taken form as a distinct religious movement, it is becoming more and more markedly a kind of syncretism, a putting together of religious elements drawn from widely universal sources and it patently seeks nothing less than a universal religious fellowship in which the values of all true faith are recognized and which is to be under the control of what science has to say about the world without and psychology of the world within. In a sentence New Thought is an outstanding aspect of the unconquerably religious in human nature, seeking to subdue to its own ends and inform with its own spirit the new material which science, psychology and comparative religion have put at our service in the last two generations.

If New Thought diverges from the accepted Christian theology in many ways, it runs parallel in other regions with what is enduringly true in the Gospels, and it runs parallel also with not a little of that endeavour after theological reconstruction which is loosely known as the New Theology. We are generally under a compulsion to reconstruct our creeds and adapt our religious thinking to whatever is true about us in our understanding of our world and its history and its mechanism and the laws of our own lives. Theology must take account of a creative evolution and a humanity which has struggled upward from far-off beginnings along a far-flung front and the findings of Science and the intimations of Psychology.

It will need a deal of pioneering to find roads through these new regions and such adventurous souls as seek new paths, with a daring disregard for ancient landmarks and a true passion to find religious meanings in new facts and forces, are really serving us all. There is the danger, however, that in the very freedom of their speculation they may be too impatient of old experiences and hallowed certainties, for these old experiences themselves are deeply rooted and testify to realities which we may be compelled to let in by the window, once we have put them out at the door.

IX

THE RETURN OF THE EAST UPON THE WEST

THEOSOPHY AND KINDRED CULTS

Historic Forces Carried Early Christianity West and Not East. The Far-Reaching Results of This Process

CHRISTIANITY in its beginning belonged neither to the East nor the West; it was born where they met and its subsequent development was greatly governed by the direction of the dominant tides of historical development. But from the beginning of the Christian era the main currents of human action flowed West and they carried Christianity with them. It is, therefore, outstandingly an occidental development. This is not to minimize the influence of the East in the earlier phases of Christianity. There was doubtless a measure of give and take, some blowing of the winds of the spirit in changing directions across vast regions and a confused time, which carried the germinal forces from one religion to another. But in the main, Christianity, to use Gardner's fine phrase, was baptized into the forms and forces of the West. I say in the main, for Asia Minor was in the time of St. Paul the meeting place of manifold religions and his first Gentile converts brought with them into their new faith a very great deal of what their old faiths had made them.

There was, generally, in the Apostolic world a very great longing for a spiritual deliverance and a mystic temper which easily took over and transformed those elements in Christianity which lent themselves to mystic interpretations. Something of this we discover in the Pauline Epistles themselves; Paul's use of the word " mystery " shows how he adapted his teaching to the understanding of those to whom he addressed himself. To quote Gardner: " In the growth and spread of popular superstition, if we may call them by so harsh a name, we may well discern a gradual preparation for Christianity. . . . These religions stand toward Christianity, to continue my biological comparison, as the wings of a penguin stand toward those of an eagle, and it is surely no slight on Christianity to say that it met the blind longings of a pagan nation and showed them a path toward which they had, for long generations, been trying to find their way. The religious needs which were very imperfectly met by the initiations and ceremonies and prayers of the cults of the pagan saving deities found a complete and perfect satisfaction from faith in an exalted Christ.[1]

Christianity could not do this really very great thing without at the same time being affected by that which it, in a measure, took over and completed. The influence of Asia upon Christianity is, therefore, a very

---

[1] " The Growth of Christianity," Gardner, p. 136. For fuller treatment with suggestive detail see Fraser " The Golden Bough," chapter 37.

real influence.   One can only wonder what would have happened had the course of empire been East instead of West.   Christianity might then have been carried into India and China and through long centuries been given so distinctly an oriental content as to have taken on a character radically different from its Western form.   But this did not happen.   To follow Gardner's figure still farther, it was baptized into Greek philosophy and Roman imperialism and the power of the nascent nations of western Europe, and into the medieval spirit, and so we have become its heirs. More than that, the East took its own way, uninfluenced by the West, until two entirely different types of culture, civilization, religion and approach to reality had been developed, as far apart as the East is from the West, and each, until almost our own time, substantially uninfluenced by the other.

The West Rediscovers the East; the East Returns Upon the West

Given the contacts of the modern world this massive isolation of cultures could not continue. The East and the West were bound to meet and religion was bound to be affected by their meeting. Western Christianity has for more than a hundred years now been sending its missionaries to the Orient and oriental religions are beginning to send their missionaries to the West. More justly the return of the East upon the West is not so much in a missionary propaganda, though there is a measure of that, as in a more subtle indoctrination of Western speculation by the fascination and mystery of the Eastern cults. It is not possible to follow this process in detail but it has gone on long enough now for us to begin to see the outcome of it and to appraise its force. It began with New Thought. One discovers oriental names on the programs of New Thought conventions; the Vedanta Philosophy was expounded by East Indian speakers at the Greenacre conference in Maine in the late nineties; B. F. Mills was lecturing on Oriental Scriptures in 1907; and a lecture on the Vedanta Philosophy appears on the program of the second convention of the International Metaphysical League held in New York City in the year 1900. The New Thought movement in England naturally reflected the same tendency to look for light to Eastern speculation even more markedly than the American movement.

All this was natural enough because New Thought, once divorced from inherited Christianity and committed to pure speculation about the sources and meanings of life, was sure to find out that the Orient had been doing just this for a thousand years. Two things happened. First, New Thought welcomed Eastern teachers to its conventions in the hope of receiving thereby some measure of enlightenment, and second, many of these seekers, finding that the East had a wealth of speculation compared with which the West is poor indeed, took over the Eastern cults bodily, gave themselves up to their study and became their ardent devotees and missionaries.

Generalizations are always dangerous and though the East has, until the West began to exploit it, re-

mained practically unchanged, the West has changed
so often that whatever one may say about it must immediately be qualified. But, on the whole, Eastern
and Western life are organized around utterly different
centers. The West in its present phase is predomi-
nantly scientific. Our laboratories are perhaps the
distinguishing hall-mark of our civilization. We are
always asking questions of the outside world; we are
hungry for facts; we are always seeking to discover
the law and direction of physical force; we have taken
small account, comparatively, of our own inner states,
but we have taken immense account of the universe
of which we are a part and the forces which play
around us. Our realities are what we touch and see.
We have given to our sight an immense increase of
searching power through the microscope and telescope,
but we are slow to venture beyond what they reveal
to us. We have increased the sensitiveness of our
touch through the instruments of our laboratories.
We have organs to sensibly register the vibrations
of an etheric force and even to weigh light. But we are
slow to recognize any range of reality not thus revealed to us.

We have gained in such ways a really illuminating
understanding of the physical universe; we have formulated its laws, chronicled its sequence and made it in a
marvellous way the instrument of our material well-
being. If we have speculated at all it has been rather
in the direction of the ultimate nature of matter and
force, as these have supplied us material for speculation, than in any other direction. We have been gen-

erally and soundly suspicious of conclusions which
cannot be verified by the scientific method, and so have
built about ourselves restraining limitations of thought
which we are wholesomely unwilling to pass. We
have found our real joy in action rather than medita-
tion. Our scientific achievements have supplied material for our restless energy and our restless energy
has urged us on to new achievement.

True enough, there has been of late signs of a
changing temper. We are beginning to discover that
science has marked limitations; there are ranges of
reality of which our laboratories can make no possible report which we are beginning to take into account. But in a large way the matured Western outlook upon life has been conditioned by the scientific interpretation of the universe.

Chesterton's Two Saints

The East has taken an entirely different line; its
laboratories have been the laboratories of the soul.
The East has had little concern about outside things;
it has had an immense concern for its own inner life.
The East has made little attempt to master outer
forces; it has been generally content to let them have
their way with it, realizing, maybe, that after all what
the outside world can do for the inner life is negligible
compared with what the soul can do for itself. Race
and climate and the sequence of history have all con-
spired to produce this temper. The history of the
East is a strange combination of drive and quiescence;
its more vigorous races have had their periods of

conquest and fierce mastery, but sooner or later what they have conquered has conquered them and they have accepted, with a kind of inevitable fatalism, the pressure of forces which they were powerless to subdue to their own weakening purposes. They have populated their lands to the limit and accepted the poverty which a dense population without scientific resource, on a poor soil and in a trying climate, inevitably engenders. The more helpless have fallen back upon fate and accepted with a pathetic resignation their hard estate, asking only to be freed from the weariness of it. "It is better," says an Eastern proverb, "to sit than to stand, it is better to lie than to sit, it is better to sleep than to lie, and death is the best of all."

There is an immensity of weariness and disillusionment in such an interpretation of life, which needs no comment. But the Eastern mind is subtle and speculative, possessing a peculiar penetrating power; and, for the want of any other field in which to act, it turned in upon itself.

Chesterton has both hit and missed the immense difference between the East and the West in one of his brilliant paragraphs.[1] "No two ideals could be more opposite than a Christian saint in a Gothic cathedral and a Buddhist saint in a Chinese temple. The opposition exists at every point; but perhaps the shortest statement of it is that the Buddhist saint always has his eyes shut, while the Christian saint always has them very wide open. The Buddhist saint has a sleek

[1] "Orthodoxy," p. 243.

and harmonious body, but his eyes are heavy and sealed with sleep. The medieval saint's body is wasted to crazy bones, but his eyes are frightfully alive. There cannot be any real community of spirit between forces that produced symbols so different as that. Granted that both images are extravagances, are perversions of the pure creed, it must be a real divergence which could produce such opposite extravagances. The Buddhist is looking with a peculiar intentness inwards; the Christian is staring with a frantic intentness outwards. If we follow that clue steadily we shall find some interesting things."

But to follow Chesterton's own method, the saint with the open eyes may still be blind while the saint with his eyes shut may really see a vast deal, and the East has seen much. Whether what it sees be true or not, is another matter, but there is no denying the range of his conjecture. The Eastern saint has sought to answer for himself and in his own way those compelling questions which lie behind all religion— Whence? and Whither? and Why? He, too, has sought to come into right relations with the power which manifests itself in the universe and he has sought, with an intensity of effort to which the West is strange, for a real communion with the power he has discovered. And above all, he has sought deliverance.

Why the West Questions the East

He has not been so conscious of the need of forgiveness, since forgiveness plays no great part in his understanding of the sequences of life, but he is anxious enough to be set free from pain and weariness and at his best he has traced the relation of moral cause and effect far more analytically than his Western brother. He has, indeed, introduced greatly speculative elements in his balancing of life's accounts, but the West has done that also, for the accounts of life persistently refuse to be balanced unless something beyond ordinary experience is taken into account. The longing of the East for deliverance has, on the whole, however, been less theological and more simple than the longing of the West. The West has been led to turn to the East for teaching and deliverance through a combination of forces. I have noticed already the very direct way in which New Thought, once committed to free speculation about life and God, found congenial guidance in the Eastern cults, but other elements enter. The West has begun to share something of the disillusionment of the East; so many things which promised to deliver us have seemingly failed us. Our sciences have immeasurably enlarged our knowledge and increased our power; they have added to our material well-being; they have worked their miracles for us; but they have brought us neither peace nor true happiness. They have instead added their own disturbances to our other perplexities and they have ultimately simply extended the frontiers of the mysterious and given a new and vaster quality to our problems.

Our democracies and our humanitarian movements have shown us that the keys both to liberty and progress are still in human nature and not in forms of organization and government. As our civilizations have grown older and particularly as they have wasted themselves in war, some shadow of the age-old weariness of the East has begun to fall across our Western world. We have also reacted strongly against materialism in thought and life; we have begun to see, as has been said, how the need and force of personality have the right to assert themselves against the dominance of things. We are beginning to recognize the right of religion and philosophy to suggest terms to science, and all these tendencies have combined to produce a considerable group of people who, having found, for one reason or another, no real satisfaction in their inherited Christianity, have welcomed the Eastern solution of the problems of life, or else have positively turned to the East in the hope of discovering what Western Christianity has not been able to give them. One should add also that the pure love of speculation which is one of the phases of modern thought has made an opening in the West for the East. If unlimited speculation is the main business of life, the East has certainly everything to offer us, and for warning, as we shall presently see, as well as for guidance.

Pantheism and Its Problems

The older Eastern religions are, to begin with, Pantheistic. We have seen how religion generally in its development takes form and content from its governing conception of God. We have seen also that there are three governing conceptions of God: He is conceived as Transcendent or Immanent, or else He is simply identified with the range and force of the universe. Pantheism is generally the creation of brooding wonder and uncritical thought; Pantheism feels rather than thinks; it accepts rather than seeks to explain. It may be devout enough but its devotion is passive rather than active. Pantheism is never scientific in the accepted sense of that term; it has little concern for law; it explains by personalizing the forces with which it has to deal; it is akin to the temper which finds some animating spirit in all natural phenomena. The flow of waters, the growth of things, the drift of clouds across the sky are all, for Pantheism, simply the revelation of the action of some indwelling spirit or other, without which they could neither exist nor go on.

At its worst Pantheism issues in a grotesque mythology and an inconceivable multiplication of divinity; the gods in the Hindu Pantheon are numbered by the thousands. At its best Pantheism issues in a kind of mystic poetry and creates a devotee sensitive as Tagore to the fugitive gleams of beauty through the murk of things, voicing his prayers and insights in rare phrases which are, on the whole, in arresting contrast to the actuality of life about him. Western devotion has been caught by the mystic and poetical character of Pantheism and is, on the whole, strangely blind to its actual outcome in the life of its devotees.

We all feel the suggestion of it in certain of our tempers. If we should take out of much of our finest poetry suggestions akin to the suggestions of Pantheism at its best, we should leave even Western poetry strangely poor, and we have beside, particularly in the contemplation of rare natural beauty, a feeling of kinship with the spirit which clothes itself in dawn and twilight, or speaks through the rhythmic beat of sea waves, or lifts itself against the skyline in far blue mountain summits, which helps us to understand this old, old faith. And if modern cults had done nothing more than appropriate the poetry of Pantheism they would have lent only a touch of oriental colour to the somberness of Western life.

But Theosophy and kindred cults have gone farther, since Pantheism itself must go farther. Directly you have identified creation and the creative power so intimately as Pantheism does, then you are under bonds, if you have any curiosity at all or any speculative force, to try to explain the ways in which a God, who is just to begin with all that there is, has managed to reveal Himself in such an infinitude of minute and sometimes ungodlike ways. So Pantheism has its own scheme, not of creation, for there is no place in Pantheism for creation, but rather of emanation. Eastern thought substitutes for the cosmogony of the Old Testament which simply carries the world back to a creative God and seeks to go no farther, and for the methods of Western science which carries creation back to ultimate force and is unable to go any farther, an entirely different system.

How the One Becomes the Many

A paragraph in Mrs. Besant's " The Ancient Wisdom" (page 41) may help us here. "Coming forth from the depths of the One Existence, from the One beyond all thought and all speech, a Logos, by imposing on Himself a limit, circumscribing voluntarily the range of His own Being, becomes the manifested God, and tracing the limiting sphere of His activity thus outlines the area of His universe. Within that sphere the universe is born, is evolved, and dies; it lives, it moves, it has its being in Him; its matter is His emanation; its forces and energies are currents of His life; He is immanent in every atom, all-pervading, all-sustaining, all-evolving; He is its source and its end, its cause and its object, its centre and circumference; it is built on Him as its sure foundation, it breathes in Him as its encircling space; He is in everything and everything in Him. Thus have the Sages of the Ancient Wisdom taught us of the beginning of the manifested worlds."

It is not, of course, fair to say that here is something entirely different from the line of Western scientific and philosophic thought or wholly alien to elements in modern Christianity.[1] The real problem of modern Theism is to connect what science discovers with what faith assumes. The broader generalization of science resolves action and existence into the unities of an underlying and self-conserving force which grows more and more subtle and tenuous as we follow it

[1] Indeed this is a better commentary on the prologue to the Gospel of John and certain passages of Colossians than most of the orthodox theologies, and the self-limitation of God is the key to the moral freedom of the individual.

from molecules to atoms, from atoms to eons and electrons, and even discern beneath these something more impalpable than themselves, and there must be some way in which a creative power conceived by faith in terms of personality has released the forces which have built themselves into the universe. The difference is, however, that Christian Theism refuses completely to identify God and His universe.

There is, after all, a profound distinction between creating and becoming. Theosophy undertakes to explain for us how " the One beyond all thought and all speech " has become us and our universe. It attempts also to provide a way by which we, who are entangled, to our pain and sorrow, in the web of things thus woven, may escape from it and lose ourselves again in the One. It takes the wheel for its symbol in more senses than one. Everything is a turning and returning and we ourselves are bound upon the wheel, carried down or up and finally to be set free, only by the acceptance of a certain discipline of life.

Theosophy, then, is both speculative and practical. Its speculations take an immense range necessarily; it is no simple thing to follow the One from the depths of His hidden existence to our earth-born lives and the forces which flow about them. Only an expert deeply versed in Eastern literature would be able to say whether Mrs. Besant follows her Eastern masters faithfully in reporting their conclusions, but she has plainly availed herself of many of the terms and suggestions of modern science in interpreting them to us. If one could use a figure borrowed from electricity,

the One is " stepped-down " through a series of planes
and manifestations. Theosophy makes much of sevens
—no use to ask why—and bridges the gulf between
ultimate and present realities by a series of seven
planes in which what is coarsest in the plane above
becomes the germ of what is finest in the plane beneath. Even so, the One does not directly touch even
the highest of these seven planes. (Theosophy is,
first of all, a study in descents and not in ascents; ascent comes later.) There are between the One and
the topmost plane three emanations (but perhaps we
would better let Mrs. Besant speak to us herself):
" The self-unfolding of the Logos in a threefold
form: the first Logos the root of all being, from Him
the second manifesting the two aspects of life and
form, then the third Logos, the universal mind, that
in which all archetypically exists, the source of beings,
the fount of fashioning energies." [1]

Evolution and Involution

It would seem to the uninitiated that all this is a
kind of smoke-screen of words to conceal our real
ignorance of what we can never know and really have
no need to know. It is evidently just an attempt to
bridge the abyss between the immaterial and the material. If Theosophy wishes to bridge this abyss with
conjecture, well and good, but its conjectures really
leave us more deeply perplexed than we should be if
we frankly recognized and accepted the limitations of

[1] " The Ancient Wisdom," p. 41.

our ignorance. Once within sight of the topmost of her seven planes, Mrs. Besant goes on a little more definitely though she confesses " of what occurs on the two higher planes of the universe, the seventh and the sixth, we can form but the haziest conception." Each plane has what she calls its own " spirit matter "; this spirit matter becomes coarser as we descend; each plane is an emanation from the plane above it and the spirit matter of each plane winds one more veil around those emanations of the immaterial One in whom or which the whole process took its beginning.

Theosophy does not speak of evolution as it attempts to account for our material world, it speaks of involution. Here it reverses what is most distinctive in modern Western religious thought as far as modern Western religious thought has accepted evolution. For us evolution, if we seek to give it a Theistic content, is God making manifest, in the vast ascent of form and existence, an always fuller revelation of Himself. Our familiar phrase " the self-revelation of God " posits a power which can never for a moment be contained in all that is, but which may always be more clearly known as we follow His creative record from stage to ascending stage. A grass blade is a richer revelation than a crystal, a bird than a grass blade; personality is almost infinitely richer than the lower forms, some personalities are more perfectly the instruments of the divine self-revelation than others, and Christian faith accepts in Jesus Christ the supreme self-revelation of God in terms of human experience.

Theosophy Undertakes to Offer Deliverance to the Entangled Soul

But Theosophy reverses all this. As the One comes down from emanation to emanation and from plane to plane He is always more deeply entangled in the veil of things, until on our last and lowest plane He is seven times enwrapped and smothered. We must not, however, confuse this last and lowest plane with our little world, or even our universe; these are but sensible aspects of it and they are really the manifestation of the deeply enwrapped Divine trying to struggle up and out again and so building our realities about us and eventually bringing us, with all our conscious powers, into being. (Here the theosophist has more in common with the evolutionist than one or two of the preceding paragraphs would seem to indicate.) If we follow the figure of the wheel our present plane, the last and lowest of them all, is really the turning point of the wheel; now it begins to turn back upon that from which it descended, and according to Theosophy our practical human task is so to avail ourselves of its upward movement as to be carried back with it toward the high planes of perfect being.

Theosophy undertakes to account for personality as it accounts for our sensible universe and along much the same line of speculation. Just as the whole physical plane on which our world exists has really somewhere deep wrapped up within it some emanation of the One from whom everything flows out, so our true selves, which have really come down from the One and should thence return, are wrapped up so deeply as also to be near lost and smothered with, nevertheless, the power to get themselves unwrapped. Our wrappings are our bodies, but we do not begin to understand Theosophy if we think of body in the ordinary sense; our physical body is only one and that the coarsest of the seven veils, for there are seven here also, in which the true soul is enmeshed. We have really seven bodies and we are not any one of them though each of them is useful and each one of them puts us in touch with a certain order of existence. Some of these bodies are mortal, others of them belong to the truly enduring order.

Now we are lost here unless we recognize the profound difference between all our usual ways of thinking or talking and the wisdom of Theosophy. Theosophy begins at the top and comes down, at least until it reaches our present world; it also begins at the inside and works out. We think of our physical bodies as the instruments, on one side at least, through which the physical world communicates with us, but for the theosophist they are only instruments through which we communicate with the world. Not quite so, however, for Theosophy recognizes the give and take of experience. The soul may slip out of the physical body in sleep and it—our physical body—is at the best a stupid, imprisoning, misleading sort of a husk which has its practical uses but ought by no means to be taken too seriously.[1] Its coarse matter may be refined by discipline and diet and apparently the physical

[1] For a striking modern phrasing of this see Edward Carpenter's Free Verse "The Stupid Old Body."

body of a vegetarian is a finer instrument than the physical body of one who feeds on the flesh of animals.

But Becomes Deeply Entangled Itself

The physical body has also an etheric double which duplicates in a more subtle way the constitution of the physical body. This is the vehicle of the life force, whatever that means. The physical body and its double are in a rough way the vehicles of the give and take of physical existence, but for the experiences of pain and pleasure and for the dwelling place of the passions, desires and emotions, we have an astral body. Here the theosophist makes much use of vibrations and colours, and apparently our changing play of emotion is reflected in a play of colour which puts the chameleon to shame and makes us in our most excited moment rivals of the rainbow itself. The astral body shows upon occasion browns, dark reds and greens and their combinations, lit from time to time with flashes of scarlet. Our better feelings reveal themselves in finer colours; rose indicates love, blue, religious feeling, yellow, intelligence, and violet, spirituality. The Theosophist believes that we can be trained to see all this and illustrates it in coloured plates which are, to the uninitiated, not over convincing. Beside the body of physical existence and the astral body we possess also a mental body. This is the seat of thought and mental action. In a sentence, maybe, the theosophist is trying to say that we have a body for each phase of personality through which we come into contact with the finer realities of the ascending planes of existence, and that the matter of these bodies is more subtly refined as we pass from mere sensation to higher spiritual states.

So within the astral body there is the mental body which, says Mrs. Besant, is of finer material than the astral as the astral is finer than the physical. This is the body which answers by its vibrations to our changes of thought. The mental body may be refined by fitting disciplines as it is coarsened by evil thoughts. These thoughts may become "veritable diseases and maimings of the mental body incurable during its period of life." These bodies we discard in due time, the physical at death and the astral when ready to enter the heaven world. What becomes of the mental body Mrs. Besant does not say.

Beyond these are bodies which belong to man's timeless existence, curiously named and obscurely defined. There is apparently a causal body which is possibly the vehicle of will and, more involved still, a super-spiritual body which is the reality of God deep within us, and the carrier and vehicle of our supreme and enduring personal values. All this is a curious enough mingling of psychology, a subtle materialism, and unbounded speculation; it is equally beyond proof and denial, though for the proof of it the theosophist offers the testimony of those whose senses are so refined by peculiar disciplines as to see in and about physical form a play of light and colour which are themselves the revelation of mental and emotional states. We literally go about, according to this testimony, "trailing clouds of glory" or of gloom. While for the denial of it there is the deep-seated protest of Western reason, that personality, complex as it is, cannot possibly be so bafflingly complex as this.

The West Accepts Suffering as a Challenge and Looks to Personal Immortality for Victory

We are, therefore, according to the theosophist, emanations from the Divine; deeply enveiled and much enshrouded within us is a timeless and changeless self descended from the mysterious All which lies back of all things and under high compulsion to seek again, in some vast turning of the wheel of Being, that from which we sprang. Theosophy becomes more understandable in its practical reaction upon life, for this many veiled self is deeply involved in forces and states to which it is not really akin, and since it suffers greatly in being so involved the end of existence is, in discipline and ascent, to be set free from the pain and weariness of conscious existence, and to be absorbed in the changeless peace of that ultimate reality out of which we have issued and back again to which we are destined to go. We cannot be insensible to the vast scope of such a speculation as this for in one form or another there are, in all religion and in the deeper yearnings of life, elements akin to it.

The order of which we are a part bears hard upon the soul. No one who meditates deeply upon the strangeness of human destiny can fail to recognize the arresting estate of sensitive personality enmeshed in laws and forces which drive on with so little apparent consideration for those who are caught in the turning of their wheels, or ridden down in their drive. Western faith has generally seen in this situation a challenge to personality to assert its own supremacy over the impersonal and subject its encompassing order to the high purposes of the soul. If we are wounded in the fight we take our wounds as good soldiers; if the forces which face us are challengingly strong we fall back upon our deeper resources and in the end assert our own vaster powers.

We accept the conditions of the struggle as a part of the discipline of life and in our braver moments win from the fight itself those elements of personal steadfastness which, matured in character, give moral meaning to the endeavour, and though we anticipate an ultimate release and blessed compensation for the present travail of our souls, we find that release and those compensations in a personal immortality which attends the termination of the individual life in the present order, and continues that life conscious, free and triumphant in an immortal order, and even there we ask neither to be released from effort nor denied progress. We challenge the fortunes of the Unknown in the poet's phrase, and seek " other heights in other lives, God willing."

The East Balances the Accounts of Life in a Series of Reincarnations

But just as the East casts the glamour of its speculation over the processes by which we have come to be where and what we are, so it casts the glamour of its speculation over the process of our release. The

West stakes everything on the issue of one individual life even if death ends it, or else it assumes a conscious continuity of life rich in memory and persistent in individuality in whatever progress lies beyond the grave. Those whom Dante saw ascending from terrace to terrace of the Mount of Purgation were in all stages continuously and truly themselves. They knew the faults for which they made atonement and looked back with unclouded vision along all the stages by which they had climbed. The East makes little of the continuity of individual life and everything of the sequence of individual lives. It offers for the solution of our problem of ultimate destiny and also for its solution of the problem of pain and sorrow and manifest inequality in human states, two simple and unescapable laws—the law of moral consequence and the law of reincarnation. The East and the West both believe that " whatsoever a man soweth that shall he also reap " but the West believes he gathers his harvests of pain or punishment in a continuity of conscious existence, the vaster part of which is lived beyond death, with no rebirth and with no travelling again the light or shadowed ways of earth and time. The Christian West believes also in redemption which is just that sharing of God in the process which makes faith and repentance definite and saving elements in the struggle of the soul.

The East believes in a series of reincarnations, each reincarnate state taking its character from the quality of the life before. The fact that the doors of recollection are shut and locked between each incarnate

existence makes no difference to the East. If a man
has lived well and justly and followed his light, he will
hereafter be born higher up; if he has loved darkness
because his deeds are evil, he will be born into some
low estate; he may descend into the beast or ascend
into the saint. He will pay for present injustice with
future suffering—

> " Or reach a hand through time to catch
> The far-off interest of tears "

even though he have no conscious remembrance of the
faults for which he atones, or the sorrow for which
he is recompensed. If he is steadfast through countless rebirths, the slow turning wheel will bear him
higher and higher until he begins to ascend the successive planes, discovering in each plane for which
he has fitted himself a new wealth and reality of existence, until at last he is lost in the Infinite Existence
and his struggle is ended.

Perhaps the word " struggle " as here used is wrong.
Deliverance for the East is not so much struggle as
acquiescence. For the theosophist desire is the master
mischief maker. Desire leads us in wrong directions,
complicates our spiritual problems and thrusts us
against the turn of the wheel. We are rather, according to the theosophist, to reduce desire to its simplest
terms, thereby freeing ourselves from restlessness,
above all taking care not to hurt or embitter others.

Theosophy Produces a Distinct Type of Character

There is no denying that here is a faith capable of

producing a distinctive type of character. It tends at its best toward an extreme conscientiousness and an always excessive introspection; it creates also a vast and brooding patience. " In countries where reincarnation and karma [the law of Cause and Effect] are taken for granted by every peasant and labourer, the belief spreads a certain quiet acceptance of inevitable troubles that conduces much to the calm and contentment of ordinary life. A man overwhelmed by misfortunes rails neither against God nor against his neighbours, but regards his troubles as the result of his own past mistakes and ill-doings. He accepts them resignedly and makes the best of them. . . . He realizes that his future lives depend on his own exertions and that the law which brings him pain will bring him joy just as inevitably if he sows the seed of good. Hence a certain large patience and philosophic view of life tending directly to social stability and to general contentment." [1]

If such a faith as this be informed with humaneness and be deeply tempered with the principle of sacrifice, it may, and does, result in a distinct type of real goodness. It is possibly a good faith for helpless and more or less despairing folk, though it likely creates many of the evils from which it desires to escape. The very reach and subtlety and even splendour of its speculation will make a strong appeal to minds of a certain type.

Two elements in the whole system doubtless account for what hold it has upon the Western mind.

[1] " The Ancient Wisdom," Besant, p. 273.

It does offer, to begin with, a coherent explanation of the problem of pain and sorrow. As we have seen more than once in this study, Western Christianity has been deficient just here. The accepted explanations of the shadowed side of life have not been great enough to meet the facts. Practically every cult we have studied has found its opportunity just here. Christian Science solves the problem by denying the essential reality of pain and disease. New Thought believes in an underlying and loving good to which life may be so attuned as to bring us generally into the current of health and happiness. Theosophy accepts pain, sorrow and all unhappy forces and explains them as the inevitable result of wrong action either in this or a previous existence.

Theosophy a " Tour de Force " of the Imagination

Christian Science saves the justice and affirms the love of God by making Him just a God with apparently no concern for and no participation in the shadowed side of life. New Thought saves the love and justice of God by discovering in pain and unhappiness our lack of harmony with Him. Theosophy meets the whole shadowed order along its full front and explains everything in terms of compensation. Now there is much in this to appeal to our modern temper. Directly we recognize the scales in which the consequences of our actions are weighed as being so sensitive that not even a thought can be thrown in the one balance without disturbing the equilibrium, directly we recognize ourselves as involved in a sweep of law from whose consequences there is no possible escape, we have at least a consistent scheme in which there is room for no evasion, and if we balance the manifold inequalities of one life by what has been done or left undone in some previous life, we are always able to add weight enough to the scales to make them hang level. True enough, there is nothing to guide us here but imaginative ingenuity, but it is always possible to imagine some fault in a previous existence which we pay for in pain or loss or disappointment, or some good deed done in a previous existence which accounts for our happy fortune in this. And so justice is saved if only by a tour de force of the imagination. (Mrs. Besant, for example, explains the untimely death of a child as a penalty due the parents for unkindness to a child in an earlier incarnation.)

The speculative aspects of Theosophy also appeal to tempers which love to dream without accepting the laborious discipline of a truly reasoned speculation. To quote a phrase of Macaulay's quoted in turn by William James in one of his letters, there is a type of mind " utterly wanting in the faculty by which a demonstrated truth is distinguished from a plausible supposition," and there has been amongst us of late a marked increase of this type of mind. There has been up to our own time no great amount of such speculation as this in the West. It is not native to the occidental temper and it has been held in control by our scientific approach to the facts of our world and our experiences therein. We have demanded for our speculations generally the demonstration of fact and this

has heretofore held us to a rather narrow range, but
that widening of the frontiers of the possible which
has attended the new psychology with its emphasis
upon the subconscious, along with the rather baffling
character of psychic phenomena, has opened the flood
gates and released a tide of speculation which goes far
beyond the proved fact and accepts no limits but its
own ingenious audacity. We have already seen how
evident deficiencies in the discipline of present-day education and the loose state of mind too much in evidence amongst us has contributed to all this. There
are everywhere a great number of perplexed people
who want to believe something and find it far easier
to believe in dreams and guesses and cloud-built systems than in restraining facts or even the rather clearly
demonstrated realities of the moral order, and such as
these have found a wealth of material in Eastern speculation.

A Bridge of Clouds

In trying to appraise the truth of Theosophy we
have to disentangle the system and the needs and the
seekings which lead its adherents to accept it. These
needs and seekings are, after all, near and familiar;
they are only our old questions Whence? and
Whither? and Why? Theosophy is at least the attempt to really answer some of the questions which
Western science is either content or compelled to leave
unanswered. The creative point of contact between
personality and matter and force is deeply enwrapped
in mystery. Orthodox Christianity has been content

to affirm the facts of creation without asking any questions at all as to its methods. It has affirmed the omnipotence of the Creator and has found in His omnipotence a satisfactory resting place. God is great enough to do what has been done and the detail of it is rather an affair for God than man. Scientific speculation generally has gone back as far as it can go in the resolution of its forces and laws and recognized its own limitations, leaving the rest to the theologian and the philosopher. The result has been a gap which has not been bridged over. Theosophy has undertaken to bridge that gap. But, examined more carefully, one sees that the abyss has been crossed by nothing more solid than a fabric of cloudy speculation. True enough these speculations are ingenious and touched with suggestive light, but they are strangely insubstantial. After all they do absolutely nothing more than our Western affirmation of the immanence of God in life and force and law, and our Western thought has the advantage alike in simplicity, in scientific basis and reverent self-restraint.

We might as well recognize, and be done with it, that there are questions here which in all human probability are insoluble. There are elements of mystery in life and the universe beyond our present and likely our future power to definitely resolve. In the end faith can do nothing more than rest in God and accept as an aspect of life itself the necessary limits of our position. Our organized knowledge all too quickly brings us to regions where faith and faith alone completes the inquiry. But on the other hand, a faith which too far outruns either in the reach or audacity of its speculation those elements which organized knowledge supplies and reason validates, loses itself in futilities or else misleads us altogether. Eastern speculation is too far beyond either ordered knowledge or right reason to be of any practical use in the fruitful conduct of life. Believing too much does just as much harm as believing too little.

Theosophy's seven planes and ascending emanations and sevenfold veils and all the rest really explain nothing. On the other hand they tempt their faithful to take conjecture for reality; they create a credulous and uncritical temper; they are hostile to that honest dealing with fact which is just one condition of getting on at all. A brave confession of ignorance is often more truly reverent than knowing too many things which are not so. As we approach more nearly the reality of things as they are we find them always unexpectedly simple. The burden of proof is always upon the murky and the complex. Those who try to escape the difficulties in which our deeper understanding of the world order and our own personalities involve us, by taking refuge in Eastern occultism are on the wrong line.

The Difficulties of Reincarnation

The same criticism holds true of Reincarnation. It is involved in hopeless difficulties. There are apparent injustices and inequalities in life—so much is beyond debate—but we have in general, if we are honest enough to follow it through, the clue to even these.

We are all parts of a struggling and, we trust, ascending order, an order which on the whole is not so greatly concerned for the individual as we are concerned for ourselves. We are hampered by our ignorance and we are deeply involved one with the other. The orthodox theology which blames everything upon sin as an abstraction is not convincing, but sin as the projection of wrong desires, through self-will, into the field of human action is a fact to be constantly reckoned with. The individual and social consequences of it are enormous, nor can they be confined either to one individual or one generation. Heredity continues weakness as well as strength. A vast deal of our bitter reaping is due to the wrong or foolish sowing of others, though fortunately we share the good as well as the bad. The laws of heredity will account for a vast deal in any one generation; the laws of social action and reaction for a great deal of the rest, and there is finally not a little for which we ourselves are responsible. A good many of our problems ought to be approached from the point of view of the well-being of humanity generally and not our own individual destiny.

We may safely trust our individual destiny to brave and unselfish living. I ought not to test what I do or leave undone by its effect upon me in some future reincarnation; I ought to test it by the effect which it has now upon the world of which I am a part, upon the generation which is to follow me and upon the quality of my own present life. True enough, the theosophist and myself find ourselves here in substan-

tial agreement as to many of the things which a man
ought practically to do to secure a happier future, but
I maintain that the motives just named are far more
solid and worthy motives than the camouflaged selfishness of Theosophy, and they are certainly in far deeper
accord with the ascertained facts of life. If we recognize that the more shadowed side of life is partly the
result of social and individual development conditioned
by weakness, ignorance and sin, if we recognize that
the present reaps what the past has sown, if we recognize that we suffer for the faults of others and that no
one of us may hope to climb far until his neighbour
climbs with him, if we recognize that pain and suffering are disciplinary, illuminating, educative, and
finally, if we recognize that we do possess the power
to take all the more difficult elements in experience
and subdue them to an increased wealth of personality, we have really all the elements in hand for the
solution of the problem of pain and sorrow in terms
of action and understanding, and we do not need a
series of reincarnations to help us out.

Reincarnation really explains, as it claims to explain,
neither the exceptional individual nor the apparently
unmerited sufferings of the individual, and it has beside inescapable difficulties of its own. It has to parallel the course of human existence with a range of
supernal existence for which there is absolutely no
proof; it has to numerically equalize birth and death
—and these are not equal in an increasing terrestrial
population—or else it has to assume, as it does of
course, on other planes a storehouse of souls from

which to draw. And more than that, it involves itself in a perfect tangle of heavenly bookkeeping.
Here is the best Mrs. Besant can do to explain the
difficulties of reincarnation. " We have seen that man
during his passage to physical death loses, one after
the other, his various bodies, . . . These are all
disintegrated and their particles remixed with the materials of their several planes. . . . At this stage,
then, only the man himself is left, the labourer who
has brought his harvest home and has lived upon it
till it is all worked up into himself. The dawn of a
new life begins." [1]

To condense, he now proceeds to build up for himself a new body for his coming life on the lower
mental level. " This again exactly represents his desire nature, faithfully reproducing the qualities he
evolved in the past; . . . thus the man stands
fully equipped for his next incarnation. . . .
Meanwhile action external to himself is being taken
to provide him with a physical body suitable for the
expression of his qualities. . . . All this is done
by certain mighty spiritual Intelligences often spoken
of as the lords of Karma because it is their function
to superintend the working out of causes continually
set going by thoughts, desires and actions. They hold
the threads of destiny which each man has woven, and
guide the reincarnating man to the environment determined by his past. The race, the nation, the family
thus determined, what may be called the mould of the
physical body . . . is built within the mother's

[1] " The Ancient Wisdom," p. 202—passim.

womb by the agency of an elemental, the thought of the Karmic lords being its motive power." The difficulties which this statement evades are enormous, its conjectures are even more enormous.

This is the subversion of all the facts of biology and heredity to a capricious scheme, built up just to answer a few practical questions—Why do we differ? Why do we suffer? Why are we happy? Surely there are far more simple and reasonable answers to these questions than the answer of Theosophy, and the willingness of so many people to rest in such an answer as this can prove only one of two things—the capacity of the mind for credulity or the arresting failure of those whose business it is to interpret life to the perplexed, to have even begun their task.

Immortality a Nobler, Juster and Simpler Balancing of Life's Account-Book

If there be a want of opportunity in our present existence for a true balancing of the scales of justice, and if some future existence be needed to make things right, then the Christian doctrine of immortality has an immense advantage over the reincarnations of Theosophy. We have no right to underestimate the difficulties of a reasonable faith in immortality, but they are simplicity itself as compared with the difficulties of reincarnation, for reincarnation must answer every question which the possibility of immortality raises and answer even more difficult questions of its own. It is far simpler to believe that having survived the shock of death we go on with the same essential individuality we had before death, than to believe that having survived we are sent back again through the gates of birth and are really reincarnated in another individuality. More than that, the Christian belief in immortality is more ethical. The action and reaction of life have real meaning for me only as I know and remember. No theosophic evasion can take the force out of this.

If I consciously connect to-day's pain with yesterday's pain with the folly or fault of a previous existence of which I am really unconscious, the chain has been broken and no speculative question can supply the missing link. Very likely the accepted Christian doctrine of the finality of life after death has given Theosophy an opportunity in the West. Protestantism particularly has allowed absolutely no place after death for repentance, has offered no new chance to the adventuring soul; its Hell and its Heaven have been final states. Catholicism has eased the strain of this with purgatory, a belief wholly without Scriptural basis, but nevertheless evolved in answer to great necessities of life. We need neither purgatory nor reincarnation; we need only the recognition of what is so centrally a part of any conception of immortality as to make one wonder why we have so greatly missed it; the reasonable confidence, that is, that we really go on very much as we left off here.

If there be in a future existence—and there must be if there be a future existence—any room for repentance born of a clearer recognition of fault and new and holier purposes born of a clearer understanding of the true values of life, then we shall go on in a truly moral process of growth, availing ourselves always of the teachings of experience and working toward the true well-being of our souls, and if the mercy and justice of God be not the figment of our imagination those who have been hardly dealt with here will be given new opportunity, the deficient and the handicapped released from what weighed them down will find a new departure, and the justices of eternity complete what time began. All this will be accomplished not in a series of existences, separated one from the other by abysms of forgetfulness, but in a remembered continuity of life deepening through endless growth. If this be only faith and speculation it is at least a far more reasonable faith and speculation than the alternative which Theosophy offers. Theosophy is a side issue in the real solution of the problems of life.

Pantheism at Its Best—and Its Worst

Finally, though this is possibly unfair, Eastern Pantheism generally must be tested by its fruits. We ought not, if we are to deal justly with it, to ignore its better side. The East at its best has been strong in a type of life wanting in the West; the East has been rich in patience and gentleness and in consideration for every kind of life, even the ant in the dust or the beast in the jungle. The East at its best has weighed conduct in delicate balances and traced the play of cause and effect in character far, far beyond the West; it has been content with simple things and found its true wealth in the inner life. It has willingly, for the sake of truth and goodness, subjected itself to disciplines, some of which are admirable, others of which are loathsome. It has at its best ventured everything for the well-being of the soul, even when it has misconceived that well-being. It has had little of the hard driving quality of the West. Not a little of the teaching of Jesus fits in better with the temper and devotion of the Orient than the competitive materialism of the Occident. It is easily possible to pass not a little of the Gospels through the interpretation of Eastern mysticism and find therein arresting correspondences. For example, a little book called " At the Feet of the Master " by a young Indian student, has in it a wealth of insight and an understanding of the balanced conduct of life which is wanting in a good many of the Western interpretations of life, but none the less, things must be judged by their massed outcome and the massed outcome of Eastern Pantheism does not commend itself.

The larger part of the religious literature of the East is upon a distinctly lower level than those parts of it which are brought to us by its devotees, and when Pantheism—and the basis of all Eastern speculation is Pantheistic—comes down from its high places and begins practically to express itself in worship and the conduct of the crowd, then it is such as to give us pause. What Kipling calls " the sculptured horrors " of the carved fronts of the temples in Benares are no accident; they are simply the logical outcome of a faith which lifts the whole to the level of the divine and has nothing beyond to correct what is by what

ought or ought not to be. Almost inevitably Pantheistic religions unduly exalt those powers which make
for fertility of field and the increase of life. As they
do this they have on their side the elemental forces in
human nature. When we begin to make gods of what
after all must be sternly subordinated to higher things,
and the East has done this in spite of its mystics and
its dreamers, then we are not only in danger of sculp-
turing symbolic horrors on the fronts of our temples
but of setting up therein strange altars to strange gods
who are best worshipped by strange rites. All this,
inevitably enough, has given to Eastern worship a
more than earthly character, and has invested with the
sanction of religion forces which it must always be
the business of religion to subordinate and control.

Along with all this has gone a grotesque mythology
and an inconceivable multiplication of divinity.
Since no one but an expert can hope to understand the
complexities of a faith like this, the East has developed a priestly class which bears harder upon its devotees and at the same time more contemptuously
separates itself from them than perhaps any priestly
class in the world. If the East is to return upon the
West in substituting a refined and more or less mystic
Pantheism for the sterner forms of Western faith,
we ought at least to understand what it is which, with
all its implications, is beginning to set up its altars
amongst us. No one can follow the theosophic religion of the West without recognizing how largely
Western Theosophy avails itself of Western science
and informs itself with what Christianity has given to

the West. If these were taken out of it it would be hopeless. Since, therefore, its speculations carry us beyond reason or science, since its solution of the problems of life is far too complex, since whatever is good in it may be found more richly and simply in what we already possess and since the practical outcome of it in the East itself is an arrested civilization which has many depths but few heights, one must inevitably conclude that Theosophy has no real meaning for those who possess already the knowledge which we have so laboriously gained and the faith and insight which Christianity has brought us.

X

SPIRITUALISM

PRACTICALLY all the newer cults are quests in one general direction but down more or less specific roads. Christian Science and New Thought are endeavours after health and well-being and the endeavour also to reconcile the more shadowed experiences of life with the love and goodness of God. Theosophy and kindred cults are quests for illumination and spiritual deliverance along other than the accepted lines of Christian " redemption." Spiritualism is practically the quest for the demonstration of immortality through such physical phenomena as prove, at least to those who are persuaded by them, the survival of discarnate personality.

All these movements involve in varying degrees the abnormal or the supernormal. They imply generally another environment for personality than the environment which the ordered world of science supplies, and other laws than the laws of which it takes account. They are one in affirming the mastery of the psychical over the physical. They either affirm or imply faculties which do not depend upon the senses for their material; they suggest a range of personality which, if the facts which they supply are sound, demands a very considerable recasting of our accepted beliefs about ourselves.

Christian Science and New Thought confine themselves largely to the present term of life, though Christian Science affirms strongly enough that death is an error of the mortal mind. New Thought places a shifting emphasis upon immortality. Spiritualism centers wholly upon the phenomena of the discarnate life, upon the power of the discarnate to communicate with us and upon our power to receive and interpret their communications.

Spiritualism, or Spiritism the name its adherents prefer, is, however, by no means so simple as this definition of it. It may be anything from the credulity which accepts without question or analysis the trick of a medium, to the profound speculation of Meyer or Hyslop or the new adventures in psychology of Émile Boirac and his French associates. It may be a cult, a philosophy or an inquiry; it may organize itself in forms of worship and separate itself entirely from the churches. It may reinforce the faith of those who remain in their old communions. Spiritism has a long line of descent. The belief that the spirit may leave the body and maintain a continued existence is very old. Mr. Herbert Spencer finds the genesis of this belief in dreams. Since primitive men believed themselves able, in their dreams, to wander about while the body remained immobile and since in their dreams they met and spoke with their dead, they conceived an immaterial existence. The spirit of a dead man, having left the body, would still go on about its business. They, therefore, set out food and drink upon his grave and sacrificed his dogs, his horses or his wives to serve him in his disembodied state. All this is familiar enough and perhaps the whole matter began as Mr. Spencer suggested, though it by no means ends there.

The animism which grew out of this belief characterizes a vast deal of early religion, penetrates a vast deal of early thinking. Primitive man lived in a world constantly under the control of either friendly or hostile spirits and the really massive result of this faith of his is registered in regions as remote as the capricious genders of French nouns and the majestic strophes of the Hebrew Psalms, for the genders are the shadowy survivals of a time when all things had their spirits, male or female, and the Psalms voice the faith for which thunder was the voice of God and the hail was stored in His armoury. It would take us far beyond the scope of our present inquiry to follow down this line in all its suggestive ramifications. Animism, medieval witchcraft and the confused phenomena of knocks, rappings and the breaking and throwing about of furniture and the like reported in all civilized countries for the past two or three centuries, supply the general background for modern Spiritualism. (The whole subject is fully treated in the first and second chapters of Podmore.)

The Genesis of Modern Spiritualism

Modern Spiritualism does not, however, claim for itself so ancient an ancestry. In 1848 mysterious knockings were heard in the family of John D. Fox at Hydesville, N. Y. They appeared to have some purpose behind them; the daughters of the family finally worked out a code: three raps for yes, one for no, two for doubt, and lo, a going concern was established. It is interesting to note that mysterious noises had been about a century before heard in the family of the Wesleys in Epworth Rectory, England. These noises came to be accepted quite placidly as an aspect of the interesting domestic life of the Wesleys. It has usually been supposed that Hattie Wesley knew more about it than she cared to tell and, as far as the illustrious founders of Methodism were concerned, there the matter rests.

But the Fox sisters became professional mediums and upon these simple beginnings a great superstructure has been built up. The modern interest in Spiritualism thus began on its physical side and in general the physical phenomena of Spiritualism have become more bizarre and complex with the growth of the cult. Raps, table tiltings, movements of articles of furniture, playing upon musical instruments, slate writing, automatic writing, of late the Ouija Board, materialization, levitation, apparent elongation of the medium's body, are all associated with Spiritism. It was natural that the voice also should become a medium of communication, though trance mediumship belongs, as we shall see, to a later stage of development.

Incidentally the movement created a kind of contagious hysteria which naturally multiplied the phenomena and made detached and critical attitudes unduly difficult. For reasons already touched upon, America has been strongly predisposed to phases of public opinion which in their intensity and want of balance have the generally accepted characteristics of hysteria. Some of them have been religious, great awakenings, revivals and the like. These in their more extreme form have been marked by trances, shoutings and catalepsy and, more normally, by a popular interest, strongly emotionalized, which may possess a real religious value. Other religious movements have centered about the second coming of Christ and the end of the world. Many of these peculiar excitements have been political. The whole offers the psychologists a fascinating field and awaits its historian.[1] Yet the result is always the same. The critical faculty is for the time in abeyance; public opinion is intolerant of contradiction; imposture is made easy and charlatans and self-appointed prophets find a credulous following. Movements having this genesis and history are in themselves open to suspicion.

It Crosses to England and the Continent

The American interest in Spiritualism from 1848 to 1852 belongs distinctly to this region. The Fox sisters have been generally discredited, but what they began carried on. In 1852 a Mrs. Hayden and a little later a Mrs. Roberts introduced raps and table turnings to England. There, and more particularly on the Continent, Spiritualism met and merged with a second line of development which in turn reacted upon American Spiritualism, and, in America, released movements on the surface wholly unrelated to Spirit-

[1] Sidis has a résumé of Social Epidemics in part three of his work on the "Psychology of Suggestion."

ism. In France to a degree and in Germany strongly Mesmerism lent itself to spiritistic interpretations. I quote Podmore, who is commenting upon the trance utterances of a Mrs. Lindquist: " It is to be noted that the ascription of these somnambulic utterances to spirit intelligences was in the circumstances not merely easy but almost inevitable. The entranced person was in a state obviously differing very widely from either normal sleep or normal wakefulness; in the waking state she herself retained no recollection of what happened in the trance; in the trance she habitually spoke of her waking self in the third person, as of some one else; the intelligence which manifested in the trance obviously possessed powers of expression and intellectual resources in some directions far greater than any displayed by the waking subject. Add to this that the trance intelligence habitually reflected the ideas in general and especially the religious orthodoxy of her interlocutors; that on occasion she showed knowledge of their thoughts and intentions which could not apparently have been acquired by normal means; that she was, in particular, extraordinarily skillful in diagnosing, prescribing for, and occasionally foretelling the course of diseases in herself and others—the proof must have seemed to the bystanders complete." [1]

The Beginnings of Trance-Mediumship

We have here plainly enough the beginnings of trance mediumship. It needed only unstable personalities, capable of self-induced trance states, so to

---

[1] " Modern Spiritualism," Podmore, Vol. I, p. 77.

widen all this as to supply the bases of spiritistic faith and the material for the immensely laborious investigation of the Society for Psychical Research. In the main, however, French interest in Mesmerism and animal magnetism took a more scientific turn and issued in the brilliant French studies in hypnotism. Spiritualism has made little headway in Catholic countries. The authority of the Church is thrown so strongly against it as to prohibit the interest of the credulous and the penetrating minds of the southern European scientists have been more concerned with the problems of abnormal personality than the continued existence of the discarnate.

The interest in Germany took another line. There was less scientific investigation of hypnotism and trance states as abnormal modifications of personality and far more interest in clairvoyance and spirit existence. Men whose names carried weight accepted the spiritistic explanation of phenomena ranging from broken flower pots to ghosts. Very likely the German tendency toward mysticism and speculation explains this. Jung followed Swedenborg and the mystics generally in affirming a psychic body, but was a pioneer in associating it with the luminiferous ether in a range of speculation which in our time supplies an hypothetical scientific basis for the environment of the discarnate. (So Sir Oliver Lodge.) Podmore concludes that the foundations of modern Spiritualism were laid by the German magnetists of the first half of the nineteenth century.

The movement developed along these lines till 1875.

Once broadly in action it touches at one point or another the whole region of the occult. Many spiritualists found in Theosophy, for which existence is the
endless turning of a wheel, a cycle of death and rebirth, a pseudo-philosophic support for their belief.
Spiritualism appealed naturally to the lovers of the mystic and the unusual and it associated itself, to a degree,
with extreme liberalism in the general development
of religion. (On the whole, however, as far as religion goes, Spiritualism has created a religion of its
own.) Its advocates were likely to be interested in
phrenology, advanced social experiments, or modification of the marriage laws. Spiritualistic phenomena themselves became more varied and complex;
trance mediumship became a profession with a great
increase of performers; slate writing was introduced
and finally materialization was achieved. All this
might mean that the spirits were growing more adept
in "getting through," the mediums more adept in
technique, or else, which is more likely, that latent
abnormal aspects of personality were being brought to
light through suggestion, imitation and exercise. But
no concerted effort was made by trained and impartial
observers to eliminate fraud, collect data and reach
dependable conclusions. This has been finally attempted by the Society for Psychical Research and the
results of their laborious investigations are now at the
service of the student of the occult.

The Society for Psychical Research Begins Its Work
    The weight which attaches to the names of many

English and some American members of the Society, the carefully guarded admission of some of them that there is in the whole region a possible residue of phenomena which indicate communication between the living and the discarnate and the profoundly unsettling influence of the war, really account for the renewed interest in Spiritualism in our own time. In 1875 a few Englishmen, one of them a famous medium—Stainton Moses—formed a Psychological Society for the investigation of supernormal phenomena. (In general all this account of the history of Spiritualism is greatly condensed from Podmore and Hill and the reader is referred to their works without specific reference.)

This first group dissolved upon the death of one of its members—though that would seem to have been a good reason for continuing it—and in 1882 Professor (afterward Sir) William Barrett, who had already done some experimenting and had brought hypnotism and telepathy to the notice of the British association for the advancement of science, consulted Stainton Moses with the view of founding a society under better auspices and the Society for Psychical Research was organized, with Professor Henry Sidgwick as first president. The Society undertook, according to its own statement:

I. An examination of the nature and extent of any influence which may be exerted by one mind upon another, otherwise than through the recognized sensory channels.

2. The study of hypnotism and mesmerism, and an inquiry into the alleged phenomena of clairvoyance.

3. A careful investigation of any reports, resting on testimony sufficiently strong and not too remote, of apparitions coinciding with some external event (as for instance a death) or giving information previously unknown to the percipient, or being seen by two or more persons independently of each other.

4. An inquiry into various alleged phenomena apparently inexplicable by known laws of nature, and commonly referred by Spiritualists to the agency of extra-human intelligences.

5. The collection and collation of existing materials bearing on the history of these subjects.[1]

They sought also " to approach these various problems without prejudice or prepossession of any kind and in the same spirit of exact and unimpassioned inquiry which has enabled science to solve so many problems, once not less obscure nor less hotly debated."

As a matter of fact the region is the most obscure which inquiry has ever been called to enter. A noble rationality pervades the whole normal material order, causes can be controlled, effects anticipated, laws formulated and above all, the hypotheses of science are, if true, always capable of a luminous and splendid verification. The disciplined intellect moves through it all with a sense of " at-homeness " which is itself a testimony to profound correspondences between the human mind and the order with which, during its long, long unfolding, it has been associated in inti-

[1] " Spiritualism," Hill, p. 100.

macies of action and reaction too close to be adequately set forth in words. But the mind does not rest easily in the region which Spiritism claims for its own.

The Difficulties It Confronts

Of course this is to beg the whole question. The more scientifically minded spiritualists might fairly enough answer that they are attempting to discover the laws of the occult and reduce an anarchical system to order, that our feeling of strangeness in these regions is only because of our little contact with them. There are, they claim, undeveloped aspects of personality which we have had as yet little occasion to use, but which would, once they were fully brought into action, give us the same sense of rapport with a supersensible order that we now have in our contact with the sensible order. The crux of the whole contention is probably just here and in view of what has heretofore been accomplished in discovering and formulating the laws of the physical universe and in reducing an immense body of apparently unrelated facts to order, there is doubtless possible a very great systematization of psychical phenomena, even the most obscure. Nor may we readily set bounds to the measure of human development. But at any rate the statement with which this paragraph began is true. The region which the Society for Psychical Research set out to explore is obscure and is, as yet, so far from yielding to investigation that the investigators are not even agreed as to their facts, let alone the conclusions to be drawn from.

The proceedings of the Society literally fill volumes (thirty-two) ; it would require a specialist to follow them through and an analysis here impossible, rightly to evaluate them. When such careful investigators as Hill and Podmore, dealing with the same body of fact, differ constantly and diametrically in their conclusions, it is evident that the facts so far collected have not cumulative force enough to establish in the generality of disciplined minds a substantial unanimity of conviction. There are far too many alternatives in the interpretation of the facts and, in general, the personal equation of the investigator colours the conclusions reached. Of course this is, in a measure, true in every field of investigation, but it is outstandingly true in psychical research.

William James Enters the Field

For some years the Society was mainly occupied with hypnotism and thought transference, with occasional reports on " apparitions, haunted houses, premonitions, automatic writing, crystal vision and multiple personality." Professor William James' experiment with Mrs. Piper carried the Society over into the field of trance mediumship. James had a sound scientific interest in every aspect of the play of human consciousness and was earlier than any of his contemporaries awakened to the psychological value of abnormal mental states. He also loved fair play. He made his first report on Mrs. Piper in 1886. He was unable, he said, " to resist the conviction that knowledge appeared in her trances which she had never gained by the ordinary waking use of her eyes, ears and wits. . . . What the source of this knowledge may be, I know not, and have not a glimmer of explanatory suggestion to make, but from admitting the fact of such knowledge I can see no escape."

In a letter to Flourney dated August 9, 1908, James says of later investigations: " It seems to me that these reports open a new chapter in the history of automatism. . . . Evidently automatism is a word that covers an extraordinary variety of fact." The reports of Mrs. Piper's sittings fill a large place in the Society's records. Dr. Richard Hodgson and Professor Hyslop were finally led to accept her trance utterances and writings as spiritistic revelations. Podmore, after a most careful analysis, concludes that " Mrs. Piper's trance utterances indicate the possession of some supernormal power of apprehension, at least the capacity to read the unspoken and even unconscious thoughts and emotions of other minds." [1] He is willing to admit that if any case in the whole history of Spiritualism points at communication with the spirits of the dead, hers is that case, but he adds, " to other students of the records, including the present writer, the evidence nevertheless appears at present insufficient to justify the spiritualistic view even of a working hypothesis." " I cannot point to a single instance in which a precise and unambiguous piece of information has been furnished, of a kind which could not have proceeded from the medium's own mind,

[1] " Modern Spiritualism," Podmore, Vol. II, pp. 342–343.

working upon the materials provided in the hints let drop by the sitter." [1]

The Limitations of the Scientist in Psychical Investigation

It is impossible in this study to follow through the records of the Society. A representative group of its members, some of them men whose names carry weight in other regions, have been led by their investigations to adopt the spiritistic hypothesis. Significantly, however, it is generally the scientist and not the psychologist who commits himself most strongly to Spiritism. He is strongly impressed, as was Sir William Crookes, by phenomena of one sort or another which do not come under his laws, and he assigns to them causes which lie altogether out of his field. Indeed the temper and training of the scientist handicap him in all psychical investigations. He has only one of two alternatives: to explain what he sees in terms of what his laboratories have told him, or else in terms of forces with which he is not familiar. His training in careful experimentation may fit him to test and isolate physical phenomena, but if they cannot be explained in terms of the forces and laws with which he is familiar his conclusions are no more authoritative than the conclusions of any other reasonably intelligent man. He may, therefore, lend the weight of a great name to conclusions—or conjectures—entirely outside his own province. The element of trickery in the ordinary

[1] "Modern Spiritualism," Podmore, Vol. II, p. 345.

professional séance is notorious.[1] The ordinary
physical phenomena of spiritism have almost without
exception been duplicated by conjurers—many of
whom have mystifying tricks of their own no medium
can duplicate and even the most unusual phenomena,
such as Home's apparent ability to handle fire unburnt
and his levitation can be paralleled in savage rites or
the performance of Indian fakirs, to which no professedly spiritistic explanation is attached. In many
instances a trained conjurer would be far more apt to
detect fraud than a trained scientist. He would at
least know where to look for a probable explanation.

The Society for Psychical Research Gives Intellectual Standing to Their Investigations

If the explanations of the whole group of phenomena is not in the known resident forces about us it
is presumably in powers or aspects of personality not
yet fully known. Here the psychologist is a better
witness than the scientist and it is significant that
psychologists have been slower to accept the spiritistic
hypothesis than the scientist. Hyslop is an exception
but the extent to which Hyslop has of late gone in
some of his reported utterances would seem to indicate
that he has passed far beyond the bonds of the scientific. And indeed, the whole tendency of those who
let themselves go strongly with the spiritistic tide is
exactly in this direction. It ought, however, to be said
that even these members of the S. P. R. who have

[1] Carrington, "The Psychical Phenomena of Spiritualism,"
pp. 6 and 7.

become spiritistic have generally been savingly conservative in their conclusions.

At any rate, the work of the Society for Psychical
Research has given intellectual standing to what was
before a sort of hole and corner affair under suspicion
twice: first, because of the character of those involved,
second, because of the character of what they revealed.
It is difficult for one not predisposed toward the occult and even strongly prejudiced against it to deny in
alleged spiritistic phenomena a challenging residuum
which may in the end compel far-reaching modifications in the conclusions both of science and psychology. By one set of tests this residuum is unexpectedly
small. One of the canons of the S. P. R. is to reject
the work of any medium once convicted or strongly
suspected of fraud. There is a vast literature in this
region through whose outstanding parts the writer has
for a good while now been trying to find his way, often
enough ready to quote the Pope in the Ring and the
Book.

> " I have worn through this sombre wintry day
>   With winter in my soul . . .
>   Over these dismalest of documents "

The reports of sittings cover weary pages of murky
statement; the descriptions of the discarnate life are
monotonously uniform and governed almost without
exception by old, old conceptions of planes and
spheres. There is always a preponderance of the
trivial—though the advocates of spiritism claim, and
the justice of this claim must be allowed, that this is
inevitable and that only through the veridical character

of the inconsequential can the consequential be established. Moreover, the impartial student working over the records should at least recognize the pathetic importance which those, believing themselves to be in touch with their own dead, naturally attach to even the most trivial instances. This sense of really being in touch, itself entirely subjective, probably carries over ninety-nine out of every hundred who finally become spiritists. It would be foolish to ignore the contributive force of this sense. In one form or another it is the last element in our recognition of our friends, and it never can be judged externally. But on the other hand a recognition of the unwarranted lengths to which—with lonely longing behind it—it may carry even the best poised minds, must give us pause in accepting any conclusion thus reached.

The Very Small Number of Dependable Mediums

Spiritistic literature is endlessly diffuse, but on the other hand the more dispassionate students rest their case on an unexpectedly small body of undiscredited evidence. Mrs. Piper, Home and Stainton Moses are the mediums with whom the case of the S. P. R. really stands or falls. Home was never detected in fraud and was non-professional. Sir William Crookes' experiments in these physical phenomena were carried on with him as medium. His work, however, was generally done for a small group of already convinced followers and their testimony, while sincere and generally consistent, may often have been influenced in ways of which they themselves were not conscious.

Podmore thinks them to have been unduly suggestible and offers hallucinations as an alternative hypothesis. Stainton Moses was respected in his private life, a teacher, a clergyman and a private tutor. His specialties were the introduction of a great variety of articles—apports as they are called—at his sittings, levitation, table-tipping and automatic writing and the direct voice. His control was known as " Imperator " and this ghostly commander fills a large place in the S. P. R. literature. " Imperator " had a strong homiletic instinct (remember that Moses was a clergyman) and communicated first and last through automatic writing, a considerable exposition of the spiritualistic creed, the larger part of which could have been preached from any liberal pulpit with no other effect on the hearers than to win their assent to blameless commonplaces—or, possibly, put them to sleep.

Mrs. Piper affords the strongest evidence of what Podmore calls " Some supernormal power of apprehension " in the entire history of trance mediumship. She was for years under the constant observation of a capable group by no means unanimously sympathetic with the spiritistic hypothesis, and has never been detected in fraud. She contributed a very great amount of information to her sitters which she apparently could not and did not obtain from known sources. There are no physical phenomena in connection with her work. The records of her séances fill a large place in the proceedings of the S. P. R. and the case for spiritism could be more safely rested with her than any other medium.

But the point here is that these three—Home, Moses and Mrs. Piper—supply the larger part of material which the really trained investigators of the last forty years are at all willing to take seriously. If there have been only three mediums in forty years who have commanded the general confidence—and Podmore does not feel absolutely sure of Home—of the group whose judgment the rest of us have to depend upon, we have a situation in which the average untrained seeker dealing with the average medium can have no sound confidence at all. The whole region is shot through and through with uncertainties, deceits and alternative hypotheses.

Spiritism a Question of Testimony and Interpretation

It is all fundamentally a matter of testimony. We have, or we have not, a body of fact for which we are in debt to observation. The observation may be first hand—as in Sir Oliver Lodge's sittings where he reports what he saw and heard. It may be second hand as the cases reported in the larger part of the authoritative literature of psychic phenomena. (Second hand, that is, for the authors and those who depend upon them.) Trustworthy observation is probably more difficult here than in any region of investigation. The whole situation is unfavourable; low lights and high emotion, the instinctive tendency to read into the facts a desired content even in watching them, the possibility of hallucinations and forms of hypnosis, all combine to render human testimony unreliable and introduce errors of observation. Nowhere can we be less sure of our facts and even when the facts are admitted the interpretation of them still remains, and here the room for difference is equally great. At best we are dealing with forces not yet subdued to law, phenomena for which normal experience supplies no parallel. It is all a region of intimations and possible permissions, but never for a moment of inevitable conclusions. One must go slow enough in offering any opinion at all. The writer recognizes and accepts, to begin with, a preponderance of dependable testimony for physical phenomena not to be explained in terms of any force with which science is now familiar.

In this he goes beyond Podmore who would eliminate all physical phenomena from the problem, and fully as far as Carrington. But Sir William Crookes never admitted entire error in this region,[1] and the conclusions of Geley (though he cites in part Eusapia Palladino, who is more or less discredited) point in the same direction. His studies of materialization are so vivid as to be uncanny and his photographs a series of documents which still await explanation.[2] There would seem to be a possible exercise of personal force not dependent upon muscular pull or pressure, bodily movements operating against known laws and even the building of this mysterious force into complete or fragmentary body-like forms.

On the psychical side there is dependable evidence for information conveyed by supernormal means

[1] See Carrington, "The Physical Phenomena of Spiritualism," p. 377.
[2] Geley, "From the Unconscious to the Conscious."

across considerable spaces—possibly long distances and the power to secure and report information not gained in any normal way. These are bare statements capable of great amplification. But they cover the ground.

Three Possible Explanations of So-Called Spiritistic Phenomena

Admitting the facts, there are three possible explanations. First, the Daimonistic. There are, according to this theory, in the unseen world—wherever and whatever that may be—an order of beings akin to ourselves, either less or more highly developed, mischievous or benign. This is an old, old belief; it has pervaded animistic religions, fathered witchcraft, persisted in the belief of demoniac control, enriched folk lore, filled the friendly silences of the night with terror and haunted humanity. Now it has found its renaissance in the full blaze of Twentieth Century Science.

" It seems not improbable," says Sir William Barrett, " that many of the *physical* manifestations witnessed in a spiritualistic séance are the product of human-like but not really human intelligence—good or bad daimonia they may be, *elementals* some have called them, which aggregate round the medium; drawn from that particular plane of mental and moral development in the unseen which corresponds to the mental and moral plane of the medium." [1] This is, with little enough alteration, the very point from which we set out in the remote dawn of our endeavour to interpret the mystery of the world about us. The only

[1] " On the Threshold of the Unseen," p. 113.

difference is that Sir William has his daimon for a tipping table and the savage had his for a flowing spring. Sir William may be right but primitive man was wrong. The whole trend of science heretofore has been to eliminate capricious and isolated elements from observed phenomena and include them in a sweep of law for whose operation the resident forces in the universe and human personality are seen to be sufficient. The daimonistic hypothesis has always up to this time been proved not only unnecessary but positively misleading. It belongs to a region where proof and disproof are equally impossible, but the weight of experience and especially all our truer understandings of ourselves and our world, dearly bought through the intellectual travail of our race, are against it. To accept it is really to turn back the clock and populate the unseen again with the creation of our fears or our fancies. It is at the best the too easy solution of a challenging problem, at the worst an aspect of that renaissance of superstition which is one of the strangest characteristics of our own time.

The second explanation is spiritistic. There are unseen presences but they are the discarnate who seek in the more trivial phenomena to bring themselves to our attention and in the more important to assure us of their continued existence and satisfy their longing and ours in renewed personal contacts. Given a faith in immortality, this explanation is natural enough— even inevitable. If the discarnate still live they must remember and desire. Death does not end affection on our side. It should not end affection on their side.

There must be, moreover, what one may call a discarnate status—an order, that is, of relationships and activities in which discarnate personality realizes and expresses itself. Our racial curiosities about the state of the dead are quenchless. Every religion has its creeds, its dreams, its assurances. From the Nirvana of the Buddhist to the ardent paradise of the Mohammedan, faith and longing have built their structure and peopled it with their dead. Great ranges of literature are coloured by such speculations. Christian hymnology is instinct with them and not a little of our noblest poetry. We have set our hells over against our heavens and opposed their terror to celestial splendours. Modern Spiritualism has to head it the whole drive of such speculations as these. For if the generality have been content to leave the solution of the very great difficulties which any faith in immortality involves, to the demonstrations of eventual experience, and rest in what is really the poetry of their faith, others either more curious or more credulous seek the testimony of the senses. Such as these naturally find what they seek in the phenomena of trance mediumship. They believe that the discarnate are constantly seeking to penetrate the veil between their order and ours and avail themselves of every opportunity to recall themselves to the memory of the incarnate.

Myers' Theory of Mediumship

F. W. H. Myers undertakes to describe how this may be done from the point of view of the spirit.

"Seeking then for some open avenue, it discerns something which corresponds to a *light*—a glimmer of translucency in the confused darkness of our material world. This 'light' indicates a *sensitive*—a human organism so constituted that a spirit can temporarily *inform* or *control* it, not necessarily interrupting the stream of the sensitive's ordinary consciousness; perhaps using a hand only, or perhaps, as in Mrs. Piper's case, using voice as well as hand, and occupying all the sensitive's channels of self-manifestation."

There are, naturally, in all this unescapable elements of speculation. As a matter of fact anything which we may imagine about the discarnate life may be almost unbelievably wide of the mark. Memory more than anything else is the binding force in personality. We know ourselves to be in the morning what we were when we went to sleep the night before, simply because memory reassembles immediately the continuing elements of our individual existences. More than that, we are greatly helped by our surroundings; everything which meets us in the morning has associations by which memory is served and, therefore, by the almost automatic process of putting together what we remember and surrendering ourselves to the suggestions of what we see and meet we find our places in a waking, working world and go about our business.

If we were to awake in a totally strange world where nothing was in any degree at all similar to the world in which we went to sleep, we might find ourselves so sadly puzzled as to doubt our own identity, even though memory persisted in its identifying suggestion.   And if in addition to this we found ourselves without the contribution of physical sensation to which we have always been used—sightless, soundless, touchless—one can easily imagine a shock in the face of which even the most strongly centered personality would give way.   And yet such changes as this probably only faintly indicate the adjustments which the discarnate are called upon to meet.   It is as if we were asked to argue or to imagine from one dimension to another.

These are difficulties, of course, which attend any conception of immortality, but we usually escape them by refusing to follow through what they involve and taking refuge in a free poetic imagination sustained by faith and enriched by tradition.   In the face of all this Myers' supposition, ingenious as it is, can do no more than repeat the more prosaic assumption which is the basis of spiritism, and that is that the discarnate naturally desire to communicate with those whom they have left, one hardly dares say behind them for even that simple word introduces suppositions which may have no meaning at all, and would naturally avail themselves of any possible opportunity.   The whole process, if it be a process, must lie in the region of suggestion.   If there be a telepathy between the living it is not impossible that there should be a telepathy between the living and the discarnate.

Telepathy: Between the Living or the Living and the Discarnate?

There might be thus a kind of eager pressing of the

departed against the doors which had been shut and not quite locked behind them, taking the form of more or less obscure suggestion to which the medium would be sensitive and so recreate in ways at which we can only guess some hint of the voice or presence of the discarnate. The suggestion would come from the other side. The form in which it is given to our world would be the contribution of the medium. As far as there is any possible explanation of the facts of trance mediumship as a revelation from the dead it is somewhere here.

Telepathy between the living is fairly well enough established to make this a not impossible hypothesis, and even materialization might be accounted for in the same way. Sir Oliver Lodge is inclined to discover in the luminiferous ether an environment in which discarnate personality could function. But this is pure supposition, though others have adopted it. Walker, for example, in his extremely suggestive work on Monism and Christian Theism. But he suggests the ether only as a help to the imagination in meeting the difficulties of an immortal existence—the old Heaven and Hell having been made astronomically and geologically impossible. But if Einstein should upset the hypothesis of the ether all this would go the way of the Heaven and Hell of Dante.

We cannot eliminate, however, in a supposition so vague as this the contributive elements supplied by the friends themselves to whom the communication is supposed to be addressed and by whom it is certainly interpreted, for if the trance medium is open to suggestion from the discarnate side, the medium must be equally open to suggestion from the living, a suggestion likely to be very much stronger, more distinct, more compelling.

The real crux of the whole problem is the disentanglement of these possible lines of suggestion and the assignment of them to their true sources. We may, the writer believes, eliminate as far as their evidential value is concerned, all physical phenomena. In doing this we need not necessarily deny the reality of some of the physical phenomena but the larger part of the residue which might possibly be left after the elimination of fraud on the part of the medium and unintentional misrepresentation on the part of the witnesses is so utterly meaningless as to have no value at all. The only physical phenomena which can have any direct bearing on spirit communication are the tappings and table tippings which can by a deal of ingenuity be made to spell out a message or answer questions yes or no. The same question as to the source of the suggestion enters here. Even if we admit the taps to spell out a message, we have still to decide from whom the message comes and the messages alleged to be contributed through the voice are so much more full and intelligible as to leave the whole question standing or falling with the credibility of voice trance mediumship.

Controls

The usual machinery of a séance creates suspicion. Most mediums have controls. Nothing is more capricious than these controls. They may be people who really never existed at all. The genesis of Mrs. Piper's control, Dr. Phinuit, is suggestive. " It would appear that Mrs. Piper in 1884 had visited for advice a professional clairvoyant whose leading control claimed to be a Frenchman named Finné, or Finnett." [1] When Mrs. Piper was later seen by William James, a French doctor had succeeded in obtaining almost exclusive control and his name was reported to be Phinuit. Beyond debate, as far as name goes, here is a kind of transmuted suggestion. The Finnett of the French clairvoyant, who may or may not have really lived, becomes the Phinuit of Mrs. Piper, for whose existence there is apparently no testimony at all.

The controls have sometimes been Indians and indeed almost any one may appear as a control—Longfellow, for example, or Mrs. Siddons, or Bach or Vanderbilt. In a region where disproof and proof are equally impossible this element of capricious control is suspicious. It is much more likely to be some obscure casting up of the medium's mind, through lines of association of which the medium is utterly unconscious, than to represent the personalities so named. In Raymond the control is one Moonstone, or a little Indian girl called Freda or Feda, who speaks of herself in the third person and who reports a great many silly things in a very silly way.

It is possible, of course, to say that these thus named are spirit mediums as necessary for the transfer of suggestion from the discarnate order as mediums seem to be in the incarnate order, and that abnormal

[1] Podmore's " Modern Spiritualism," Vol. II, p. 333.

personalities are as much needed on one side as the other through the abnormality of the whole process. But this is patently to beg the question. There is room in the whole process for the trivial, even the inconsequential. As the advocates of spiritism have urged, identification very often turns on apparently trivial things but it is difficult to justify the very great element of the capricious and actually foolish which enters so largely into the records of all sittings. It would seem as if death robbed grave personalities of their gravity, the strong of their force and the wise of their wisdom, and this is so hard to believe as to make us wonder whether we are not really dealing with something which belongs to an entirely different region and is open to an entirely different line of explanation.

But beyond such considerations as these, which may or may not have force, there remains the graver question still—the question of the identification of the sources from which the intelligible residue of communications is received. If we fall back upon suggestion there are always two general sources of suggestion—the incarnate and the discarnate, and among the incarnate themselves there are manifold sources of suggestion. The sitter may be unconsciously supplying the material which the medium is receiving, recasting and giving back again, or the medium may be reporting what is received from other incarnate sources than the sitter. (This, of course, when we have eliminated all that might possibly be contributed by the medium.)

The Dilemma of Spiritism

Anything, therefore, which is known to the living may be the source of the medium's information. Only those things, therefore, which are utterly unknown to the living anywhere, which cannot possibly have been known by the medium himself or herself, can be finally and conclusively a testimony to communications from the dead. But unless the information thus received is known to the living, its truth or falsity can never be proved or disproved. This is the dilemma which spiritism is finally brought to face and from this dilemma there is absolutely no escape. It does not forbid the conclusions which may be drawn from a seeming preponderance of evidence, but it does forbid absolute certainty, for, to repeat, if the information is to be verified it must be verified by the living, which proves that some one does possess it and may have communicated it—if we assume such communication to be possible—to the medium. On the other hand, if no one at all possesses the information, then we may never be sure that it is real information, or anything else than a creation of an excited imagination.

There is one test here which, if it were really made under absolutely dependable conditions, conditions, that is, in no wise open to suspicion or misunderstanding, might be final. If a message written before death and so sealed as to be unknown to any one save the one who wrote it, could be correctly reported, it would have, everything else being right, an immense force. (Though even here clairvoyance—for which, on the whole, there is a pretty dependable evidence—might afford the true explanation.) F. W. H. Myers left such a message as this. In January, 1891, he sent Sir Oliver Lodge a " sealed envelope, in the hope that after his death the communication contained in the envelope would be able to be given by means of a medium. Many different messages obtained by a well-known medium, Madame Verrall, and coming supposedly from Frederick Myers, led them to believe that they represented this communication. The envelope was opened in December, 1904, and ' it was found that there was no resemblance between its actual contents and what was alleged by the script to be contained in it.' " [1]   If there is any authentic case of this final test being successfully maintained, the writer does not know it. There are instances of hidden articles discovered, but these tests by no means possess the same force of testimony.

We may assume, then, that we have no absolute demonstration of spirit communication. We have only a very complex group of phenomena capable of varying explanations. Any fair-minded student of the whole subject must recognize that men who have had ample opportunity for first hand investigation, not hasty in their conclusions and in some instances of very great intellectual force, have taken an opposite view. They have felt the testimony to be both sound and sufficient. There is an unescapable personal equation here which probably finally determines diver-

[1] Boirac, " The Psychology of the Future," p. 278.

gent attitudes. As has been said before, those generally who have accepted the spiritistic explanation have been led to do so through communications in which they discovered some personal note or touch, to which they themselves would be hospitably susceptible and which would have far less weight with those whose affections and previous associations were not thus involved. This does not necessarily prove their conclusions to have been false. Perhaps just this personal element is necessary to give final meaning to what otherwise is so perplexing and even contradictory. The dogmatism which shuts the door squarely in the face of spiritism is as unreasonable, as unscientific, as the credulity which opens the door wide and accepts everything which comes through.

The Influence of Spiritism Upon Its Adherents

There are other considerations which bear more or less indirectly upon this difficult matter, but which have their weight. In general, those who have wholeheartedly accepted spiritism have been unable thereafter to maintain the balanced detachment which they urge upon others. They tend to become unduly credulous; they force their explanation beyond its necessary limits; they tend to become persons of the ideé fixe type; they become sponsors for extravagant stories, and, in general, lead those who are influenced by their position or name far beyond the limits which impartial investigation, even on the part of those sympathetic, has as yet justified. Those descriptions of the discarnate state, moreover, which reach us through mediums are undependable.

There is a machinery of planes and spheres and emanations and reincarnations which is not at all peculiar to spiritism but belongs to the fringes of the occult in every manifestation of it, which is perpetually recurrent in modern spiritualistic literature. We are on the frontiers of a region where the reason which steadies us in the practical conduct of life and guides us in an order with which we are familiar through age-old inheritances, has no value at all. Our very terminology ceases to have any meaning. A generous creative imagination may build for itself what cities it will of habitation, furnish them as it desires and try to conceive, as it has power, the experiences and progressions of the discarnate, but to invest these imaginations with evidential accuracy is to break down all the limits between the dependable and the undependable.

And finally, though this is rather a commonplace observation than an aspect of our investigation, there is little to be gained in the necessary business of solid living by such an interweaving of the two worlds as spiritism carries with it. One life at a time is plainly enough all that we are equal to. Those who surrender themselves to such conclusions and inquiries are in very great danger of being so detached from the actualities of the present order as to become themselves errant and eccentric spirits, finding their true interests in endless séances and investigations which have no practical bearing upon life as it now is.

The Real Alternative to Spiritism

The writer's observation of the effect of much going to mediums upon those whom he has personally known leads him to distrust the whole matter and possibly to react too strongly against it. A discriminating critic has said that Spiritualism is not Spiritualism at all, but a subtle materialism, in that it is the effort to verify the reality of the spiritual in terms of the material. It is, therefore, just one more unexpected aspect of the hard skepticism of the time, which trusts nothing it cannot hear, or see, or touch. A faith which is not solidly established in reason, which does not continue and complete in its own regions what we know and understand, is a cloud-built faith, but a faith, on the other hand, which refuses to adventure beyond the limits of the senses is a faith too largely empty of any noble content.

If the phenomena under examination, then, cannot be explained in terms of animism and if the spiritistic hypothesis is gravely open to question, what explanation is left? In what follows the writer has been greatly influenced by the suggestion of the students of abnormal personality generally, and partly by the work of certain Frenchmen who, with French logic and brilliancy of insight, are working toward far-reaching psychological restatements and even to recasting of the accepted scientific understandings of matter and force. Maeterlinck says somewhere in substance that our universe is as tightly sealed as a sphere of steel and that whatever happens inside must be explained in terms of its own resident forces, and, in general, the whole of science and the weight of experience are on Maeterlinck's side. Of course this assumes that a good many things have been put inside this sphere to begin with. Speaking in terms of religion, this does not shut God out of the world, but it does shut up life and experience to conformity with their own laws and forces them to explain their phenomena in terms of their own content.

In a sentence, just as the resident forces of the outside world have been heretofore sufficient, in the measure that we have been able to discover them, to explain all the phenomena of the outside world, it is reasonable to believe that the content of personality is sufficient to explain all personal phenomena, whether normal or abnormal, and that it is to ourselves and not to the discarnate that we have to look for the explanation of the phenomena of alleged spiritism.

The Investigations of Émile Boirac

The men who are working along this line, particularly Geley and Émile Boirac, by no means deny the phenomena, but they offer another solution. Boirac, particularly, finds his point of departure in hypnotism and suggestibility. Now here is a continuation of the line of approach and interpretation which cleared up the whole confused matter of mesmerism. We have already seen how the French investigators found the explanation of what Mesmer and those who followed him have been able to accomplish, not in magnetic influence or any such thing, but in the remarkable changes produced in personality by exterior or auto-

suggestion, and just as this was the key to the phenomena of mesmerism, it is more likely than anything
else to prove the key to the explanation of the phenomena of spiritualism, for these are really nothing
more than simply aspects of the trance state, however induced.

It is not necessary to follow, in this connection,
Boirac's analysis of the phenomena attendant upon the
trance state, or to consider his theories as to hypnosis
itself. He believes that there are in our personalities
hidden forces which, in the normal conduct of life, are
not brought into action. They are no necessary part
of our adjustment to our working environment; on
the whole they complicate rather than simplify the
business of living and they are best—though this
is not his statement but the writer's conclusion from
the whole matter—they are best left unawakened.
What we are normally is the outcome of the adjustment of personality to those creative and shaping
forces in response to which life is most happily and
usefully carried on. But when the waking self and
normal self is for the moment put in abeyance and new
forces are evoked from the " vasty deep " of our souls,
we are capable of an entirely different set of manifestations. First of all, those usually associated with
the hypnotic state which do not need to be further considered here—a great docility to suggestion, unconsciousness to pain and the like. We have also the
possibility of powers which Boirac calls magnetoidal.
" These appear to involve the intervention of forces
still unknown, distinct from those that science has so

far discovered and studied, but of a physical nature
and more or less analogous to the radiating forces of
physics: light, heat, electricity, magnetism, etc." [1]

Under this general head he considers Animal
Magnetism, what is known generally as mesmerism,
the power, that is, to create hypnotic states in others;
the phenomena of Telepathy " comprising numerous
varieties, such as the transmission or penetration of
thought, the exteriorization of the sensitiveness,
psychometry, telepathy, clairvoyance or lucidity, etc.,"
and finally states " where physical matter appears to
exert over animate beings, especially human beings, an
action that does not seem to be explicable by any
physical or chemical properties already known." He believes also that there is in human beings a radiating influence susceptible of being exercised at a distance over
other animate beings or else upon inanimate objects.
He finds in trance mediumship all the elements which
enter into any hypnotic state. " The trance is produced and developed spontaneously, without the intervention of any visible operator, under the sole effect
of the nervous and mental conditions in which the
medium is placed, and among which the *belief in spirits* and the expectation of their intervention would appear to play a considerable part." [2] The italicized

[1] Boirac, " The Psychology of the Future," p. 24. Some recent
French investigations seem to indicate that this force—Myers'
Telekinesis—operating through barriers, changes the magnetic
properties of that through which it passes. Carrington, the most
skeptical student in this region, is inclined to admit its existence.
See " The Physical Phenomena of Spiritualism," p. 359.

[2] Boirac, " The Psychology of the Future," p. 271.

words " a belief in spirits " are extremely significant. In the entranced personality there is the suggestion, already strongly established, that whatever is experienced during the trance will be due to spirit intervention or revelation. This introduces the element of expectant attention. We know on the physical side of what expectant attention is capable. It becomes a real factor in all faith healing; it may produce, either for the better or the worse, far-reaching changes in physical states and it is perfectly possible for such an expectant attention once fully in action in the trance —given of course, to begin with, the attitude and interests of the medium in a waking state—to create all the machinery of controls, revelation and the like, which characterize trance mediumship.

Boirac finds, therefore, in spiritism a complex determined by certain particular nervous and mental states into which there enter, in one form or another, almost all the facts of abnormal psychology and he believes that science, faithful to the principle of economy, should consider the alleged phenomena of spiritism, until proved to the contrary, reducible to facts of the preceding orders. He does not call the spiritistic hypothesis impossible; he does believe it ought not to be called in until every other explanation has been examined and found inadequate and he is not inclined to believe that we have as yet exhausted other possible explanations.

One man's authority here is by no means final. F. W. H. Myers has taken into consideration many of the facts upon which Boirac dwells and on the whole has reached a different conclusion. But, in general, the more deeply we advance into the region of abnormal personality and the phenomena of hypnotic and related states, the more reason there seems to be for believing that there are resident in human personality powers which, if at once evoked and released, are sufficient to account for all mediumistic revelations without assuming that they come from the discarnate.

Geley's Conclusions

Geley has gone much farther in some directions here than any one else. He is more concerned with the physical phenomena. He has a striking series of photographs of materialization, the authenticity of which it is difficult to doubt. He finds an ascending series in abnormal psychology from neuropathic states to mediumship with gradations which intensify the abnormal or the supernormal, but in which the continuity of development is never broken. His analyses here are both keen and suggestive and tend to confirm the conclusions of other students that we have resident in human personality elements which are adequate to the explanation of any phenomena which have been as yet presented.

As far as the physical phenomena go, he cites experiments which seem to reveal " threads of substance and rigid rods, sometimes visible, sometimes invisible, proceeding from the fingers of the medium " and serving as a real mechanism for the movement of distant and sometimes quite heavy articles. He argues from this that there is a possible exteriorization of power which may itself be governed by ideas and believes also that such facts as this will eventually compel us to recast our conceptions of matter and force and profoundly affect biology and all evolutionary theories. The whole matter is necessarily obscure, but such studies do give a new direction and a larger significance to our whole subject matter.

In substance the spiritistic hypothesis is inadequate; it is too simple, too easy. We are evidently only upon the threshold of the whole subject. All conclusions are necessarily inconclusive; there is no region in which one has less right to be dogmatic. The bearing of it all upon immortality seems to the writer to be not at all where the spiritists place it. If human personality has in itself such latent powers, if there are these extensions of a mysterious force which operate beyond our normal mechanism, if there are contacts of consciousness deeper than consciousness itself in which information is given and received outside normal methods of communication, we are led to conceive that what for want of a better name we call spirit has an unexpected range and force. We are by no means so shut in by the walls of the material and the sensible as we have heretofore supposed. There is a transcendence of spirit over matter and materially imposed conditions which must give us pause. If, in the murky ways which have been brought to our attention, spirit can transcend matter, we have at least one more reason for affirming its supremacy and one more suggestion of a force or a reality which may be able to survive even the dissolution of matter itself.

In other words, here is a line of testimony, richly
suggestive, though by no means clear, to the power of
the soul to make its own conditions, and what is immortality but just this?

The phenomena of so-called spiritism, while not as
yet justifying Spiritualism, certainly make a dogmatic
materialism increasingly different. Those of us who
are as anxious for a sustaining faith in immortality
as any of our comrades in the great quest may possibly be, but who are as yet unwilling to accept their
conclusions, may nevertheless find in this subject matter which is common both to us and to them, the permission to believe that that which is most distinctly
ourselves possesses enduring possibilities. If it may
from time to time break through in curious ways the
walls which now shut it in, may it not in some very
real way pass through the gate which Death opens
and still continue in such a richness of consciousness
and identity as to organize for itself another life beyond the grave?

The Meaning of Spiritism for Faith

Faith may find its permissions and witnesses in
many regions. The writer believes that faith in immortality finds an added permission in this region also.
Beyond debate, there are laws which we now but
dimly discern and possible forces which only now and
again touch the coasts of our present experience, as
tides which sweep in from distant and mysterious seas.
Beyond debate, we may not confine the interplay of
mind with mind to purely physical channels, and un-

der exceptional circumstances effects may be produced whose causes we have not yet been able to tabulate. Our conscious lives are rooted deeper than we dream. They reach out in directions which we do not ourselves know. It may well be, therefore, that they ascend to heights whose summits we do not see, and possess a permanence independent of the body which they inhabit, or the things of seeming sense which surround them, and it may be also that what is now occult and perplexing and capricious may in the future become as truly an organized science as the alchemy and the astrology of the Middle Ages have become the chemistry and astrology of our own time. Beyond this one may assert the wholesome commonplace that the main business of living is in the region of the known and the normal. It is for our own well-being that the veil hangs dark between this world and the next. An order in which there was constant passing and repassing would be impossible. It would be either one thing or the other. It does demoralize us to be always searching after the secrets of the unseen. Might it not demoralize those who have passed through the veil to be always trying to come back? Surely the most fitting preparation for what awaits us hereafter is the brave conduct of life under those laws and conditions which are the revelation of the whole solid experience of our race. Beyond this it is difficult to go and beyond this it is not necessary to go.

XI

MINOR CULTS: THE MEANING OF THE CULTS FOR THE CHURCH

Border-land Cults

THE cults which we have so far considered are the outstanding forms of modern free religious movements, but they do not begin to exhaust the subject matter. Even the outstanding cults have their own border-lands. New Thought is particularly rich in variants and there are in all American cities sporadic, distantly related and always shifting movements—groups which gather about this or that leader, maintain themselves for a little and then dissolve, to be recreated around other centers with perhaps a change of personnel. The Masonic Temple in Chicago is said to be occupied on Sundays all day long by larger or smaller groups which may be societies for ethical culture or with some social program or other, or for the study of Oriental religions. One would need to attend them all and saturate himself far more deeply than is possible for any single investigator in their creeds or their contentions to appraise them justly. Their real significance is neither in their organization, for they have little organization, nor in their creed, but in their temper. They represent reaction, restlessness and the spiritual confusion of the time. They can be explained—in part at least—in terms of that social deracination to which reference has already been made. They represent also an excess of individualism in the region of religion and its border-lands.

An examination of the church advertisement pages in the newspapers of New York, Detroit, Chicago or San Francisco reveals their extent, their variety and their ingenuity in finding names for themselves. On Sunday, February 25th, the Detroit papers carried advertisements of Vedanta, Spiritist and Spiritualist groups (the Spiritist group calls itself " The Spirit Temple of Light and Truth "), The Ultimate Thought Society, The First Universal Spiritual Church, The Church of Psychic Research, The Philosophical Church of Natural Law, Unity Center, The Culture of Isolan, Theosophy, Divine Science Center, and Lectures on Divine Metaphysics. Their leaders advertise such themes as: The Opulent Consciousness, The Law of Non-Attachment, Psychic Senses and Spirituality, The Continuity of Life, The Spiritualism of Shakespeare, The Voiceless Code of the Cosmos, The Godlikeness of Divine Metaphysics in Business. Their themes are not more bizarre, it must be confessed, than some of the topics announced for the orthodox churches. (Indeed the church advertisement page in cities whose churches indulge generously in display advertisements is not altogether reassuring reading.) But, in general, this list which can be duplicated in almost any large city is testimony enough to a confusion of cults and a confusion of thought. As far as they can be classified, according to the scheme of this study, they are variants of New Thought, Theosophy and Spiritualism. If they were classified according to William James' "Varieties of Religious Experience" they would be seen as mystical rather than rational, speculative rather than practical.

Fort Newton, who speaks of them perhaps more disrespectfully than they deserve as "bootleggers in religion," finds in these lesser movements generally a protest against the excessively external in the life of the Church to-day and a testimony to the quench-less longing of the soul for a religion which may be known and lived out in terms of an inner experience. But this certainly is not true of all of them.

Bahaism

There is, however, one other larger and more co-herent cult, difficult to classify, which deserves a more extended notice. That is Bahaism, which, as it is now taking form, is a leaven rather than a cult. It is an attempt after spiritual unity and the reduction of religion to very simple and inclusive forms and a challenge to the followers of religions widely sepa-rated on the surface to be more true to what is deepest in their faith. It has a long and stirring history and curiously enough is drawn from Mohammedan sources. Its basal literatures are Arabic and Persian, "so numerous and in some cases so voluminous that it would hardly be possible for the most industrious student to read in their entirety even those which are accessible, a half dozen of the best known collections in Europe."

We find its genesis, historically, in certain expectations long held by Persian Mohammedans akin to Jewish Messianic expectations held before and at the time of Christ. There has been, we know, a tradition of disputed succession in Mohammedanism ever since the death of the prophet. Persian Mohammedans believed the true successor of Mohammed to have been unjustly deprived of his temporal supremacy and they trace a long line of true successors whose divine right would some day be recognized and reëstablished. Perhaps we might find a parallel here among those Englishmen who believe that the true succession of the English throne should be in the house of the Stuarts, or those royalists in France who champion the descendants of one or the other former reigning houses. But the Persian faithful have gone farther than that. They believe that the last true successor of Mohammed who disappeared in the tenth century never died, but is still living in a mysterious city, surrounded by a band of faithful disciples and " that at the end of time he will issue forth and ' fill the earth with justice after it has been filled with iniquity.' " A parallel here would be the old stories of Frederick Barbarossa who waits in his cave for the proper time to come forth and reassert his imperial power. This curious Persian belief has worked itself out in a time scheme much like the time schemes of other Apocalyptic beliefs, the detail of which is difficult enough.

But in substance this hidden and true successor of the prophet has had from time to time those through whom he reveals himself to the faithful and makes known his will, and these are known as Babs or gates; "the gate, that is, whereby communication was reopened between the hidden one and his faithful followers." The practical outcome of this would be that any one who could convince Persian Mohammedans that he was the Bab or "gate" would possess a mystic messianic authority. Such a confidence actually established would give him an immense hold over the faithful and make him a force to be reckoned with by the Mohammedan world.

The Bab and His Successors

As far as our own present interest is concerned, the movement dates from 1844 when a young Persian merchant announced himself as the Bab. If we are to find a parallel in Christianity he was a kind of John the Baptist, preparing the way for a greater who should come after him, but the parallel ends quickly, for since the Mohammedan Messiah did not appear, his herald was invested with no little of the authority and sanctity which belonged to the hidden one himself. The career of the first Bab was short—1844 to 1850. He was only twenty-four years old at the time of his manifestation, thirty when he suffered martyrdom and a prisoner during the greater part of his brief career. The practical outcome of his propaganda was a deal of bloody fighting between antagonistic Mohammedan factions. The movement received early that baptism of blood which gives persistent intensity to any persecuted movement. His followers came to regard him as a divine being. After his execution his body was recovered, concealed for seventeen years and finally placed in a shrine specially built for that purpose at St. Jean d'Acre. This shrine has become the holy place of Bahaism.

During one period of his imprisonment he had opportunity to continue his writings, correspond with his followers and receive them. He was thus able to give the world his message and we find in his teachings the germ of the gospel of Bahaism. Before his death he named his successor—a young man who had been greatly drawn to him and who seemed by his youth, zeal and devotion to be set apart to continue his work. To this young man the Bab sent his rings and other personal possessions, authorized him to add to his writings and in general to inherit his influence and continue his work. This young man was recognized with practical unanimity by the Babis as their spiritual head. Owing to his youth and the secluded life which he adopted, the practical conduct of the affairs of the Babi community devolved chiefly on his elder half-brother Baha'u'llah. What follows is a confused story of schism, rival claimants and persecution but the sect grew through persecution and the control of it came in 1868 into the hands of Baha'u'llah.

During the greater part of his life Baha'u'llah was either an exile or a prisoner. From 1868 until his death in 1892 he was confined with seventy of his followers in the penal colony of Acca on the Mediterranean coast. Meanwhile the faith which centered about him changed character; he was no longer a gate or herald, he was himself a " manifestation of God " with authority to change all earlier teaching. He really universalized the movement. Beneath his touch religion becomes practical, ethical, less mystic, more universal. He was possessed by a passion for universal peace and brotherhood. He addressed letters to the crowned heads of Europe asking them to co-operate in peace movements. It has been suggested that the Czar of Russia was influenced thereby and that we may thus trace back to Baha'u'llah the peace movement which preceded the war.

Pilgrims came and went and through their enthusiasms the movement spread. After his death there was the renewal of disputes as to the proper succession and consequent schisms. The power came finally into the hands of Abdul-Baha who was kept under supervision by the Turkish government until 1908. He was freed by the declaration of the New Constitution and carried on thereafter with real power a world-wide propaganda. He had an unusual and winning personality, spoke fluently in Persian, Arabic and Turkish and more nearly than any man of his time filled the ideal rôle of an Eastern prophet. He died in November, 1921, and was buried on Mt. Carmel—with its memories of Elijah and millenniums of history—his praises literally being sung by a most catholic group of Mohammedans, Jews and Eastern Christians.

The Temple of Unity

Bahaism as it is held in America to-day is distilled out of the writings and teachings of Baha'u'llah and

Abdul-Baha. Naturally enough, in the popularization of it its contradictions have been reconciled and its subtleties disregarded. What is left fits into a variety of forms and is in line with a great range of idealism. The twelve basic principles of Bahaism as announced in its popular literature are:

The Oneness of Mankind.
Independent investigations of truth.
The Foundation of all religions is one.
Religion must be the cause of unity.
Religion must be in accord with science and reason.
Equality between men and women.
Prejudice of all kinds must be forgotten.
Universal Peace.
Universal Education.
Solution of the economic problem.
An international auxiliary language.
An international tribunal.

A program inclusive enough for any generous age. These principles are substantiated by quotations from the writings of Abdul-Baha and the teachings of Baha'u'llah. Many things combine to lend force to its appeal—the courage of its martyrs, its spaciousness and yet at the same time the attractiveness of its appeal and its suggestion of spiritual brotherhood. Since the movement has borne a kind of messianic expectation it adjusts itself easily to inherited Christian hopes. There are real correspondences between its expected millennium and the Christian millennium.

How far its leaders, in their passion for peace and their doctrine of non-resistance and their exaltation of the life of the spirit, are in debt to the suggestions of

Christianity itself, or how far it is a new expression of a temper with which the Orient has always been more in sympathy than the West, it would be difficult to say, but in some ways Bahaism does express—or perhaps reproduces—the essential spirit of the Gospels more faithfully than a good deal of Western Christianity as now organized. Those members of Christian communions which are attracted to Bahaism find in it a real hospitality to the inherited faith they take over. It is possible, therefore, to belong to the cult and at the same time to continue one's established religious life without any very great violence and indeed with a possible intensification of that life.

It is difficult, therefore, to distinguish between Bahaism as it is held by devout groups in America, so fas as ethics and ideals go, from much that is distinctive in the Christian spirit, though the influence of Bahaism as a whole would be to efface distinctions and especially to take the force out of the Christian creeds.

Chicago, or rather Wilmette, is now the center of the movement in America and an ambitious temple is in the way of being constructed there, the suggestion for whose architecture is taken from a temple in Eska-bad, Russia. This is to be a temple of universal religion, symbolizing in its architecture the unities of faith and humanity. "The temple with its nine doors will be set in the center of a circular garden symbolizing the all-inclusive circle of God's unity; nine pathways will lead to the nine doors and each one coming down the pathway of his own sect or religion or trend of thought will leave at the door the dogmas that separate and, under the dome of God's oneness, all will become one. . . . At night it will be brilliantly lighted and the light will shine forth through the tracery of the dome, a beacon of peace and unity rising high above Lake Michigan."

This study has led us into many curious regions and shown to what unexpected conclusions the forces of faith or hope, once released, may come, but surely it has revealed nothing more curious than that the old, old controversy as to the true successor of Mohammed the prophet should at last have issued in a universal religion and set the faithful to building a temple of unity on the shores of Lake Michigan.

If this work were to be complete it should include some investigation of the rituals of the cults. They are gradually creating hymns of their own; their public orders of service include responsive readings with meditations on the immanence of God, the supremacy of the spiritual and related themes. In general they dispense with the sacraments; they have no ecclesiastical orders and hardly anything corresponding to the Catholic priesthood or the Protestant ministry, though the Christian Science reader has a recognized official place. They meet in conferences; they depend largely upon addresses by their leaders. Spiritualistic movements organize themselves around séances. They use such halls as may be rented, hotels, their own homes; they have not generally buildings of their own save the Christian Science temples which are distinctive for dignity of architecture and beauty of appointment in almost every large city.

General Conclusions; the Limitations of the Writer's Method

It remains only to sum up in a most general way the conclusions to which this study may lead. There has been a process of criticism and appraisal throughout the whole book, but there should be room at the end for some general statements.

The writer recognizes the limitations of his method; he has studied faithfully the literature of the cults, but any religion is always a vast deal more than its literature. The history of the cults does not fully tell their story nor does any mere observation of their worship admit the observer to the inner religious life of the worshippers. Life always subdues its materials to its own ends, reproduces them in terms of its own realities; there are endless individual variations, but the outcome is massively uniform. Religion does the same thing. Its materials are faiths and obediences and persuasions of truth and expectations of happier states, but its ultimate creations are character and experience, and the results in life of widely different religions are unexpectedly similar. Both theoretically and practically the truer understanding or the finer faith and, particularly, the higher ethical standards should produce the richer life and this is actually so. But real goodness is everywhere much the same; there are calendared saints for every faith.

There is an abundant testimony in the literature of the cults to rare goodnesses and abundant devotion, and observation confirms these testimonies. Something of this is doubtless due to their environment.

The Western cults themselves and the Eastern cults in the West are contained in and influenced by the whole outcome of historic Christianity and they naturally share its spirit. If the churches need to remember this as they appraise the cults, the cults need also to remember it as they appraise the churches. Multitudes of Catholics and Protestants secure from a religion which the cults think themselves either to have corrected or outgrown exactly what the cults secure— and more. Such as these trust God, keep well, go happily about their businesses and prove their faith in gracious lives. There is room for mutual respect and a working measure of give and take on both sides.

The writer is inclined to think the churches at present are more teachable than the more recent religious movements. For a long generation now the churches have been subject to searching criticism from almost every quarter. The scientist, the sociologist, the philosopher, the publicist, the discontented with things as they are and the protagonist of things as they ought to be, have all taken their turn and the Church generally, with some natural protest against being made the scapegoat for the sins of a society arrestingly reluctant to make the Church's gospel the law of its life, has taken account of its own shortcomings and sought to correct them. The cults are as yet less inclined to test themselves by that against which they have reacted. But this is beside the point. The movements we have been studying can only be fairly appraised as one follows through their outcome in life and that either in detail or entirety is impossible. But it is possible to gain from their literature a reasonable understanding of their principles and interrelations and this the writer has sought to do.

The Cults Are Aspects of the Creative Religious Consciousness of the Age

Certain conclusions are thus made evident. These movements are the creation of the religious consciousness of the time. They are aspects of the present tense of religion. Since religion is, among other things, the effective desire to enter into right relationships with the power which manifests itself in the universe there are two variants in its content; first, our changing understanding of the power itself and second, our changing uses of it. The first varies with our knowledge and insight, the second with our own changing sense of personal need. Though God be the same yesterday, to-day and forever, our understandings of Him cannot and ought not to be the same yesterday, to-day and forever. Our faith is modified by, for example, our scientific discoveries. When the firmament of Hebrew cosmogony has given way to interstellar spaces and the telescope and the spectroscope plumb the depths of the universe, resolving nebulæ into star drifts, faith is bound to reflect the change. The power which manifests itself in the universe becomes thereby a vaster power, operating through a vaster sweep of law. Our changed understandings of ourselves must be reflected in our faith and our ethical insights as well. And because there is and ought to be no end to these changing understandings, religion itself, which is one outcome of them, must be plastic and changing.

What we ask of God is equally subject to change. True enough, the old questions—Whence? Whither? and Why? are constant. As we know ourselves to be living in a world which is less than a speck in an immensity wherein the birth and death of suns are ephemeral, we may rightly distrust our own value for the vaster order. We shall, therefore, the more insistently ask Whence? and Whither? and Why? But, none the less, there is always a shifting emphasis of religious need. Our own time is manifestly more concerned about well-being in the life that now is than a happy issue in the life which is to come. Temperament also qualifies experience. The mystic seeks conscious communion with God as an end in itself; the practical temper asks the demonstration of the love of God in happy material conditions. In general, action and reaction govern this whole region. The Puritan was supremely concerned about his own salvation and the struggle consequent thereto; his descendants were chiefly interested in the extension of knowledge and the conquest of the physical order and we react against this in a new return upon ourselves and the possibilities of personality.

Now these changing understandings of the power which manifests itself in the universe on the one side and our own changing senses of need on the other, give to religion a constantly fluctuating character and what is most distinctively religious in any period must be the outcome of the combination of these two variants. What an age asks of the God whom it knows colours the whole of its religious life. These cults and movements do not wholly represent the creative religious consciousness of our time, of course; a great deal of that same creative religious consciousness has given new quality to the organizations and orthodoxies of the churches. But within the frontiers of historic Christianity it has been rather the working over of the deposit of faith than an actual adventure in the making of religion. The cults and movements have not been thus limited. They have challenged old understandings, broken away from the older organizations and taken their own line, using such material as seems proper for their purpose.

They are not wholly independent of the past; some of them have taken the immemorial speculations of the East for their point of departure though introducing therein a good many of the permissions or conclusions of modern science and something of the spirit of Christianity itself. Those taking their departure from Christianity have claimed rather to reinterpret and modernize it than to supplant it by their own creations. Yet when all this is recognized these cults and movements are particularly the creation of our own time. So accepted, they reveal strongly the persistence of religion. All these conjectures and confidences and reachings through the shadows are just a testimony that few are content to go on without some form of religion or other.

All religion has, in one phase or another, gone through much the same process. There has been for every religion a time when it took new form out of older elements, a time when the accepted religions had little enough sympathy for and understanding of what was taking place about them while those committed to new quests were exultant in the consciousness of spiritual adventure and discovery and heard the morning stars sing together for joy. What is thus begun must submit always to the testimony of time. In the end a religion is permanent as it meets the great human needs and adjusts itself to their changing phases. It is imperial and universal as it meets these needs supremely. If in addition it be capable of organization, if there be within it room for expansion, and if, on the whole, it justifies itself by the outcome of it in life and society it will persist, and if it persists through a long period of time and creates for itself literatures, dogmas and authorities, it becomes as nearly fundamental as anything can be in this world. It creates cultures, shapes civilizations, colours art, establishes ideals and fills the whole horizon of its devotees.

If a religion is to endure it must meet a wide range of need; it must be plastic and yet invest itself with the sanctions of History. For the conservative it must possess the note of authority and at the same time promise freedom to the liberal. It must persuade the forward-looking that it holds within itself the power to meet changing conditions. It must offer a satisfying experience to the mystic and the practically minded and deliverance to the despairing. It must be able to build into its structure new sciences and philosophies and yet it must touch the whole of life with some sense of the timeless, and above all, it must include the whole of life, nor depend upon particularized appeals or passing phases of thought. Historic Christianity has more nearly met all these tests than any other religion, for though under the stress of meeting so great a variety of needs and conditions it has organized itself into forms as different as Latin Catholicism and the Society of the Friends, so losing catholicity of organization, it has secured instead a catholicity of spirit and a vast elasticity of appeal which are the secret of its power and the assurance of its continuing and enduring supremacy.

Their Parallels in the Past

Now by such tests as these what future may one anticipate for such cults as we have been studying? Are they likely to displace the historic forms of Christianity, will they substantially modify it, or will they wear away and be reabsorbed? Evidently one of these three things must happen. This is not the first time in the Western world that historic and authoritative Christianity has been challenged. We should have, perhaps, to go back to the fourth century to find an exact parallel and then we should find in the vast and confused movement of Gnosticism an unexpected parallel to a great deal of what is happening about us. Gnosticism was the effort of a reason excessively given to speculation, undisciplined and greatly unrestrained by any sense of reality to possess and transform the Church. Various forces combined to build its fabric of air-born speculation and though for the time it gave the patristic Church the hardest fight of its existence, the discipline of the Church was too strong for it. Its own weaknesses proved eventually its undoing and Gnosticism remains only as a fascinating field of study for the specialist, only a name if even so much as that for the generality of us and valuable chiefly in showing what speculation may do when permitted at will to range earth and sky, with a spurious rationalism for pilot and imagination for wings.

There have been, beside, in the history of the Church many other movements possessing a great staying power and running in some cases for generations alongside the main current of religious development, until they finally disappeared with the changing centuries. Arguing from such historical precedents as these one might easily assume a like fate for the Gnosticism of our own time, and yet a note of caution is needed here for there are divisive religious movements which have as yet neither failed nor been absorbed in that from which they took their departure. The expectation of the Catholic Church that Protestantism will spend its force and be lost again in the majestic fabric of Latin Catholic Christianity as it is continued amongst us, is as far from realization today, or farther, than at any time in the last 300 years. We need to remember also that conditions change. The right of individual initiative and judgment once secured in the region of religion is not likely ever to be lost. A good many divergent movements have literally been whipped back into line or else put out in fire and blood. Nothing of that sort is likely to happen now.

No student of history should be blind to the sequence of action and reaction. A period of excessive dependence upon authority may follow a period of undue self-assertion, but it is not likely that we shall ever find recreated exactly the conditions of the past or that religion can hereafter be held, as it has heretofore, in relatively well marked channels under the stress of accepted authorities. Prophecy is hazardous business but it is safe to assume that these modern religious cults and movements represent the beginnings of a freer, more diffused, less formal religious faith. The peculiar cults themselves may reach their term but the temper which produced them is likely to continue and with other groupings of forces produce something in the future which will at least be their parallel.

The Healing Cults Likely to be Adversely Influenced by the Scientific Organization of Psycho-therapy

As far as the fortunes of the distinctive cults themselves go, one's conclusions may be less tentative. For the most part the foundations upon which they are built are not big enough to carry an ample and secure structure. They have been made possible not only by marked limitations in historic religion itself, but also by contemporaneous tempers which, one may sincerely hope, are self-limiting, and this is said not through undue prejudice against the cults themselves, but simply because one is loath to believe that the want of critical faculty which has made some of these cults possible will not in the end yield to experience and a really sounder education. Since, moreover, some of them—and Christian Science, preëminently—depend upon faith and mental healing, whatever helps us to a clearer understanding of the nature and limits of psycho-therapy will greatly affect their future. All faith healing cults have heretofore depended very greatly upon the atmosphere of mystery with which they have been able to surround themselves. The fact that they have been able to secure results with no very clear understanding of the way in which the results have been secured has invested them with awe and wonder, so essential to every religion.

But as psycho-therapy itself becomes organized, works out its laws, develops its own science and particularly as the knowledge of all this is extended and popularized, they will lose their base of support. For this reason the writer believes that the final explanation of all faith and mental healing in terms of some form of suggestion which is just now strongly in evidence will prove a distinct service to us all.

The intimate association of religion and healing has, on the whole, been good neither for religion nor health. Of course, this statement will probably be sharply challenged but it is maintained in the face of possible challenge. As far as religion goes it has withdrawn the interest of the religious, thus influenced, from the normal expressions of the religious life to border-land regions; it has stressed the exceptional rather than the sweep of law, and the occult rather than the luminously reasonable. Where it has failed in individual cases, as it is bound to fail, it has left those thus disillusioned without any sound basis for their faith and generally has driven them away from religion altogether. It has tempted religious teachers to win a hearing by signs and wonders. Even the Founder of the Christian religion grew weary of this, as the records show plainly enough, in that He saw His true work to be thereby not helped but hindered, and if this be true of the Founder it is by so much the more true of His followers.

On the scientific side this temper has hindered honest thinking, laborious investigation and that specialization which is absolutely necessary to the furtherance of any great division of human effort. Medicine made little progress until it got itself free of the Church. Specifically the average minister is neither by training nor temperament fitted for healing work and those laymen who have assumed that office have generally been wanting in balance and self-restraint. This is not to deny the reality of a power not ourselves making for health and well-being generally, or the power of faith, or the efficacy of prayer. Least of all is God, upon this understanding, to be shut out of life. But the power not ourselves which makes for faith and healing is best known through laborious investigation, the discovery of methods and obediences to ascertained law. When we have clearly come to see the nature of psycho-therapy, the occult authority of healing cults will in the end yield to this understanding and the cults themselves be greatly weakened or displaced.

One must recognize, on the other hand, the staying power of any well-established religious system. Through nurture and those profound conservatisms which hold more tenaciously in the region of religion than anywhere else, it is possible to continue from generation to generation the unreasonable or the positively untrue, and this holds in the Church as well as outside it. None the less, the most coherent systems must reckon with their own weaknesses. Christian. Science may have before it a long period of solid going or even marked growth, but its philosophy will at last yield to the vaster sweep of a truer philosophic thought. Its interpretations of historic Christianity will come up again and again for examination until their fallacies become apparent and its force as a system of psycho-therapy will be modified by simpler and more reasonable applications of the same power.

New Thought Will Become Old Thought

New Thought is likely to take a different course but it also will have to reckon with changing sciences and philosophies. What is New Thought to-day will be old thought to-morrow; it will be challenged by new expressions of the spirit which begot it. It will endure, therefore, only as it is open, flexible and possesses a great power of accommodation. But as long as understandings and ideals are fluid, as long as religion is under bonds to take account of all the elements which must be incorporated in it in order to enlarge and continue it, as long, in short, as the human spirit outgrows fixed forms in any region there is likely to be in religion itself something corresponding to the New Thought of to-day, but this will be true only as New Thought is not a cult at all but something larger—a free and creative movement of the human spirit.

Of all these cults it has made the soundest contribution to religion as a whole. It is also more easily assimilated, more easily absorbed. Its own distinct field will be limited by the increasing hospitality of Christian thought to contemporaneous truth. A wholly open-minded church will go a long way toward taking from New Thought its raison d'être. Its future depends, therefore, very largely upon the open-mindedness of the older and more strongly established forms of religion.

The future of Spiritualism is greatly open to conjecture. We have already seen the alternatives which Spiritualism is called upon to face and the uncertainties which attend its conclusions. A fuller understanding of the possibilities of abnormal personality and the reach of automatism are likely to work against Spiritualism. If we find ascertainable causes for its phenomena resident within personality itself there will be no need of calling in the other world in order to explain what is happening in this. On the other hand, if there should evidence an increasing and tested body of facts which can be explained only in terms of spiritistic communications, Spiritualism will naturally make headway. But we are certainly standing only upon the threshold of a scientific interpretation of spiritistic phenomena and until the whole region has been very much more carefully worked through and far more dependable facts are in hand, one can only say that Spiritism is a hypothesis which may or may not be verified, and attend the outcome.

It is hard to believe that Theosophy and kindred speculation will ever get a strong hold upon the practical Western mind. It owes what force it has either to an excessive love of the speculative on the part of a few, or else to that particular temper which always wants something else and something new, or else to wearinesses and misunderstandings of the more shadowed side of life. Theosophy is greatly at the mercy of the positive, practical temper; it will always find a prevailing competitor in the Christian doctrine of immortality. Whatever, moreover, explains the apparent inequalities of life in more simple and reasonable terms will cut the roots of it. The movement toward religious syncretism of which Bahaism is just now the expression will not be so easy to dispose of. There will always be a temper impatient of the past, eager for unity, anxious for something big and interpenetrating. Historically this temper has from time to time emerged, particularly in the latter phases of Roman paganism, and there is likely to be a larger interchange of religious faith and understanding in the future than there has been in the past.

In general, this desire for a universal religion, simple and wanting in distinctive characters, follows a weakening of conviction, a loss of passion for accepted forms. If anything should deepen again amongst us in religion what corresponds just now to the passion for nationality these more general religious quests would suffer. A strong feeling for a church or a creed or one's own movement would displace them. They have, on the other hand, in their favour the general tendency of all religion toward simplicity, the reduction of faith, that is, to a few broad and generally shared elements. But there is no reason to anticipate a speedy breakdown of what one may call particularist religion and the substitution therefor of a faith built up out of many diverse elements and held in common by widely separated tempers.

There is Likely to be Some Absorption of the Cults by a Widening Historic Christianity

If the past supplies analogy or suggestion there will be some tendency for the cults and movements to be reabsorbed by the dominant religious forms from which they have broken off. A careful analysis of this statement would involve the consideration of a finality of Christianity as now held in the Western world. That is impossible in the range of a study like this. Any general statement is of course coloured by the temper of the one who makes it and to a certain extent begs the whole great question. But a careful and dispassionate examination of present-day cults would seem to indicate that they really have nothing to offer which the dominant Christianity does not possess either explicitly or implicitly. There is a solidity of human experience behind its forms and creeds which cannot be lightly left out of account. They represent the travail of twenty centuries and

have behind them far older confidences and hopes.   If
Christianity should widen itself to the full limit of its
possibilities, it would leave little room for that which
seeks to supplant it and would meet the needs which
have begotten the cults in far richer and more reasonable ways.

As far as the cults are mistakenly distinctive, as far
as they cannot stand a careful examination, they represent what must be corrected and cannot be absorbed.
Christianity can absorb New Thought far more easily
than Christian Science. Theosophy in its extremer
forms it cannot absorb at all. It is more hospitable
to the quest for a universal religion for it seeks itself
to be a universal religion and can never achieve its
ideal unless it takes account of the desire for something big enough to include the whole of life, East as
well as West, and to make room within itself for a
very great variety of religious tempers.

But Christianity is Being Influenced by the Cults

If Christianity is not to reabsorb the cults in their
present form, it must, as has been said over and over
again, take account of them and it is not likely to go on
uninfluenced by them. Already it has yielded in some
directions to their contentions. If it feels itself challenged by them it must meet that challenge not so much
by intolerance as by the correction of conditions which
have made them possible, and here its most dependable instruments are education and self-examination.
There is need of a vast deal more of sheer teaching in
all the churches. The necessity for congregations and

the traditions of preaching conspire to make the message of the Church far less vital than it ought to be. Preaching is too much declamation and far too much a following of narrow and deeply worn paths.

The cults themselves represent a craving for light, especially in the regions of pain and loss. Historic Christianity has lost out because it has made religion too self-centered, not that the cults are a corrective here, for they are even more self-centered—that is one of their great faults. The individual is not the center of the world; he is part of a larger order concerned for great ends for which his life can only be contributory. The Church and the cults together have forgotten too largely that life is sacred only as we lose it. We need in the churches generally a braver personal note and a very much larger unself-centeredness.

It is interesting to note that the movement of the cults, with the possible exception of New Thought, has been away from rationalism rather than in the direction of it. This is a consideration to be taken into account. It would seem on the surface of it to indicate that what people are wanting in religion is not so much reason as mysticism and that for the generality religion is most truly conceived in terms not of the known but of the unknown. If the Christian Church is to meet the challenge of the cults with a far more clearly defined line of teaching, it is also to meet the challenge of the cults with a warmer religious life, with the affirmation of an experience not so much tested by crises and conversions as by the constant liv-

ing of life in the sense of the divine—to use Jeremy
Taylor's noble phrase: in the Practice of the Presence
of God. The weakness of the cults is to have nar-
rowed the practice of the presence of God to specific
regions, finding the proof of His power in health and
well-being. If we can substitute therefor the consciousness of God in the sweep of law, the immensity of
force, the normal conduct of life, in light and understanding, in reason as well as mysticism and science
as well as devotion, we shall have secured a foundation
upon which to build amply enough to shelter devout
and questing souls not now able to find what they seek
in the churches themselves and yet never for a moment
out of line with what is truest and most prophetic in
Christianity itself.

Sir Henry Jones has a paragraph in his " Faith that
Enquires " distinctly to the point just here. " The
second consideration arises from the greatness of the
change that would follow were the Protestant
Churches and their leaders to assume the attitude of
the sciences and treat the articles of the creeds not as
dogmas but as the most probable explanation, the most
sane account which they can form of the relation of
man to the Universe and of the final meaning of his
life. The hypothesis of a God whose wisdom and
power and goodness are perfect would then be tried
and tested, both theoretically and practically, and, I
believe, become thereby ever the more convincing. The
creed would be not merely a record of an old belief
to be accepted on authority, but a challenge to the
skeptic and the irreligious. The Church, instead of

being a place where the deliverances of ancient religious authorities are expounded, and illustrated by reference to the contents of one book and the history of
one nation—as if no other books were inspired and all
nations save one were God-abandoned—the Church
would be the place where the validity of spiritual convictions are discussed on their merits, and the application of spiritual principles extended; where enquir-
ing youths would repair when life brings them sorrow,
disappointment or failure, and the injustice of man
makes them doubt whether there be a God, or if there
be, whether he is good and has power, and stands as
the help of man. Recourse to their certified spiritual
guides, knowing that full and sympathetic justice will
be done to all their difficulties, ought to be as natural
to them as their recourse to the physical laboratory or
the workshop of the mechanician when an engine
breaks down." [1]

Medical Science Should Take a More Serious Account of the Healing Cults

Not only the churches but the schools and particularly Medical Science need to take account of the cults.
They constitute perhaps one of the sharpest indict-
ments of present-day education. Many of their adherents are nominally educated above the average.
They have secured for what they follow the authority
which always attaches, in the American mind, to the
fact that those who champion any movement are college bred, and yet the want of clear vision, the power
to distinguish and analyze, along with the unexpected

[1] "A Faith that Enquires," p. 82.

credulities which are thus made manifest, seem to indicate arresting deficiencies in popular education. It has left us unduly suggestible, much open to mass movement, at the mercy of the lesser prophets and wanting in those stabilities and understandings upon which a sound culture is to be built. When we consider what they are capable of believing who have had college or university training, we must conclude either that contemporaneous education is wanting in the creation of sound mental discipline, or else that we have a strange power of living in water-tight compartments and separating our faith wholly from our reason.

The cults which are organized around faith and mental healing at once challenge and in a measure indict modern medical science. In many directions all these movements are reactions against an excessive materialism; they affirm the power of personality as against its environment, testify that the central problems of life may be approached from the spiritual as well as from the physical and material side. It would not for a moment be fair to say that modern Medicine is ignoring this. There has probably always been a considerable element of mental healing in any wise medical practice. But on the whole, the marvellous successes and advances in Medical Science within the last thirty years and the very great success which has attended the definition of all diseases in terms of physical disarrangement has led physicians generally unduly to underestimate or ignore the undoubted power of faith and mind over bodily states.

Even as a matter of scientific investigation medicine as a whole has not taken this line of approach seriously enough. The Society for Psychical Research has something to teach the medical faculties just here. That Society, as we have seen, set out in the most rigorous and scientific way possible to find out first of all just what actual facts lay behind the confused phenomena of Spiritualism. They have given a long generation to just that. As they have finally isolated certain facts they have, with a good deal of caution, undertaken to frame hypotheses to account for them and so, with the aid of the students of abnormal personality, they are gradually bringing a measure of order into the whole region. Medical Science on the whole has not done this in the region of faith and mental healing. We are, therefore, far too uncertain of our facts. A good deal of this is open to correction. If a Society for Psycho-Therapeutic Research should be organized, which would follow up every report of healings with an accurate care, beginning with the diagnosis and ending with the actual physical state of the patient as far as it could be ascertained by the tests at their disposal, they could greatly clarify the popular mind, prevent a vast deal of needless suffering, save the sick from frustrated hope and secure for their own profession a distinct reinforcement and an increased usefulness.

A Neglected Force

If they thus find—as is likely—that the real force of Psycho-therapy has been largely overestimated, that imagination, wrong diagnosis and mistaken report as to the actual physical condition have all combined to produce confidences unjustified by the facts, we should begin to come out into the light. And if, on the other hand, they found a body of actual fact substantiating Psycho-therapy they would do well to add courses therein to the discipline of their schools.[1] The whole thing would doubtless be a matter for specialization as almost every other department of medicine demands specialization. Every good doctor is more or less a mental healer, but every doctor cannot become a specialist in Psycho-therapy, nor would he need to.

Temperamental elements enter here very largely. But we might at least take the whole matter out of the hands of charlatans and the half-informed and establish it upon a sound scientific basis. There is, beyond debate, a real place for the physician who utilizes and directs the elements of suggestion. They have gone farther, on the whole, in this direction in France and Switzerland than we have in America. Evidently we are standing only upon the threshold of marked advances along these lines. Psycho-therapy can never be a substitute for a medical science which deals with the body as a machine to be regulated in its processes, defended against hostile invasion or reinforced in its weaknesses, but there is also another line of approach to sickness. A catholic medical science will use every means in its power.

[1] But this is already being done.

The Cults Must be Left to Time and the Corrections of Truth

Beyond such general considerations as these there is little to be said. The Christian churches will gain nothing by an intolerant attitude toward expressions of faith and spiritual adventures beyond their own frontiers. Just as there is a constant selective process in answer to which the historic churches maintain their existences, a selective process controlled by association and temper, in that some of us are naturally Catholics and some Protestants, there are tempers which do not take kindly to inherited organization, authority or creed. Such as these are seekers, excessive perhaps in their individuality, but none the less sincere in their desire for a faith and religious contact which will have its own distinct meaning for their own lives. And if there may seem to some of us elements of misdirection or caprice or unreason in their quests, it is perhaps in just such ways as these that advances are finally made and what is right and true endures.

If nothing at all is to be gained by intolerance, nothing more is to be gained by an unfair criticism and, in general, all these movements must be left to the adjustments of time and the corrections of truth.

We began this study by defining religion as the effective desire to be in right relation with the power which manifests itself in the universe. How vast this power is we are just beginning to find out. How various we are in our temperaments and what unsuspected possibilities there are in the depths of personality we are also just beginning to find out. There is possible, therefore, a vast variation of contact in this endeavour to be in right relation with the power which faith knows and names as God. In an endeavour moving along so wide a front there is room, naturally, for a great variety of quest. When we have sought rightly to understand and justly to estimate the more extreme variants of that quest in our own time, we can do finally no more than, through the knowledge thus gained, to try in patient and fundamental ways to correct what is false and recognize and sympathize with what is right and leave the residue to the issue of the unresting movements of the human soul, and those disclosures of the Divine which are on their Godward side revelation and on their human side insight, understanding and obedience.

Printed in the United States of America

JOHN HENRY JOWETT, D.D.

God Our Contemporary

A Series of Complete Addresses $1.50.

Among the pulpit-giants of to-day Dr. Jowett has been given a high place. Every preacher will want at once this latest product of his fertile mind. It consists of a series of full length sermons which are intended to show that only in God as revealed to us in Jesus Christ can we find the resources to meet the needs of human life.

SIDNEY BERRY, M.A.

Revealing Light $1.50.

A volume of addresses by the successor to Dr. Jowett at Carr's Lane Church, Birmingham, the underlying aim of which is to show what the Christian revelation means in relation to the great historic facts of the Faith and the response which those facts must awaken in the hearts of men to-day. Every address is an example of the best preaching of this famous "preacher to young men."

FREDERICK C. SPURR

Last Minister of Regent's Park Chapel, London.

The Master Key

A Study in World-Problems $1.35.

A fearless, clearly-reasoned restatement of the terms of the Christian Gospel and its relation to the travail through which the world is passing. Mr. Spurr is a man in the vanguard of religious thought, yet just as emphatically as any thinker of the old school, he insists on one Physician able to heal the wounds and woes of humanity.

RUSSELL H. CONWELL, D.D.

Pastor Baptist Temple, Philadelphia.

Unused Powers $1.25.

To "Acres of Diamonds," "The Angel's Lily," "Why Lincoln Laughed," "How to Live the Christ Life," and many other stirring volumes, Dr. Conwell has just added another made up of some of his choicest addresses. Dr. Conwell speaks, as he has always spoken, out of the experimental knowledge and practical wisdom of a man, who having long faced the stark realities of life, has been exalted thereby.

GAIUS GLENN ATKINS, D.D.

Minister of the First Congregational Church, Detroit, Michigan.

The Undiscovered Country $1.50.

A group of addresses marked by distinction of style and originality of approach. The title discourse furnishes a central theme to which those following stand in relation. Dr. Atkins' work, throughout, is marked by clarity of presentation, polished diction and forceful phrasing.

TIMELY ESSAYS AND STUDIES

NEWELL DWIGHT HILLIS

Author of "Great Books as Life-Teachers."

Great Men as Prophets of a New Era

$1.50.

Dr. Hillis' latest book strikes a popular chord. It fairly pulses with life and human sympathy. He has a large grasp of things and relations, a broad culture, a retentive memory and splendid imagination, and there are few writers to-day with so large an audience assured in advance. The subjects include: Dante; Savonarola; William the Silent; Oliver Cromwell; John Wesley; John Milton; Garibaldi; John Ruskin, etc.

THOS. R. MITCHELL, M.A., B.D.

The Drama of Life

A Series of Reflections on Shakespeare's *"Seven Ages."* Introduction by Nellie L. McClung.

$1.25.

A fresh, stimulating discussion of old themes. Mr. Mitchell handles his subject with unusual directness, bringing to its discussion clarity of thought and lucidity of expression which has already won the enthusiastic endorsement of Sir William Robertson Nicoll, Chas. W. Gordon, D.D., (Ralph Connor) Archdeacon Cody and Prof. Francis G. Peabody.

D. MACDOUGALL KING, M.B.

Author of "The Battle with Tuberculosis."

Nerves and Personal Power

Some Principles of Psychology as Applied to Conduct and Health. With Introduction by Hon. W. L. Mackenzie King.

$2.00.

Premier King says: "My brother has, I think helped to reinforce Christian teaching by showing wherein recent medical and scientific researches are revealing the foundations of Christian faith and belief in directions hitherto unexplored and unknown.—The world needs the assurance this book can scarcely fail to bring."

REV. R. E. SMITH   *Waco, Texas.*

Christianity and the Race Problem

$1.25.

A sane, careful study of the Race problem in the South, written by a born Southerner, the son of a slave-owner and Confederate soldier. Mr. Smith has lived all his life among negroes, and feels that he is capable of seeing both sides of the problem he undertakes to discuss.

PROBLEMS OF TODAY

GEORGE McCREADY PRICE, M.A.
Poisoning Democracy
A Study of the Present-Day Socialism. $1.25

Professor Price shows that the conditions prevailing today are due largely to the acceptance of various socialistic and evolutionary theories termed "New" Theology. No more terrific moral and religious indictment of Socialism has ever been presented.

ALBERT CLARKE WYCKOFF
The Non-Sense of Christian Science
$1.75

A deadly, withering attack on Christian Science enfilading its every position. Mr. Wycvoff's searching analysis of the pretensions, errors, follies, and non-sense of so-called Christian Science should prove as convincing as it is unanswerable.

ALLEN W. JOHNSTON
The Roman Catholic Bible and the Roman Catholic Church
Foreword by David J. Burrell, D.D. $1.25

A book that examines the cardinal doctrines as taught by the Church of Rome, such as the Invocation of Saints, Purgatory, Indulgences, Worship of Mary, the Holy Eucharist, etc. etc., and indicates the dissimilarity between this body of teaching and Holy Writ.

New Editions.

I. M. HALDEMAN
Can the Dead Communicate with the Living?
$1.25

"Needless to say, Dr. Haldeman holds no brief for Spiritism. A book that is awakening everyone to the peril of 'spiritualism' among Christians."—*Christian Work.*

JAMES M. GRAY, D. D.
Spiritism and the Fallen Angels
From a Biblical Viewpoint.
$1.25

"Beginning with a review of the present-day revival of Spiritism and how to meet it, Dr. Gray harks back to origins, the baleful influence of the cult from the earliest recorded history of the human race."
S. S. Times.

G. B. F. HALLOCK   *Editor of "The Expositor."*

A Modern Cyclopedia of Illustrations for All Occasions

Nineteen Hundred and Thirty-eight Illustrations. $3.00.

A comprehensive collection of illustrative incidents, anecdotes and other suggestive material for the outstanding days and seasons of the church year. The author, well-known to the readers of *"The Expositor,"* has presented a really valuable handbook for Preachers, Sunday School Superintendents and all Christian workers.

JAMES INGLIS

The Bible Text Cyclopedia

A Complete Classification of Scripture Texts. New Edition.   Large 8vo, $2.00

"More sensible and convenient, and every way more satisfactory than any book of the kind we have ever known. We know of no other work comparable with it in this department of study."—*Sunday School Times.*

ANGUS-GREEN

Cyclopedic Handbook to the Bible

By Joseph Angus. Revised by Samuel G. Green.
New Edition.   832 pages, with Index, $3.00.

"The Best thing in its line."—*Ira M. Price, Univ. of Chicago.*

"Holds an unchallenged place among aids to the interpretation of the Scriptures."—*Baptist Review and Expositor.*

"Of immense service to Biblical students."—*Methodist Times.*

The Treasury of Scripture Knowledge

Introduction by R. A. Torrey

Consisting of 500,000 Scripture References and Parallel Passages. 788 pages. 8vo. Cloth. $3.00.

"Bible students who desire to compare Scripture with Scripture will find the 'Treasury' to be a better help than any other book of which I have any knowledge."—*R. R. McBurney, Former Gen. Sec., Y. M. C. A., New York.*

A. R. BUCKLAND, Editor

Universal Bible Dictionary

511 pages. 8vo. Cloth. $3.00.

Dr. Campbell Morgan says: "Clear, concise, comprehensive. I do not hesitate to say that if any student would take the Bible, and go through it book by book with its aid, the gain would be enormous."

CHURCH WORK

ROGER W. BABSON   *Author of "Fundamentals of Prosperity," etc.*

New Tasks for Old Churches

Cloth, $1.00. Paper, ✠ 60c.

Suggestions for the solution of to-day's problems, clear-cut and courageous. Babson has little sympathy with the arguments of self-interest of business men or with the out-worn methods of the church in industrial communities. His sole interest is in the physical, social, and spiritual salvation of the men, women, and children in our indus-trial centres.

PRES. WILLIAM ALLEN HARPER

Author of "The New Church For The New Time" etc.

The Church in the Present Crisis

$1.75.

Hon. Josephus Daniels says: "Dr. Harper has ably pre-sented the demand that the church shape the thought and life of the future. The world, having tried everything else, is becoming convinced that no Golden Rule alone will be the savior. Dr. Harper wisely stresses study of the Bible, the Christian leaven in education, the duty to look difficult problems in the face and solve them by application of the Christian religion. It is a book of faith with wise directions and guidance.

REV. ALBERT F. McGARRAH

Author of "Modern Church Management."

Money Talks

Stimulating Studies in Christian Stewardship. $1.25.

Ministers and laymen, who desire to present convinc-ingly the principles and practices which should govern Christians in getting and using money, will find here a wealth of fresh material, popular in style, yet deeply inspiring in tone. A companion volume to "Modern Church Finance" and "Modern Church Management."

LYMAN EDWYN DAVIS, D.D., LL.D.

Editor "Methodist Recorder."

Democratic Methodism in America

A Topical Survey of the Methodist Protestant Church. $1.50.

A history of the Methodist Protestant church from its founding in 1830, pointing out the various links in the chain of circumstances which lead to the organization of the Methodist Protestant Church and the fundamental principles which prompted and justified the movement. It constitutes a vigorous and ably-argued plea for "mutual-rights" Methodism.

P. WHITWELL WILSON *Author of "The Christ We Forget"*

The Church We Forget

A Study of the Life and Words of the Early Christians. 8vo, cloth, net

The author of "The Christ We Forget" here furnishes a companion-picture of the earliest Christian Church—of the men and women, of like feelings with ourselves, who followed Christ and fought His battles in the Roman world of their day. "Here again," says Mr. Wilson, "my paint-box is the Bible, and nothing else—and my canvas is a page which he who runs may read."

C. ALPHONSO SMITH, Ph.D., LL.D.

Head of the Department of English in the U. S. Naval Academy, Annapolis, Md.

Key-note Studies in Key-note Books of the Bible   12mo, cloth, net

The sacred books dealt with are Genesis, Esther, Job, Hosea, John's Gospel, Romans, Philippians. Revelation. "No series of lectures yet given on this famous foundation have been more interesting and stimulating than these illuminating studies of scriptural books by a layman and library expert."—*Christian Observer.*

GEORGE D. WATSON, D. D.

God's First Words

Studies in Genesis, Historic, Prophetic and Experimental. 12mo, cloth, net

Dr. Watson shows how God's purposes and infinite wisdom, His plan and purpose for the race, His unfailing love and faithfulness are first unfolded in the Book of Genesis, to remain unchanged through the whole canon of Scripture. Dr. Watson's new work will furnish unusual enlightment to every gleaner in religious fields, who will find "God's First Words" to possess great value and profit.

EVERETT PEPPERRELL WHEELER, A. M.

Author of "Sixty Years of American Life," etc.

A Lawyer's Study of the Bible

Its Answer to the Questions of To-day. 12mo, cloth, net

Mr. Wheeler's main proposition is that the Bible, when wisely studied, rightly understood and its counsel closely followed, is found to be of inestimable value as a guide to daily life and conduct. To this end Mr. Wheeler examines its teachings as they relate to sociology, labor and capital, socialism, war, fatalism, prayer, immortality. A lucid, helpful book.